D1625980

*The Lotus Sutra
in Japanese Culture*

# The Lotus Sutra
# in Japanese Culture

*Edited by*
George J. Tanabe, Jr.
*and*
Willa Jane Tanabe

*University of Hawaii Press*
*Honolulu*

94 93 92 91 90 89   5 4 3 2 1

Published with the support
of the Kamigata Bunka Kenkyūkai
at the University of Hawaii
and by grants from Sumitomo Metal
Industries, Ltd., Suntory Limited,
Matsushita Electric Industrial Co., Ltd.,
Sumitomo Bank, Ltd., and Kansai
Electric Power Co., Inc.

Photographs provided by Miya Tsugio
and Willa Jane Tanabe.

**Library of Congress Cataloging-in-Publication Data**

The Lotus sutra in Japanese culture / edited by George J. Tanabe, Jr.
    and Willa Jane Tanabe.
        p.   cm.
    'The essays in this volume were selected from papers presented at
the first International Conference on the Lotus Sutra and Japanese
Culture held at the University of Hawaii in 1984"—Pref.
    Includes bibliographies and index.
    ISBN 0-8248-1198-4
    1.   Tripiṭaka. Sūtrapiṭaka. Saddharmapuṇḍarīkasūtra—Criticism,
interpretation, etc.—Japan—Congresses.   2.   Japan—Civilization—
Buddhist influences—Congresses.   I.   Tanabe, George Joji.
II.   Tanabe, Willa J. (Willa Jane), 1945–      .   III.   International
Conference on the Lotus Sutra and Japanese Culture (1st : 1984 :
University of Hawaii)
BQ2057.L66   1989                                88–36735
294.3'85—dc19                                        CIP

*To Masao Ichishima*

# CONTENTS

# PREFACE

The essays in this volume were selected from papers presented at the first International Conference on the *Lotus Sutra* and Japanese Culture held at the University of Hawaii in 1984. A second conference was held at Risshō University (Tokyo) in 1987, and a third is being planned at the University of British Columbia. This series of meetings attests to the ongoing interest that scholars in Japan and the West have for the topic of this book.

Like other classics, the *Lotus Sutra* has been translated many times. Each scholar has his or her preferred translation, and we have not insisted that the contributors to this volume use any particular one. Citations of passages and chapter titles therefore vary from author to author, but are sufficiently clear so that the reader will not be confused, even if the reader's copy of the *Lotus Sutra* is different from that used by an author.

Romanization of Japanese words is based on *Kenkyūsha's New Japanese-English Dictionary* except where customary Buddhist pronunciations depart from ordinary usage. Chinese words are rendered according to *Mathews' Chinese-English Dictionary*. A few bibliographic abbreviations are used: *T* for *Taishō shinshū daizōkyō*, *ZZ* for *Dai Nippon zokuzōkyō*, *DNBZ* for *Dai Nihon Bukkyō zensho*, and *DZ* for *Dengyō Daishi zenshū*.

The conferences and this volume have been supported by a number of individuals and organizations. We received grants for the first conference from the Kamigata Bunka Kenkyūkai (Honolulu), the Social Science Research Council (New York), Nichiren-shū Headquarters (Tokyo), the Tendai Mission of Hawaii, Kokuchūkai (Tokyo), Risshō Kōseikai (Hawaii), and the University of Hawaii Japan Studies Endowment, which is funded by a grant from the Japanese government. Without the cooperation of the East-West Center, Taishō University (Tokyo), Risshō University (Tokyo), the Korean Studies Center (University of Hawaii), and our own departments of art and religion, the conference on which this volume is based could not have been realized.

It is, of course, individuals who make institutions cooperate, and we are particularly grateful to Bishop Senchū Murano of the Nichiren Mission, Bishop Ryōkan Ara of the Tendai Mission, Rev. Nobu Masuda of Risshō Kōseikai, and our colleagues George Akita, Agnes Niyekawa, Patricia Steinhoff, John Wisnosky, and Fritz Seifert. We also wish to thank Barbara Ruch of Columbia University for constant support from the very beginning and Patricia Crosby of the University of Hawaii Press for her expert guidance in helping us conclude the publication phase of the project. To George Akita we express our thanks a second time for arranging a publication grant from the Kamigata Bunka Kenkyūkai.

Finally we wish to express our appreciation to the participants of the 1984 and 1987 *Lotus* conferences. It has been a pleasurable association sustained over several years by our common interest in the remarkable relationships this one text has with Japanese culture. On behalf of the participants, we would like to dedicate this book to Professor Masao Ichishima of Taishō University, who, at so many times and in so many ways, helped make this cooperative project possible.

*The Lotus Sutra*
*in Japanese Culture*

# Introduction

GEORGE J. TANABE, JR.
WILLA JANE TANABE

In the opening scene of the *Lotus Sutra,* great sages, deities, and kings gather by the tens of thousands to hear the Buddha speak. After the multitude showers him with reverent offerings, the Buddha offers some preliminary words and then enters a state of deep concentration. The heavens rain flowers and the earth trembles while the crowd waits for the sermon. Then the Buddha emits a glowing light from the tuft of white hair between his brows and illuminates the thousands of worlds in all directions of the universe. The bodhisattva Maitreya, wanting to know the meaning of this sign, asks Mañjuśrī, who searches back into his memory and recalls a similar display of light:

> You good men, once before, in the presence of past Buddhas, I saw this portent: when the Buddhas had emitted this light, straightway they preached the great Dharma. Thus it should be understood that the present Buddha's display of light is also of this sort. It is because he wishes all the living beings to be able to hear and know the Dharma, difficult of belief for all the worlds, that he displays this portent.[1]

Everything that is happening now, recalls Maitreya, happened in that distant past when the Buddha preached the *Sutra of Innumerable Meanings* and entered *samādhi* as the universe trembled and rained flowers. Those wondrous signs were followed by the Buddha's preaching of the *Lotus Sutra.* Now, therefore, the Buddha must be ready to preach the *Lotus Sutra* again—and as the first chapter comes to an end, the crowd waits in great expectation.

The text which we know and can read as the *Lotus Sutra* thus begins by mentioning the *Lotus* sermon first preached in the distant past and says that the same sermon is about to be preached again to the expectant multitude. As with the *Sutra of Innumerable Meanings,* the content of the first *Lotus* sermon is not revealed, and the difference between the first preaching and the one that is about to take place lies, the reader suspects, in the prospect of hearing its substance explicitly for the first time.

In chapter 2, however, the Buddha immediately gets up from his seat and expounds on the difficulty of making wisdom understandable to those who are not buddhas. Not even the best of bodhisattvas can understand the wisdom of a buddha—only buddhas can understand each other. The multitude, however, led by Śāriputra, pleads with the Buddha, who finally agrees to use a variety of expedient devices to attempt an explanation. Buddhas, after all, "appear in the world because they wish to cause the beings to understand."[2] Castigating the proud monks who, upon hearing how difficult it is to understand, had taken their leave, the Buddha praises those who remain: "You know that you yourselves shall become Buddhas."[3]

Śāriputra, therefore, is found dancing for joy as chapter 3 opens. Never before, he declares, has he heard of such a wondrous message. The narrative then enters into the first of the many parables for which the *Lotus Sutra* is famous, and thereafter concerns itself with elaborating the marvelous merits of this sutra and the responsibilities of those who embrace it: how it should be copied, revered, propagated, and explained. The status of the sutra is raised to that of an object of worship, for it is to be revered in and of itself because of the merits it asserts for itself. As praises for the *Lotus Sutra* mount with increasing elaboration, it is easy to fall in with the sutra's protagonists and, like them, fail to notice that the preaching of the *Lotus* sermon promised in the first chapter *never takes place.* The text, so full of merit, is *about* a discourse which is never delivered; it is a lengthy preface without a book.

The *Lotus Sutra* is thus unique among texts. It is not merely subject to various interpretations, as all texts are, but is open or empty at its very center. It is a surrounding text, pure context, which invites not only interpretation of what is said but filling in of what is not said. It therefore lends itself more easily than do other scriptures to being shaped by users of the text.

The fact that the preaching remains an unfulfilled promise is never mentioned, mostly because that fact is hardly noticed, or because the paean about the sermon sounds like the sermon itself. The text is taken at face value: praise about the *Lotus Sutra* becomes the *Lotus*

*Sutra,* and since the unpreached sermon leaves the text undefined in terms of a fixed doctrinal value (save, of course, the value of the paean) it can be exchanged at any number of rates. Exchange involves transformation, the turning of one thing into another, and the *Lotus Sutra* can thus be minted into other expressions of worth. That transformation process, beginning with the original text itself, did in fact take place, and the different ways in which the *Lotus Sutra* was transformed into aspects of Japanese culture are the subject of this collection of essays.

We begin with the question of whether or not there is something inherent in the *Lotus Sutra* that lends itself to transformation. Shioiri Ryōdō, one of the leading Tendai scholars today, briefly surveys the different ways in which the *Lotus Sutra* was reexpressed in Japanese literature and culture, and suggests that the answer to our question lies not merely in the traditional assumption that the *Lotus Sutra* is universally true and therefore universally applicable, but also in a critical understanding of the history of the text. While there are still debates surrounding several issues concerning the formation of the text, scholars from ancient China to modern Japan have commonly recognized that the text can be divided into several sequences. These divisions were made according to differences discerned in content, and the sutra was accordingly divided into two main parts, each with further subdivisions. Outlining the document in this way not only made it easier to read and understand, but also raised the possibility that the outline itself had its own meaning which could be derived through an analysis of its structure. Interpretation of the *Lotus Sutra* has traditionally been based on analyses of both content and structure.

Modern scholarship, relying on the traditional methods of outlining the text, has added a chronological dimension in the ascription of dates to the different divisions. Scholars differ, of course, about the exact dating of each part, but it is clear that differences in content are explainable by the fact that each part was written at different times by obviously different persons representing different religious and philosophical viewpoints. This maze of intertwining strands has been studied in detail by Japanese scholars,[4] who show that the sutra is a complex product of nearly bewildering circumstances. Yet the text coheres. And if the text was formed through a process of absorbing discrete parts from different times and places into a coherent whole, then the reverse process of applying the text to widely different situations can be equally coherent. That the *Lotus Sutra* can be reincarnated in literature, painting, politics, and so forth is thus a natural reflection of how the text itself came to be. Taking the knowledge gained from the many studies on the history of the *Lotus Sutra*, Shioiri Ryōdō steps back to offer a much needed overview of the significance of the manner in which the sutra came to be. "Both the structure and the meaning of the text," Shioiri concludes, "imply that the essential quality of the *Lotus Sutra* is that, having absorbed widely, it can be applied—infinitely, it would seem—to a great many aspects of culture." The formation and structure of the *Lotus Sutra* have their own meaning: the text, itself a tapestry of different strands, continued to weave itself into the fabric of Japanese culture long after its own formation was, strictly speaking, complete.

The same question about the *Lotus Sutra*'s easy amenability to transformation can be approached through its content as well as through its structure. The most important idea of the *Lotus Sutra*, one that accounts for a good degree of its popular veneration, is the repeated claim it makes that it is the embodiment of the underlying truth of the universe. Tamura Yoshirō, formerly of Tokyo University and now teaching at Risshō University, notes the universal persistence of the conviction that underlying all of reality must be a single, unifying principle. That truth, of course, is identified in the *Lotus Sutra* as the wonderful law of the *Lotus*. It is also referred to as the one vehicle, metaphorically taught in the famous parable of the father who lures his sons out of a burning house with promises of a magnificent cart. But what, exactly, is the content of this principle? The parable, as might be expected of a sutra featuring an unpreached sermon, asserts the existence of such a principle without specifying its substance. The task of transforming parable to specifiable principle was performed by the many commentators on the *Lotus Sutra*: Kumārajīva, for example, explained it as the "real state of all things," while Chih-i gave a systematic presentation of it as the doctrine of the "three thousand realms in one mind."

Relying on the traditional method of structural analysis, Tamura goes on to explain the idea of the eternal Buddha as the definition of the underlying principle, a definition that departs from the idea of *dharmakāya*, the more usual Mahāyāna expression of an absolute buddha.[5] The idea of the eternal Buddha is certainly one of the unique ideas of the *Lotus Sutra*, but what is unique about Tamura's analysis is that he points out the significance of human action as a kind of absolute of its own, taking its place alongside the notion of the eternal Buddha. The fundamental ideas of the *Lotus Sutra* are "the unifying truth of the universe . . . , eternal life . . . , and human activities in the real world," which correspond to the "first realm of traces, the second realm of origin, and the third realm" identified according to an analysis of the sutra's structure. While the ideas of the *Lotus Sutra* have been explained in terms of what they mean in and of themselves,[6] Tamura tries to turn the ideas inside out not just to see how "activities in the real world" are defined as ideas in the *Lotus Sutra* along with ideas like the "unifying truth" and "eternal life," but also to see how, if the truth is indeed unifying, real activities result from a sense of the absolute.

Take the case of the followers of Nichiren, certainly one of Japan's most famous *Lotus* activists. During the Muromachi period (1334–1568), his followers were concentrated among townsfolk, the *machishū*, and much of their culture, from the art of making a profit to that of writing poetry, was informed by interpretations of the general principles of the *Lotus Sutra*. Tamura's comments on the relationship between the *Lotus Sutra* and society are tantalizingly brief and suggest that further research in this area is necessary if we are to gain a better understanding of the *Lotus*-inspired ideologies of the commercial, artistic, and, it can be added, political circles of the Muromachi and Edo periods. While scholars have already pointed out the ways in which certain activities, such as those of the early Mahāyāna preachers in India, might have produced some of the ideas of the *Lotus Sutra*,[7] Tamura calls our attention to the obvious but seldom noted process in reverse: ideas breed action, and absolute ideas breed absolute actions. The *Lotus* nationalist Tanaka Chigaku, the subject of George Tanabe's chapter, is just one of many examples of those who transformed their knowledge of the *Lotus Sutra* into political action.

Knowledge is power, and it is therefore important to have power over knowledge. The idea that one can become a buddha in this existence *(sokushin jōbutsu)* is a powerful idea because of its unequivocal promise of an immediate realization of the loftiest of all the goals of Buddhism. Nothing higher could be desired by a Buddhist; nothing more elusive and difficult to attain could be experienced by a Buddhist. Centuries of Buddhist experience made it clear that becoming a buddha was reserved for the very, very few, if anyone at all. *Sokushin jōbutsu* was a manifesto that cleared the path to enlightenment of all obstacles by the power of declaration: Become a buddha in this bodily existence. That declaration, of course, had to be accompanied by right understanding and practice, which proved not to be so easy, but still the promise of such a magnificent possibility made the idea irresistible and persuasive. He who controlled it could control many.

The doctrine of *sokushin jōbutsu* is most often ascribed to Kūkai's Shingon system as one of its salient characteristics. Paul Groner, however, shows that Kūkai's rival, Saichō, also made some claim to the idea and justified his claim with the story of the dragon king's daughter from the *Lotus Sutra*. While it is not clear who first propounded the idea, it is clear that Saichō was interested in it because it provided him with another argument to establish the superiority of Tendai over Hossō. The merit of the idea, both for Kūkai and Saichō, was to be found in the advantage of immediacy: faster is better when it comes to enlightenment. The appeal of such an idea is obvious; it translates easily into persuasiveness, and therefore power in the form of followers.

Ideas such as *sokushin jōbutsu*, however, are seldom discussed in a systematic, philosophical way in the *Lotus Sutra* itself. J. W. de Jong, noting that Kumārajīva's translation of the *Lotus Sutra* is "without doubt the most famous Buddhist text in East Asia," warns against confusing the sutra with its commentaries and interpretations,[8] which give to the text more philosophical coherence than it displays on its own. Unlike the *Heart Sutra* or the *Diamond Sutra*, the *Lotus Sutra* is more an anthology of stories than a sustained argument, and this too is part of the reason for its popular veneration. It is the stories, after all, that are primary; the philosophical principles are derived from the stories and are therefore secondary as far as the ordinary believer is concerned.[9] The stories lent themselves easily to graphic transformation as paintings. Miya Tsugio, in his comprehensive typology of *Lotus* paintings, identifies two basic functions of this art. The first arose from a didactic concern for retelling the stories in pictures, and was carried out chiefly in two formats: sutra frontispieces and hanging scrolls. The frontispiece illustrations were characteristic scenes from a fascicle or chapter of the sutra, becoming in time sufficiently conventionalized to form a recognizable canon of scenes. But when the artist moved beyond the conventions of the canon and included greater detail to tell more of the story rather than merely identify the scene, a larger format than was allowable in the frontispiece became necessary. The hanging scroll paintings that resulted were called *hensō*, literally "transformations" of the story details into illustration. So much detail was included in some *hensō* that they lost their self-evident quality and required verbal explanations provided by an *e-toki*, or "picture-explaining" priest. Several levels and kinds of discourse were thus packed into the *hensō:* the pictures of the stories about the unpreached sermon became subjects of popular sermons.

Despite these layers of meaning, the final end of the paintings as well of the sutra itself was always made clear by the second type of art, which functioned as *honzon,* or objects of worship. Usually depicting a deity and his retinue, these paintings made little attempt to explain. They were used as foci of reverence directed to the deity and through it to the sutra. The religion of the *Lotus* was, to borrow a phrase from Gregory Schopen, a "cult of the book,"[10] and the *honzon* paintings do not merely illustrate figures from the book but transform them through painting into ritual emblems of the entire meaning and virtue of the text.

Both the didactic and the ritual paintings were literal in their renditions of the stories and deities. While much was assumed in the way of recognition and understanding, nothing was left to the imagination. Like the paintings, many of the poems on Buddhist sutras were didactic and literal, not attempting to do anything more than restate certain parts of the sutra in verse. While sutra poetry in Japan was largely didactic in nature and therefore mediocre in literary quality, the growth of this genre as a tradition with its own conventions made it possible for a creative poet to transform literal meanings into poetic sentiment that touched the imagination as well as the mind. The best of the *Lotus Sutra* poetry, argues Yamada Shōzen, incorporated both elements, and good *Lotus* poetry managed not only to be faithful to its ideas but also to be effective verse that alluded, as many good Japanese poems do, to other poems, thereby provoking compounded images. This meant, of course, that the reader had to be versed in the scriptural and poetic traditions so as to be able to recognize the allusions; only in this way could meanings be combined to inform a deeper imaginative appreciation of the sutra. The development of *Lotus* poetry—its conventions, occasions, forms, collections, writers, and conceptions—has been well studied, most notably by Takagi Yutaka,[11] but Yamada Shōzen is the first to analyze the poetry in terms of the religious consciousness it conveys as well as its literary quality.

A poem, after all, is a reflection of the poet, and to judge the one is to measure the other. In Yamada's analysis, the quality of the poem is directly related to the consciousness of the writer and can therefore be used to assess his depth of feeling and understanding. The popularity of writing poems on the *Lotus Sutra* makes it possible to use them as a common standard against which several poets can be judged. Yamada puts several well-known poets through this test and ranks them according to the depth of religious perception manifested in their art. Saigyō's *Lotus* poems reveal an informed and questing mind while the poems of Jien, the great Tendai cleric, demonstrate his own humanity. Fujiwara Shunzei, interestingly enough, does not fare as well by this standard.

Poetic consciousness thus measured is, for Yamada, evidence of the depth to which the *Lotus Sutra* penetrated the minds and hearts of cultured people. The acceptance of the *Lotus Sutra* can also be measured by another standard, one that gives some indication about the breadth of its influence. The life of the nation as whole was affected by what happened in the court, and playing central roles in the seemingly endless intrigues were the Tendai clerics (among those from other sects as well), who used their *Lotus* ritual skills to enhance their own power by influencing the selection of those who would wield authority over the nation. As ritualists, the priests of the Tendai sect commanded great respect from a community that made little distinction, as Neil McMullin argues, between "religion" and "politics," particularly during the Heian period. Ritual power was redeemable for political power. McMullin states his case succinctly: "the political role that the *Lotus Sutra* played in the early to mid-Heian period is that it served as the coinage by which Tendai monks purchased power." In a court ruled by the politics of marriage and lineage, a monk could gain enormous favor by being able to perform potent rituals to bring about the sex change of a fetus if it was female. Powerful aristocrats vied for such services in order to insure that their daughters, whom they had maneuvered into marrying into the imperial house, would give birth to sons, future emperors. The great Tendai cleric Ryōgen was particularly successful as a ritualist, having come to the attention of the court early in his career because of his forensic skills and knowledge of Tendai *Lotus* dogmatics. Ryōgen, a monk who came from a relatively uninfluential family, achieved spectacular success because of his mastery of the *Lotus Sutra*.

Other Tendai clerics, most of whom are nameless to us, more quietly set about the task of keeping a wide variety of records—"documents," as the translator of Kuroda Toshio's essay calls them—at Mt. Hiei. The authors of these diverse notes were known as *kike*, "chroniclers," a group that has received little attention in scholarly literature. Originally strips of paper used to record the orally transmitted teachings of the Tendai masters on Mt. Hiei, these notes and jottings came to deal with a variety of subjects that can be characterized under two headings: the doctrinal and the historical. History and theory, then, became the subjects of the chroniclers, and Kuroda shows how the genre of record keeping lent itself to editing—and from there, as every editor knows, it is but a fine line over into interpretation.

The theoretical writings of the choniclers were set in the milieu of combined Buddhist-Shinto associations. The *honji-suijaku* theories specified the complex matrix in which essence *(honji)* and its expression or hypostasis *(suijaku)* are intertwined. These theories made it possible for what we call Buddhism and Shinto to be expressed in terms of each other and formed the dominant intellectual system by which the religion from India came to sink deep roots in Japan. On a superficial level, the general rubric of essence and expression is reminiscent of other categorical pairs such as principle and phenomena and reality and appearance, but the unique context surrounding *hon* and *jaku* must not be forgotten. The ideas are clearly tied to Tendai diction, which in turn is rooted in that structural analysis by which the *Lotus Sutra* was divided into essence and expression. It is not surprising—though Kuroda's observation is certainly new and opens up an area that has hardly been studied—that the work of the chroniclers can be divided into similarly identifiable trends.

Both categories, of course, belong to a single understanding. The world, and in particular the Hiei institution, existed in a history of real time that was the proper subject for the chroniclers, but the notions by which history was understood came from the theories and interpretations of the rituals, symbols, miracles, and prophecies of a mythic time. Essence, in this case, is not so much transformed into expression as it is integrated with it. The essence of the *Lotus Sutra* can therefore function not just as a theory but as a working blueprint for the world of real time and actual places.

Such a plan, specifying an architecture of meaning, was imposed upon the ridges and valleys of the Kunisaki Peninsula in Kyūshū, an imposing volcanic dome jutting out into the Inland Sea. To one side of this 720-meter mountain is the Usa Hachiman Shrine, still in the middle of nowhere, so far away from Kyoto and yet so important as a center of the Hachiman cult and Shugendō practice. Allan Grapard details the "intertextual" process by which associations were made between the Buddha and Hachiman, the *Lotus Sutra* and the Kunisaki Peninsula. The result was a "textualized mountain" on which were stamped the structure, language, and meaning of the *Lotus Sutra.* Twenty-eight temples were established on the mountain to represent the sutra's twenty-eight chapters, and the temples were administratively divided into three sections according to the three-part division traditionally made of the sutra's structure. On the pilgrimage path connecting the temples are 69,380 Buddhist statues, one for each Chinese character of the text. The *Lotus Sutra* and the mountain were thus mutually transformed into one other, and in this envisioned landscape of intertextuality, "reading the scripture, one discovered the mountain; walking the mountain became the equivalent of reading the scripture." The implantation of the sutra into the land made it indigenous, just as the manifestation of the Buddha as Hachiman at Kunisaki accorded native status to the deity who was thereby no longer foreign.

What would happen if the method of intertextuality were applied to the field of politics? Suppose someone were to write and read the text not into geography but geopolitics? The *Lotus Sutra* would then provide more than an architecture of meaning imposed on a local mountain but a blueprint for government, a political manifesto. In the early twentieth century, the Nichiren nationalist Tanaka Chigaku (1861–1939) did just that. Tanaka envisioned more than a mountain as the embodiment of the *Lotus Sutra;* Japan itself was its incarnated essence. Using, as so many had done before, the traditional methods of analyzing the structure of the sutra, Tanaka interpreted freely to show the correlation between truth and force, and how the forceful propagation of the truth *(shakubuku)* was justifiable. Since the truth of the *Lotus Sutra* and the national essence *(kokutai)* of Japan were identical, the logic of correlation could be applied to combine *shakubuku* with national policy to produce an imperialism which justifies the use of military force precisely because it is truthful and benevolent in nature. As it was for Ryōgen, religion and politics were not separable for Tanaka, but the scale of Tanaka's political vision far exceeded the maneuverings of aristocrats and clerics at court and reached truly global proportions: the *Lotus Sutra* was to be written and read into the world at large. The political application of the *Lotus Sutra* had to be commensurate with the universality of its teaching and the eternality of its buddha, and nothing less than the transformation of the world into a single "bibliocracy," a government of the book, would suffice.

Though claimants of the universal but exclusive truth have often offered themselves as the agents for world harmony and peace, they have managed mostly to leave a trail of discord. They are not aware of what Benjamin Schwartz calls "the ultimate riddle of how the same human beings who are bound to their cultures, to their places in time, to their social strata, and to their personal psychological histories simultaneously allow themselves to believe that their own behavior and outlook can be based on a view of the way things actually are or ought to be."[12] There is a relationship between conviction and contention, and it is therefore not surprising to find the various Nichiren-related groups in conflict with each other, let alone others, over different interpretations of the *Lotus Sutra*. But the arguments and resulting conclusions did not always lead their proponents to increasingly exclusive views of the world, for the debates usually featured one party making a case for a broad interpretation over against their opponents' narrower claims. Nagamatsu Nissen (1817–1890), founder of the Butsuryūkō, officially known as Honmon Butsuryū-shū, argued that the authority to tranfer merit to the dead was not the exclusive privilege of priests, and that lay persons regardless of sex were of equal stature. Helen Hardacre's study of the *Lotus Sutra* in modern Japan describes the importance given to the lay understanding and practice of Buddhism, to the egalitarianism which does not recognize clerical privilege. Democratization, of course, requires an informed constituency, and Nissen developed a unique, multiple-choice method of testing the doctrinal understanding of his members, who could by their performance in tournament-like meetings rise in rank like *sumō* wrestlers and be spurred on to more study.

Ritual power along with understanding was also to be passed on to the people. Hardacre characterizes Kubo Kakutarō (1892–1944), who founded Reiyūkai with his sister-in-law Kotani Kimi (1901–1971), as one who saw that priests were "good for nothing but guarding the bones of the dead." Kubo, like Nissen, regarded the laity as having as much if not more authority in the matter of transferring merit to their deceased ancestors through chanting the *Lotus Sutra*. In order to facilitate this central practice, Reiyūkai developed its own *Blue Sutra*, a selection of passages from the *Lotus Sutra* combined with its own prayers. Placing power and understanding in the hands of the people has its obvious dangers, and the contentiousness that followed conviction split Reiyūkai into two irreconcilable groups. In 1938 Naganuma Myōkō (1899–1957) and Niwano Nikkyō (b. 1906) formed their own group, Risshōkōseikai, after being denounced by Kotani Kimi for their overly analytical use of the *Lotus Sutra*. Too much doctrine, it seemed, could subvert worship.

Doctrine and worship, meaning and ritual, history and mystery, ideology and power, and didactics and aesthetics have all been intertwined in the long and fascinating history of the *Lotus Sutra* in Japanese culture. The meaning of the sutra has been drawn out not only from the stories and language of the text but from its structure as well. The formation of the text spanned several centuries, and the cumulative or modular nature of that process discloses the way in which its interpretive apparatus would continually be upgraded to keep it from ever becoming obsolete. The use of the sutra as ritual object likewise goes back to its formative times and the beginnings of the "cult" which deified the book. But all scriptures are used in varying degrees for intellectual and ritual purposes, and to note the same about the *Lotus Sutra* does not indicate its uniqueness. The uncommon quality of the *Lotus Sutra* lies in the story itself whose protagonists are constantly praising a sermon that is never preached. As such, it can be read, heard, transformed, and applied in a wide variety of ways. Yet this empty text that can be fleshed out as ideas, painted for doctrinal and ritual purposes, sung as poetry, impressed upon a mountain, exchanged for political power, drafted as a blueprint for world conquest, appropriated in the service of a persuasive idea, and revered as the source for an ever-branching stream of new religions is still just one book, a classic whose "influence . . . upon the cultural life of Japan has been so pervasive that it can never be fully described."[13]

This volume of essays makes one attempt at that description.

## NOTES

1. Leon Hurvitz, trans., *Scripture of the Lotus Blossom of the Fine Dharma,* 12.

2. Ibid., 30.

3. Ibid., 47.

4. Studies on the formation and development of the text of the *Lotus Sutra* are myriad. The best collection of essays, which refer as well as make their own contributions to this body of literature, is Kanakura Enshō, ed., *Hoke-kyō no seiritsu to tenkai.* The ways in which the *Lotus Sutra* was related to various aspects of Indian, Chinese, and Japanese society and religion are examined in Sakamoto Yukio, ed., *Hoke-kyō no shisō to bunka.*

5. Whalen W. Lai has noticed the absence of the notion of *dharmakāya* in the *Lotus Sutra* in his study "The Predocetic 'Finite Buddhakāya' in the *Lotus Sutra:* In Search of the Illusive Dharmakāya Therein."

The personal quality of the eternal buddha of the *Lotus Sutra* as opposed to the impersonal *dharmakāya* is the subject of another of Lai's studies, "The Humanity of the Buddha: Is Mahāyāna Docetic?"

6. Comprehensive studies of the ideas of the *Lotus Sutra* can be found in Ōchō

Enichi, ed., *Hokke shisō;* Ōchō Enichi, *Hokke shisō no kenkyū;* and Inari Nissen, *Hoke-kyō ichijō shisō no kenkyū.*

7. See, for example, Tsukamoto Keishō, "Indo shakai to Hoke-kyō no kōshō," in Sakamoto, *Hoke-kyō no shisō to bunka,* 31–66.

8. J. W. de Jong, review of Bunnō Katō, trans., *The Threefold Lotus Sutra,* and Senchū Murano, trans., *The Sutra of the Lotus Flower of the Wonderful Law.*

9. Nomura Yōshō finds a certain limitation in the Tun-huang frescoes because they are confined to the dramatic stories and do not reflect the philosophy of the sutra. See Nomura Yōshō, "Chūgoku bunka to Hokke sango shi no renkan," in Sakamoto, *Hoke-kyō no shisō to bunka,* 97–128. The tendency among scholars to treat Buddhism mostly as a philosophical system rather than as codified myths and stories is pervasive.

10. Gregory Schopen, "The Phrase *'sa pṛthivīpradeśaś caityabhūto bhavet'* in the *Vajracchedikā:* Notes on the Cult of the Book in Mahāyāna."

11. Takagi Yutaka, *Heian jidai Hokke Bukkyō shi kenkyū,* 259–291. See also Yamagami Chusen, *Rekisei Hokke bungaku monogatari.*

12. Benjamin I. Schwartz, *The World of Thought in Ancient China* (Cambridge: Harvard University Press, 1985), 6.

13. John M. Rosenfield et al., *The Courtly Tradition in Japanese Art and Literature,* 45.

# The Meaning of the Formation
# and Structure of the *Lotus Sutra*

SHIOIRI RYŌDŌ

## The *Lotus Sutra* and Japanese Literature

Whenever the *Lotus Sutra* is mentioned, those with absolutely no interest in religion are still able to associate it with the practice of chanting the sutra's title, "Namu Myōhō Renge Kyō," while those with some interest are apt to think of it only as the scripture of the Nichiren sect and its related groups. Those with a fair amount of knowledge and education will have a certain image of Nichiren Shōnin or think of the writer Miyazawa Kenji. The *daimoku,* "Namu Myōhō Renge Kyō," and the *nembutsu,* "Namu Amida Butsu," are often mentioned together in stories and are recognized by most people as the two representative extremes of the Japanese Buddhist faith. It was not all that long ago when it was difficult for a Nichiren follower and a Nembutsu believer to get married in certain parts of Japan. Despite this popular association with Nichiren Buddhism, I would like to address the matter of the formation and structure of the *Lotus Sutra* not simply from the standpoint of the *Lotus Sutra* of the Nichiren sectarian lineage alone, but from the history of the *Lotus Sutra* as it developed and was interpreted in China and Japan.

When we look at Buddhism and Japanese culture, we cannot speak of literature, art, architecture, and crafts—from the national treasures and important cultural objects to aspects of everyday life—apart from Buddhism. It is not only on daily television and its educational programs but also in many magazines, books, and theater performances that we become aware of this. The *Lotus Sutra* has exerted an enormous influence on Japanese culture and life, and it most certainly is not a matter of one sect alone.

Shortly after Buddhism was introduced to Japan, Prince Shōtoku wrote the so-called *Commentaries on the Three Sutras* on the *Vima-lakīrti Sutra,* the *Śrīmālā Sutra,* and the *Lotus Sutra.* In his *Seventeen Article Constitution,* he took the ideas of "revering the three trea-sures" (i.e., Buddhism) and "creating respect on the basis of har-mony" as political principles, and tried to govern the country in the spirit of Buddhism. Many have speculated about the reasons for his choice of these three sutras, and it is said that since the *Vimalakīrti Sutra* explains the philosophy of emptiness and has as its hero the lay believer Vimalakīrti, who was a householder and not a priest, it was suited to Shōtoku's own desire to extend Buddhism beyond the priesthood. The *Śrīmālā Sutra* portrays a woman, Queen Śrīmālā, preaching the sutra with power received from the Buddha, and, it is said, Shōtoku probably had Empress Suiko in mind. As for the *Lotus Sutra,* there is no question that it was a popular sutra even in China at that time, and it is thought that Shōtoku himself understood the sutra as a teaching for all people, since it does not discuss difficult Buddhist doctrines but uses parables and easily understood literary expressions. He praised it indeed as "the source which is the same for all good."

At any rate, in ancient Japanese Buddhism it was considered one of the representative scriptures, and when Emperor Shōmu established provincial temples and nunneries in every province, it was stipulated that the *Lotus Sutra* would be read in the nunneries, which were called "Temples for the Eradication of Sins through the *Lotus,*" even though the sutra does not talk about the eradication of sins. The monasteries were called "Temples for the Protection of the Country by the Four Deva Kings of the Golden Light," based on the *Konkō-myō saishō-ō-kyō* (Sutra of the Sovereign Kings of the Golden Light) and the *Ninnō hannya-kyō* (Wisdom Sutra of the Benevolent Kings). These two sutras together with the *Lotus Sutra* were called the "three sutras for the protection of the country."

In the Heian period appreciation of the *Lotus Sutra* was deeply and extensively rooted among cultured persons of that time. There is, for example, a work containing poems on the *Lotus Sutra* that have been culled from more than 120 poetry collections from the Heian and Kamakura periods. This work, *Kanwa taishō myōhō renge-kyō* (The Chinese and Japanese Lotus Sutra of the Wonderful Law), which includes an appendix containing a glossary of terms and a summary of the sutra, was published in 1914 by Shimaji Daitō, the Jōdo Shin-shū scholar who wrote *Tendai kyōgaku shi* (History of Tendai Doc-trine). It is a Chinese and Japanese translation of the *Lotus Sutra,* although the Japanese translation is not done from the Sanskrit or from Chinese into modern Japanese; instead it gives the readings of the Chinese characters in Japanese word order and pronunciation, which allows for the general meaning to be grasped even though the technical terms are left in Chinese. In these more than 120 poetry collections, the number of poems that have something of the *Lotus Sutra* in their titles alone exceeds 1,360. Since the total number of poems in the selected collections has not been counted, no percentage can be given, and we cannot speak with certainty as to how they compare with the number of poems on Amida and the Pure Land, the teaching of which was popular in the middle to late Heian period. But it would still seem that the poems on the *Lotus Sutra* were exceedingly plentiful.

The poems on the *Lotus Sutra* traditionally begin with one ascribed to the priest Gyōgi (668–749):

| | |
|---|---|
| Hoke kyō o | For collecting firewood, |
| Waga eshi koto wa | Gathering herbs, |
| Takigi kori | And carrying water, |
| Na tsuke mizu kumi | My reward is |
| Tsukaete zo eshi. | The *Lotus Sutra.* |

This poem is based on the story from the "Devadatta" chapter in which the Buddha recalls a time in one of his earlier existences when a seer expounded the *Lotus Sutra* to him and thus caused him to offer fruits, firewood, water, and meals in return. Gyōgi's poem is made up of this one passage alone, but later poems on the *Lotus* were often written in sets based on the chapters or fascicles of the sutra.

The *Lotus Sutra*, as indicated on the covers of the texts which have been handed down, is made up of twenty-eight *shō* (sections), or to use the Buddhist technical term, *hon* (chapters). In Fujiwara Arikuni's *San Hoke-kyō nijūhachi bon kajō* (Introduction to Poems in Praise of the Lotus Sutra in Twenty-eight Chapters), poems were not simply written about the *Lotus Sutra* in general but dealt with the content of each chapter individually. Here we can see the degree to which the *Lotus Sutra* had become popular. There is also the Buddhist practice of the Eight Lectures on the *Lotus Sutra (Hokke hakkō),* in which lectures were given on each of the eight fascicles. Ever since Saichō (767–822), also known as Dengyō Daishi, first performed a *hakkō* on Mt. Hiei, the lectures were carried out not only at Enryakuji but at many temples in Nara and Kyoto, and the cultured people who participated and sought merit in those events came to compose *shakkyōka* (poems on the teachings of the Buddha) in which themes relating to the *Lotus Sutra* appeared. Those who do not use the *Lotus Sutra,* including Buddhist specialists who can consult Oda's Buddhist dictionary, will find difficult terms in these poem titles, the sources of which they will not know. For instance, it is easy enough to know the meaning of the phrases "everyone will become a buddha in the future" and "in the long night we engaged in the practice of emptiness," but on the question of the derivation of those passages, it is not readily apparent that they come from chapter 6, "Bestowal of Prophecy," and chapter 4, "Belief and Understanding." Furthermore, without a knowledge of the larger meaning of the passage from chapter 14, "Comfortable Conduct," which says, "In countless realms it is not possible to hear the name" of the *Lotus Sutra,* the following poem (from *Shokukokinshū*) bearing this sutra passage as its title could not have been written:

| | |
|---|---|
| Na o danimo | How can we make |
| Kikanu minori o | Promises to keep |
| Tamotsu made | The teaching |
| Ikade ka chigiri o | Whose name |
| Musubi okiken | We have not heard? |

There are innumerable other examples that illustrate the impossibility of using such terms in poetic compositions without considerable understanding of the sutra. There is a detailed study of the poetry on the *Lotus Sutra* in Takagi Yutaka's chapter titled "Hoke-kyō waka to hōmon no uta" (Poems on the Lotus Sutra and Doctrinal Poetry) in his *Heian jidai hokke Bukkyō shi kenkyū* (Studies in the History of Lotus Buddhism in the Heian Period), and I recommend this work to those who are interested. According to his statistics concerning 1,457 *Lotus* poems categorized by period, 22 percent are from the Heian period, 35 percent from the Kamakura period, 23 percent from the Muromachi period, and slightly less than 17 percent from the Edo period. In these figures we can see how the *Lotus Sutra* has been deeply imbedded in Japanese culture throughout its history.

Emperor Goshirakawa (1127–1192) compiled a poetry collection, the *Ryōjin hishō,* which contains 220 poems on Buddhism, of which 115 are on the *Lotus Sutra.* It is said that the emperor learned the then popular *imayō* songs from a certain Otsumae, a *shirabyōshi*— that is, a courtesan who danced and sang. When Otsumae was ill, he read the *Lotus Sutra* and prayed for her recovery, and it is reported that he copied a thousand *Lotus Sutras* until the first anniversary of her death. It is natural that this sutra should be so prevalent in songs and poems, and we can see what a strong influence it has had upon the arts.

That even the content of the *Lotus Sutra* was understood by Heian aristocrats is evidenced by the following facts. (In speaking of "aristocrats," I am referring not to a special upper class, but to the supporters of culture, those whom we would now call cultured or educated.) In *The Tale of Genji* there is a scene called "critical evaluations on a rainy night" in which Genji and his friends evaluate the qualities of women; this scene is an interpretive application of ideas manifested in the structure of the *Lotus Sutra,* which I shall describe later. The evaluation was carried out according to the notion of the "three rounds of preaching," which today would be described as general discussion, parable, and experiential analysis. Another example is the incident in the *Pillow Book of Sei Shōnagon* in which Sei Shōnagon wants to take leave of a sermon for some sudden reason and asks for her ox cart to be brought to the exit. A certain aristocrat then says to her that she should not become one of the "five thousand who withdrew." Such a passage indicates that the content of the *Lotus Sutra*—in this case the incident in which five thousand haughty disciples, who had no need to hear the Buddha's preaching of the *Lotus Sutra,* got up and left the assembly—had worked itself into everyday life.

In the mid-Heian period the Pure Land belief centered on Amida became quite popular, and in *Nihon ōjō gokuraku ki* (An Account of Japanese Reborn in Paradise) by Yoshishige no Yasutane (934?–997) there are many legends patterned after examples of the Chinese Buddhists considered to have been reborn in the Pure Land paradise. Eshin Sōzu (Genshin, 942–1017), a priest of Mt. Hiei, is famous for writing *Ōjōyōshū* (Essentials for Rebirth), in which he describes paradise and hell in detail and speaks of loathing the defilements of this world and desiring rebirth in paradise. In a certain sense it could be said that he perfected the Pure Land teaching on Mt. Hiei. Those who gathered around these two men heard lectures on the *Lotus Sutra,* wrote poems based on phrases from the sutra, and made the recitation of the *nembutsu* their central practice. Recitations of the *Lotus Sutra* and the name of Amida coexisted without the slightest contradiction. When I was asked by Professor Inoue Mitsusada to annotate the *Ōjōden* (Biographies of Rebirth) and the *Hokke genki*

(Miraculous Tales of the Lotus Sutra) for the Iwanami series on Japanese thought, I spent nearly a year at this task and was keenly aware of the compatibility of the two practices as I became intimate with the biographies of those reborn. The *Ōjōden* is a collection of biographies of forty-five Buddhists, beginning with Shōtoku Taishi; of the thirty-five who are said to have gained rebirth in paradise, seven are explicitly described as believers in the *Lotus Sutra*. The number can be extended to ten if we include those who I think were believers or practitioners of the *Lotus Sutra* even though there is no explicit reference to this. In a text where only three people are said to have practiced esoteric Buddhism apart from their Pure Land belief and only two were adherents of other sutras, we can see the extent to which the *Lotus Sutra* was preferred.

Following upon the *Nihon Ōjō gokuraku ki* was the *Dai Nippon goku Hoke-kyō genki* (Miraculous Tales of the Lotus Sutra in Japan) attributed to the Hiei monk Chingen, who compiled it from 1040 to 1044 in three fascicles. It contains the names of 129 *Lotus* believers, of whom 46 also recited the *nembutsu* and prayed for rebirth in paradise. Thus the *Lotus Sutra* and the Pure Land teaching coexisted together. Of the 42 biographies in *Zoku honchō ōjō den* (Biographies of Rebirth in Japan Continued) compiled by Ōe Masafusa, who completed it in 1104, ten were of those who believed in and practiced the *Lotus Sutra*, while in Miyoshi Tameyasu's *Shūi ōjō den* (Collected Biographies of Rebirth), completed in 1111, 36 of 94 were *Lotus* practitioners, as were 27 of 142 in his supplement *Goshūi ōjō den* (Collected Biographies of Rebirth Continued), completed in 1139. By the twelfth century, then, the *Lotus Sutra* and the Pure Land teaching coexisted in those who sought rebirth in the Western Paradise and believed in the *Lotus,* recited the *Lotus Sutra,* and performed the *Lotus* rite of repentance—in later times it would be said, "In the morning, the *daimoku;* in the evening, the *nembutsu.*" Or rather we should say that the *Lotus Sutra* and the Pure Land teaching were totally interfused without any contradiction whatsoever. Since the intellectual class which created and supported Japanese culture of that time was greatly influenced by the Buddhism of Mt. Hiei, and since Saichō, who established Mt. Hiei, referred to his sect as the "Tendai Lotus Sect" and the "Sect of Lotus Perfection" and vowed to establish a Buddhism in the spirit of the *Lotus Sutra* for the salvation of all Japanese people, it is natural that the *Lotus Sutra* should have penetrated deeply into the intellectual class and that Mt. Hiei, for good or ill, had a great influence.

I have dwelt upon the place that the *Lotus Sutra* has occupied particularly in Japanese literature, for this serves as a kind of introduction to my present topic, "The Meaning of the Formation and Structure of the *Lotus Sutra.*" Just as the formation and structure of the *Lotus Sutra* itself was the result of expansion and adaptation of a core text, Japanese culture took hold of the essence of what the *Lotus Sutra* intends, expressed it skillfully in Japanese literature, and provided examples of how it became a guide for living. In a certain sense it is the universality of the *Lotus Sutra* of which I speak. In concrete terms, I might say that my conclusion is that the Buddhism which takes on many different forms and beliefs irrespective of sect and relative value, and the Buddhism which has absolute significance despite these relative values are interchangeable with each other, and the expression of this conclusion can be seen in Japanese culture.

It is a well-known fact that the *Kannon Sutra,* which is recited now without regard for sect, is a part of the *Lotus Sutra.* Later I would like to touch upon the relationship between the *Lotus Sutra* and Amida Buddha, and upon the belief in Kannon (Avalokiteśvara) which appears in the *Kegon Sutra,* the *Larger Amida Sutra,* the *Meditation Sutra,* and other sutras, and came to be included in the *Lotus Sutra* in the process of its development.

Earlier I briefly mentioned Shōtoku Taishi, Dengyō Daishi, and the *Lotus Sutra.* The founder of Kōyasan, Kūkai (Kōbō Daishi, 774–835), in his work *Jūjūshin ron* (The Ten Stages of Mind), which classifies all Buddhist teachings into ten stages of profundity, says that the sublime and profound meaning of the *Lotus Sutra,* even though it is placed at the eighth level, is the same as that of the tenth and highest teaching of the Shingon school. Dōgen (1200–1253), who cited the *Lotus Sutra* extensively in his principal work, *Shōbōgenzō* (The Storehouse of the True Law), included a chapter in it called "The Lotus Turning the Lotus," in which he says, "If the mind is deluded, it is being turned by the lotus; when it is enlightened, it turns the lotus." By this he is saying that it is dangerous to understand the *Lotus Sutra* merely by grasping the outward meaning of the words. Other sectarian founders in Japan also regarded the *Lotus Sutra* highly, and there are Jōdo Shinshū scholars who think that even Shinran (1173–1262), who did not cite the *Lotus Sutra* at all in his works, based his idea of "conversion by the three vows" on the *Lotus Sutra.* What, then, is the spirit of the *Lotus Sutra,* which has had such an extensive influence on Japanese Buddhism and Japanese culture? I do not plan on dealing with the entirety of the *Lotus Sutra* in this short essay, but I do wish to examine the central spirit by which it related itself not only to other forms of Buddhism but to many aspects of culture as well.

## The Development of Sutras

Whenever the word "sutra" is mentioned in Buddhism, we think of the preaching of Śākyamuni, who was born in India some two thousand years ago and became the Buddha through his awakening to the eternal and universal truth. In fact almost all sutras begin with the words *nyoze gamon* or *mon nyoze*—"Thus have I heard from the Buddha." The "I" in this case refers to Ānanda, the disciple who memorized Śākyamuni's sermons and transmitted them during the assemblies convened after the Buddha's death by five hundred qualified disciples for the compilation of the sutras. Following this opening phrase, Śākyamuni then preaches the dharma to his many disciples gathered at certain times and places. This pattern is common to every sutra, and the names of the monks and lay people who listened to the sermons are often included, though their types and numbers differ with each sutra. These are the characteristics by which we recognize a sutra.

In this way, what we call sutras have come to be understood as the discourses which Śākyamuni preached throughout his life. With the advent of Mahāyāna Buddhism, the earlier form of Buddhism was pejoratively called Hīnayāna, the "lesser vehicle." Although there were those who claimed that the Mahāyāna sutras, which reacted against the Buddhism steeped in the stream of the Hīnayāna followers, were not the teachings of Śākyamuni, there were many who passed on Mahāyāna Buddhism as the preaching of Śākyamuni. When Buddhism entered China, the ideas and beliefs of Indian Buddhism were very difficult for the Chinese to understand, and because it was seen as a heretical foreign religion, the Indian scriptures were translated into Chinese by making use of native Chinese ideas and values. Sutras filled with a combination of Buddhism and completely new Chinese ideas were produced. By correlating the five constant virtues of benevolence, righteousness, propriety, knowledge, and sincerity with the five precepts of Buddhism, and by including the substance of filial conduct, sutras which were amenable to the Chinese sensibility appeared. Of course Chinese Buddhists also summarized the essentials of the sutras, wrote commentaries on the sutras, and expressed their understanding of Buddhism in various other ways. The result was the gradual sinification of Buddhism. Moreover, although certain sutras were clearly composed in China, they were still believed to be the preaching of Śākyamuni and reached Japan as such.

During the Edo period, however, Tominaga Nakamoto (1715–1746), a Confucian scholar in Osaka, came up with the theory of textual accretions in his work *Shitsujō kōgo* (Post-meditation Words). According to this theory, the sutras emerged after historically passing through different stages. Sutras developed as different theories were added to supercede a certain set of ideas. Buddhist scriptures, he explained, developed with the addition of the wisdom texts to the Hīnayāna compilation of the canon consisting of sutras, precepts and treatises, and to these prior ideas were added those of the *Lotus, Kegon, Nirvāṇa,* and esoteric scriptures. It is foolish, he said, for Buddhists to think that all the teachings came straight from the golden mouth of Śākyamuni. Nakamoto was clearly a scholar enriched by the modern critical spirit, and after the introduction of western learning, his accomplishment was greatly appreciated. Later Confucian and National Learning scholars shared this attitude, and the famous scholar Hirata Atsutane (1776–1843) wrote a work titled *Shitsujō shōgo* (Post-meditation Words of Laughter) in which he criticized Buddhism with expressions bordering on the abusive. Since the Meiji period Japanese Buddhist scholars have studied abroad in the West and have researched the Pali and Sanskrit texts; it is now common knowledge among Buddhists that in the *Āgamas,* which were passed down as the direct teachings of Śākyamuni, only a small part actually transmit teachings from Śākyamuni's own time, usually in the form of poetic hymns suitable for chanting. It is also believed that the composition of the texts as sutras dates from around the time of the beginning of the Christian era.

Thus the *Lotus Sutra,* as the preceding discussion indicates, was not preached by Śākyamuni himself and is thought to have resulted from gradual accretions made from about the first century B.C. Perhaps it is due to the relative clarity of these layers that in comparison to other sutras many studies of the formation of this sutra have been carried out.

## Studies of the Formation of the *Lotus Sutra*

I will not mention here the names of each researcher, but studies have shown that the ancient manuscripts of the *Lotus Sutra* in Sanskrit written in India from the fifth to the tenth centuries and the Sanskrit

*Lotus Sutra* pieced together from the many fragments which have been found are fairly complete as far as the content of the *Lotus Sutra* in current use is concerned. On the basis of these studies, it is said by scholars that the originals used for the translation of the *Lotus Sutra* into Chinese had already been developed by A.D. 150 or 220. However, as I shall indicate, even with the Chinese translations, there are several problems to be resolved if one holds to the view that the texts were completed within a single time period. It is said that several additions were made to the original corpus of the *Lotus Sutra,* which as a whole is therefore referred to as the "augmented *Lotus Sutra*" or "sutra of added sections." There are even scholars who say that up to seven additions were made to the Sanskrit texts after that. In regard to the *Lotus Sutra* translated in China, it is thought that the basic form of the text without these incremental additions was set roughly by A.D. 200, but the present state of research into the history of the formation of the *Lotus Sutra* is such that there are many scholars who divide this basic text into three sections based on both the content and the formation of the text. The extent to which these technicalities have obtruded into this discussion is perhaps regrettable, but on the basis of this research the earliest form of the *Lotus Sutra* has been identified, and in it the spirit which makes such addition and expansion possible inheres fiercely, or rather I might say that such a spirit is at the very heart of the *Lotus Sutra.* The exploration of the form of this spirit as reflected in the text is what I mean by the title of this essay.

Among the sutras in use by Buddhists today are some that were transmitted more than two thousand years ago. Even the newer ones, according to modern research in the history of the formation of sutras, developed more than a thousand and several hundred years ago. Since that time, they have taken on many different forms depending on the groups or doctrinal factions that transmitted them. In the oral traditions and manuscript copies of even the same scripture, the titles and contents manifestly differ. That there should be different Chinese words used by different translators of one and the same scripture is all the more to be expected. We cannot say that the Chinese words of the so-called sutras chanted today are the only words absolutely acceptable. Those who believe in the Pure Land teaching in Japan today, or the sects which base themselves on the Pure Land teaching, are divided into subsects. Specifically the Jōdo Sect, which claims to be a single school established on a fundamental teaching, is divided into groups such as the Seizan-ha, Zenrinji-ha, and the Fukakusa-ha. In the case of the Jōdo Shinshū Sect, there is not only the division made by the Tokugawa shogunate into the Higashi Honganji (Jōdo Shinshū Ōtani-ha) and Nishi Honganji (Jōdo Shinshū Honganji-ha), but also ten additional subsects such as the Bukkōji-ha, Kibe-ha, and Senshūji-ha. Furthermore there are the Yūzū Nembutsu Sect and the Ji Sect, and all these groups together comprise a large part of Japanese Pure Land belief. Traditionally there are twelve translations of the *Wu-liang-shou-ching* (J. *Muryō-ju-kyō*), which is one of the three Pure Land texts forming the basis of all such groups. Since the establishment of the Pure Land teaching in China, the translation by Seng-k'ai of the T'ang period has come to be used; however, there are also the *Ta o-mi-t'o-ching (Dai Amida-kyō)* by Chih-ch'ien of the Wu period, the *Wu-liang ch'ing-ching p'ing-teng chiao-ching (Muryō shōjō byōdō gakkyō)* by Chih-lou Chia-ch'an of the Later Han period, the *Wu-liang-shou ju-lai hui (Muryōju nyorai-e)* by Bodhiruci of the T'ang period, and the *Wu-liang-shou chuang-yen-ching (Muryōju shōgongyō)* by Fa-hsien of the Sung period. It is further said that twenty-eight versions of the Sanskrit text have been found, and there has yet to be a commonly accepted explanation of the relationship between these originals and the Chinese translations. The situation with other sutras is the same. Even the very short *Heart Sutra* containing 262 Chinese characters, which is a classic Buddhist text recited widely, exists in six Chinese versions. This condition is one of the reasons the Buddhist canon can boast of a magnitude unmatched by the scriptures of other religions.

In the case of the *Lotus Sutra,* six Chinese translations—three extant and three extinct—are traditionally spoken of, and they are listed in chart 1 along with the important Sanskrit texts. What I would like to address here is the matter of whether or not the "Apparition of the Jeweled Stupa" and the "Devadatta" chapters in both the Sanskrit texts and the Chinese translations were separate additions or whether they were continuous with the rest of the text. The answer will provide a clue to the development of the *Lotus Sutra.*

As can be seen in chart 2, the "Daibadatta" (Devadatta) chapter is listed as item 12 in the column for the present-day text, while in the *Shō Hokke-kyō* column that position is occupied by the "Shichi Hōtō" chapter. The *Shō Hokke-kyō* thus is composed of twenty-seven chapters. The "Daibadatta" chapter consists of the stories of Deva-datta, who opposed Śākyamuni, and Śākyamuni's assurance that the dragon king's daughter will become a buddha in the future. The *Sa-*

### CHART 1

Chinese translations
1. Cheng fa-hua-ching (Shō Hokke-kyō). Translated by Dharmarakṣa in 286. 10 fascicles, 27 chapters. *"Daibadatta"* chapter missing; continuous from *"Hōtō"* chapter.
2. Miao-fa lien-hua-ching (Myōhō renge-kyō). Translated by Kumārajīva in 406. 7 fascicles, 27 chapters. *"Daibadatta"* chapter missing; continuous from *"Hōtō"* chapter.
3. T'ien-p'in miao-fa lien-hua-ching (Tembon myōhō renge-kyō). Translated by Jñānagupta and Dharmagupta in 601. 7 fascicles, 28 chapters. *"Daibadatta"* chapter included.

Sanskrit texts
1. Nepalese texts. Complete. 8th century and later. *"Hōtō"* and *"Daibadatta"* chapters continuous.
2. Central Asian texts. Fragments. 5th to 7th centuries.
   a. Kashgar text (Petrofsky text). Nearly complete. *"Hōtō"* and *"Daibadatta"* chapters included.
   b. Khotanese text. Several fragments. Some texts with *"Hōtō"* and *"Daibadatta"* chapters included.
   c. Khadalik text. Fragment. *"Hōtō"* chapter missing. *"Daibadatta"* and *"Kanji"* chapters continuous.
3. Gilgit text (Kashmir). Three fourths extant. *"Hōtō"* and *"Daibadatta"* chapters continuous.

*t'an fen-t'o-li-ching* listed in chart 2 as item E was an independent translation of this material, and it is now thought that this was added to the original text of the *Lotus*. In the early period when the *Lotus Sutra* was translated in China, this chapter and the *gāthā* from chapter 25, "Kanzeon fumon" (Universal Gate of Avalokiteśvara)—the well-known *gāthā* of the *Kannon Sutra,* as that chapter is called—were not in the text, and this caused many problems from that time on. As mentioned earlier, this was a time when it was believed that a sutra was entirely the preaching of Śākyamuni, and therefore the legend arose that while the *gāthā* was originally in the text, a courtier in Ch'ang-an had excised and hidden it. When the *T'ien-p'in miao-fa lien-hua-ching* (item 3 in chart 1) appeared, the materials listed in chart 2 as item C, the later half of the "Yakusōyu" (Medicinal Herbs) chapter, and as item D, the first half of the "Gohyaku deshi" (Receipt of Prophecy by Five Hundred Disciples) chapter and the first half of the "Hosshi" (Preachers of Dharma) chapter, along with the Devadatta material were included in the "Hōtō" (Apparition of the Jeweled Stupa) chapter. The *gāthā* of the *Kannon Sutra* was also added at this time. This is what was said in the seventh century. It was also said at that time that there were many versions of the original

Chinese translations, and it is in consideration of those "subsequent sections" that present-day research has made progress in our knowledge of the history of the text's formation. What this means, to put it succinctly, is that the Chinese translations of the sutras which everyone recites today are most certainly not absolute entities transmitted without error from Śākyamuni.

## The *Lotus Sutra* in Twenty-eight Chapters

Having surmised that there were accretions to the text, we might now ask about the earliest form of the *Lotus Sutra* and proceed to the question of why these additions were made several times over to expand the text. Let us consider what we may call the structure or formation of the *Lotus Sutra* as set forth in chart 2.

The Chinese text of the *Lotus Sutra* which is in use in Japan today contains twenty-eight chapters in eight fascicles as indicated in column 1. The term *p'in* (J. *hon*) refers to chapters, and is a translation of the Sanskrit *varga,* which means the same part or section. In all the sutras this word has been translated by the Chinese term *p'in.* The term *chüan* (J. *kan*), usually translated as "fascicle" and sometimes as "volume," derives from the time when paper had not yet been developed in China and bamboo sticks on which writings were made were rolled into bundles. Even after people started to write on paper, they rolled the paper into scrolls and each scroll comprised what would now be called a fascicle. At any rate, the *Lotus Sutra* in use today is said to have been translated by Kumārajīva, but it is not the one from his time which had twenty-seven chapters in seven fascicles. The current version which has twenty-eight chapters in eight fascicles contains a section added from the *Tembon Hoke-kyō* (The Lotus Sutra with an Added Chapter), and this is the one in common use in Chinese and Japanese Buddhism.

I would like to give a simple introduction to the history of the formation of the *Lotus Sutra* with a concern for discovering its earliest form. As indicated in column 4, the sutra can be divided into three sections, the first and second sections being the earliest layers; the third section, as is commonly held by many scholars today, represents the additions made later to expand the sutra. By A.D. 150–220, the text was completed. The items labeled C through E in column 4 are in the *Shō Hokke-kyō* (translated in 286), while item F is in the *Tembon Hoke-kyō,* and item G is in the Sanskrit and Tibetan manu-

# CHART 2

| Fascicle | Current *Lotus* Chapter | Kumārajīva's Translation | Shō Hokke-kyō | Formation of the Text |
|---|---|---|---|---|
| 1 | 1. Jo | 1. Jo | 1. Kōzui | |
| | 2. Hōben | 2. Hoben | 2. Zengon | |
| 2 | 3. Hiyu | 3. Hiyu | 3.Ōji | |
| | 4. Shinge | 4. Shinge | 4. Shinraku | A. Latter half of Hiyu |
| 3 | 5. Yakusōyu | 5. Yakusōyu | 5. Yakusō | C. Latter half of Yakusōyu |
| | 6. Juki | 6. Juki | 6. Ju shomon ketsu | |
| | 7. Kejōyu | 7. Kejōyu | 7. Ōko | |
| 4 | 8. Gohyaku deshi | 8. Gohyaku deshi | 8. Ju gohyaku deshi | D. First half of Gohyaku |
| | 9. Ninki | 9. Ninki | 9. Ju Anan | |
| | 10. Hosshi | 10. Hosshi | 10. Yakuō nyorai | D. First half of Hosshi |
| | 11. Hōtō | 11. Hōtō | 11. Shichi Hōtō | |
| 5 | 12. Daibadatta | | " | E. Sa-t'an fen-t'o-li ching |
| | 13. Kanji | 12. Kanji | 12. Kansetsu | |
| | 14. Anrakugyō | 13. Anrakugyō | 13. Angyō | |
| | 15. Yujutsu | 14. Yujutsu | 14. Yujutsu | |
| 6 | 16. Juryō | 15. Juryō | 15. Genju | |
| | 17. Fumbetsu kudoku | 16. Fumbetsu kudoku | 16. Gofukuji | |
| | 18. Zuiki kudoku | 17. Zuiki kudoku | 17. Kanjo | |
| | 19. Hosshi kudoku | 18. Hosshi kudoku | 18. Tan hosshi | |
| 7 | 20. Jōfukyō | 19. Jōfukyō | 19. Jo hikyōman | |
| | 21. Jinriki | 20. Jinriki | 20. Jinsokugyō | |
| | 22. Zokurui | 21. Zokurui | | |
| | 23. Yakuō | 22. Yakuō | 21. Yakuō | B. Section 3 prose |
| | 24. Myōon | 23. Myōon | 22. Myōku | |
| 8 | 25. Fumon | 24. Fumon | 23. Fumon | G. *Gāthā* on Amida (Sanskrit & Tibetan texts) |
| | 26. Darani | 25. Darani | 24. Sōji | F. *Gāthā* |
| | 27. Shōgon | 26. Shōgon | 25. Jōfukujo ō | |
| | 28. Fugen | 27. Fugen | 26. Raku Fugen | |
| | | | 27. Zokurui | |

**Formation of the Text — dating / sections (vertical text):**

SECTION 1 — Verse 100 B.C. (F); Prose 50 B.C. (F), A.D. 40 (N), A.D. 50 (T)

SECTION 2 — A.D. 100 (F), A.D. 220 (N)

SECTION 3 — A.D. 150 (F)

(N) = Nakamura Hajime
(T) = Tamura Yoshirō
(F) = Fuse Hirotaka

scripts. I think that by the sixth and seventh centuries, all of these were basically completed.

The reason the first two sections are said to be the oldest is because chapter 22, "Zokurui hon," is not at the end of the sutra but in the middle. This chapter is the last one in all the translations except for Kumārajīva's version, and this had been a point of contention even in China. *Zokurui* (transmission) was also rendered as *fuzoku* (attachment), and in the Japanese translation of the Sanskrit text, it is translated as *i'nin* (entrustment). It means to confer or place the teaching in the care of another, and in the term *zoku* there is the sense of troubling or encumbering someone. The translation also includes the notion that an extraordinary effort will be required to propagate this sutra after the death of Śākyamuni, and in almost all the sutras, it was customary to place such a charge at the end of the text. Since only Kumārajīva's translation has "Zokurui" located within the text, it must have been that chapters 23 on were added to the sutra which until then had ended with "Zokurui." The placement of this chapter at the end of the other Chinese and Sanskrit texts probably means that after the additional chapters were included, this chapter was relocated to the end.

As is evident from looking at the titles, chapters 23 to 28 deal with specific beliefs and practices which were added to the *Lotus Sutra*. Chapter 23 is about the strict practice of the bodhisattva Medicine King (Yakuō Bosatsu), who, in a previous life, had made an offering to the Sun-Moon-Pure-Bright-Virtue Buddha and the *Lotus Sutra* by burning his arms. This offering involving the abandonment of one's own life, that is, the practice of self-immolation, was attached to the *Lotus Sutra*. In chapter 24, the bodhisattva Fine Sound (Myō-on Bosatsu) practices sixteen kinds of *sammai*, which is the transliteration of *samādhi*, and is therefore translated as meditation *(meisō)*. That his mind is now totally concentrated without any distraction is the result of his having made an offering in a previous existence of hundreds of thousands of kinds of music to the cloud thunder king. He is able to preach the *Lotus Sutra* to all sentient beings by transforming himself into various manifestations, thirty-four in all, such as Brahma, Śakra, a lay person, a prime minister, a *brāhmana*, a monk, a nun, a householder, a wife, a god, a dragon, a *yakṣa*, and so forth. With the statement that 84,000 sentient beings were able thereby to obtain the *samādhi* by which one can be transformed into any other form of being, reference is made to similar materials in the previous chapter. Chapter 25, "Kanzeon fumon bon" (Universal

Gate of Avalokiteśvara), contains the famous story of Kannon's thirty-three transformations through which he saves sentient beings, and this characteristic is shared in common with Myō-on Bosatsu. The belief that by being "mindful of the power of Kannon"—that is, by reciting the name of Kannon, people will be able to escape the seven misfortunes caused by fire, flood, wind, weapons, demons, punishments, and thieves; or the three poisons of greed, anger, and stupidity—is a belief which appears in many sutras. In the *Lotus Sutra* this belief is combined with the figure of Śākyamuni and the Many-treasured or Jeweled stupa. In chapter 26, "Darani hon," the virtue of reciting various *dhāraṇī* is linked with the *Lotus Sutra,* which says that those who propagate the sutra will be protected by the power of *dhāraṇī.* The objective of this chapter is the propagation of the sutra. Chapter 27, "Myō shōgon ō honji hon" (The Former Affairs of the King Fine Adornment), tells how King Fine Adornment, who was a believer in a non-Buddhist religion, was led to have faith in the *Lotus Sutra* through the practices of his two sons, Pure Storehouse and Pure Eyes. The two sons were really the Medicine King (Yakuō) and the Superior Medicine (Yakujō) bodhisattvas, and beliefs about them were thus attached to the *Lotus Sutra.* Chapter 28, "Fugen Bosatsu kambotsu hon" (The Encouragements of the Bodhisattva Samantabhadra), combines belief in Fugen with faith in the *Lotus Sutra.* Those who accept the *Lotus Sutra* in the evil age after the death of the Buddha will be protected, and Fugen will appear on a six-tusked white elephant before those who recite the sutra and meditate on it. Evil spirits will not be able to take hold of them, and Fugen will cause many people to obtain benefits and joy.

The beliefs found in chapters 23 to 28 were current in the Buddhist world of that time, and they were skillfully integrated into the *Lotus Sutra* by being set in the context of what came before and after in the text. It is with an open mind that we observe that these beliefs had no direct relationship to the earliest form of the *Lotus Sutra,* which I shall describe in a moment, and that these beliefs and stories were inserted in order to popularize the *Lotus Sutra* and proclaim its superiority. Even in the second section of the sutra, there are materials which are thought to have been added for the sake of propagating the sutra, and it is from the approach of this kind of research into the formation of the *Lotus Sutra* that we can search for its original form. It is precisely because there was this idea that an original form can assimilate various other beliefs that all these beliefs were added in turn. The existence in China of a twenty-ninth chapter, *Miao-fa lien-hua-ching tu liang t'ien-ti p'in ti erh-shih-chiu* (The Spread of the Lotus Sutra in the Heavens and on Earth) indicates the possibility of understanding the fundamental character of the *Lotus Sutra* as being one which theoretically allows the sutra to be expanded infinitely.

## The Original *Lotus Sutra*

There is a broad consensus among scholars that the later part of the *Lotus Sutra* from the "Zokurui" chapter on—that is, the third section (column 2 of chart 3)—was added to the first and second sections, which have been called the older layers or the early sections by scholars. This occurred while the early sections, comprised of the first twenty chapters up to chapter 21 ("Nyorai jinriki hon") with the exception of chapter 12 ("Daibadatta"), were in circulation. However, even the older layers did not develop all at once, and many scholars have divided them into earlier and later parts, even though the question of exactly where the line should be drawn has been a problem. Since there is contextual coherence in section 1 from the second ("Hōben bon") to the ninth ("Jugaku mugaku ninki hon") chapters, I regard this material as the original form of the *Lotus Sutra*. Later, chapters 10 ("Hosshi hon") through 21 ("Nyorai jinriki hon"), which were written as a single group with the exception of chapter 18 ("Zuiki kudoku hon"), which most scholars agree was inserted into this group, were added to section 1, and then the introduction was composed to tie both sections together. This is the theory that I hold to. There are many technical details that are problematic, but I shall overlook them since I would only compound the confusion by speaking of those complexities here. It is in chapter 10 ("Hosshi") that we first see the value placed on copying the sutra, and this can therefore be considered a development occurring after the time when the sutra, which until then had been orally transmitted, was written on leaves of the *tāla* tree. Furthermore, if I may speak very simply about the characteristics of section 2, chapter 10 and subsequent chapters emphasize the command to propagate the *Lotus Sutra* in society as opposed to the predictions given in section 1 out the future attainment of buddhahood by the disciples. In contrast to the disciples and pratyekabuddhas to whom Śākyamuni preaches in section 1, it is the bodhisattvas who comprise the audience in section 2, as they

# CHART 3

| Current *Lotus* | History of Formation | Tao-sheng | Fa-yün | Chih-i |
|---|---|---|---|---|
| 1. Jo hon | | Int. ⎤ — Three causes constituting a single cause | Int. ⎤ — Clarification of cause | Int. ⎤ |
| 2. Hōben bon | Section 1 | Correct tenets | Correct tenets | Correct tenets |
| 3. Hiyu hon | | | | |
| 4. Shinge hon | | | | |
| 5. Yakusōyu hon | | | | Secondary gate (*shakumon*) |
| 6. Juki hon | | | Meaning of cause | |
| 7. Kejōyu hon | | | | |
| 8. Gohyaku deshi juki hon | | | | |
| 9. Jugaku mugaku ninki hon | | | | |
| 10. Hosshi hon | | Propagation | | Propagation |
| 11. Ken hōtō hon | | | | |
| 12. Daibadatta hon | | | | |
| 13. Kanji hon | | | | |
| 14. Anryakugyō hon | | | | |
| 15. Jūji yujutsu hon | Section 2 | Int. ten. ⎤ — Three effects = a single effect | | Int. ten. ⎤ — Cor. |
| 16. Nyorai juryō hon | | Cor. ⎤ | | |
| 17. Fumbetsu kudoku hon | | Int. ten. Propagation | | |
| 18. Zuiki kudoku hon | | | | Propagation — Primary gate (*hommon*) |
| 19. Hosshi kudoku hon | | | Meaning of effect | Propagation after Buddha's death |
| 20. Jōfukyō Bosatsu hon | | | | |
| 21. Nyorai jinriki hon | | | | |
| 22. Zokurui hon | | | Propagation | Transmission of propagation |
| 23. Yakuō Bosatsu honji hon | Section 3 | Clarifying the propagators | | Propagation |
| 24. Myōon Bosatsu hon | | | | |
| 25. Kanzeon Bosatsu fumon bon | | | | |
| 26. Darani hon | | | | |
| 27. Myōshōgon ō honji hon | | | | |
| 28. Fugen Bosatsu kambotsu hon | | | | |

do in the introduction as well, and the central concern is the actualization of the teaching—in other words, how to practice and transmit the spirit of the *Lotus Sutra* as contained in the original form of section 1. There are, then, distinctions that can be made between sections 1 and 2 based on historical developments and changing concerns.

Other changes can be noted. According to studies of the formation of the *Lotus Sutra,* the poetic materials in section 1, which are called "hymns and praises," were written about 100 B.C. while the prose and expository materials, which are called "long lines," were composed by A.D. 40–50. The sutras were transmitted through oral recitation, as I have mentioned, and it goes without saying that it was easier to recite poetry back then just as it is easier to memorize a text now by singing it as a song. That the hymns and praises were written first is common to all the sutras. Later the poetic and prose sections were interwoven together in what appears now as a single text.

Despite the problems and complexities uncovered by specialized studies on the formation of the text, the broad outlines I have indicated are clearly discernible. It is possible to grasp the central idea of the sutra without having to consider which sections were earlier or later. Traditionally, of course, there was little interest in the history of the text. Studies and commentaries on the Chinese translations of sutras were produced shortly after the transmission of Buddhism to China, and Buddhists in China and Japan relied only on those Chinese translations without realizing that each text had undergone its own course of development, since they believed that the sutras were the actual preachings of the Buddha. Even today the sutras are appropriated and understood as single compilations. Having grasped the contents of the sutras through their studies, and believing in their respective readings of the sutras, various groups and subsects have developed whose tenets and ideas remain totally oblivious to the critical studies of the formation of the sutras. Nevertheless, the reason I have dealt with the history of the formation of the sutra at some length is because a strange coincidence can be observed between these modern studies and the traditional understanding of the *Lotus Sutra* held by Chinese Buddhists, who had no concern whatsoever with the history of the text's formation. By considering both the results of modern textual research and the traditional interpretations, we can pursue the central idea of the sutra more objectively and convincingly.

# Chinese Buddhism and The Original Section of the *Lotus Sutra*

In column 3 of chart 3 is a diagram of the *Miao-fa lien-hua-ching-su,* the oldest commentary on the *Lotus Sutra* in China, written by Tao-sheng, who was a disciple of Kumārajīva, the second translator of the *Lotus Sutra.* Tao-sheng is counted among the Four Philosophers, and it is known that he helped his master with the translation. The next oldest commentary (chart 3, column 4) which is still extant is *Miao-fa lien-hua-ching i-chi* by Fa-yün of Kuang-chai Temple, and it was this commentary that Shōtoku Taishi took as his model for his *Hoke-kyō gishō.* After that there was the *Fa-hua wen-chü,* written by T'ien-t'ai Chih-i, the founder of the T'ien-t'ai school, who reconstituted Indian Buddhism into the forms of Chinese Buddhism and is respected as the systematizer of Chinese Buddhism (chart 3, column 5). These three masters divided the text into categories that made it easy to understand the entire structure of the sutra through key phrases indicating the contents of each section, with each section itself being subdivided into detailed categories ranging from the larger to the smaller. When we compare their textual divisions with column 2 showing the formation of the text, we can discern the points at which they are similar even without knowing the phrases and their contents. First of all, we notice that all three masters divided the entire sutra into first and second halves: Tao-sheng's "three causes constituting a single cause" and "three effects constituting a single effect," Fa-yün's "meaning of cause" and "meaning of effect," and Chih-i's "secondary gate" *(shakumon)* and "primary gate" *(hommon).* On the next level below those main divisions are three further categories: the introductions, sections on correct tenets, and sections on propagation. All three masters regarded the section on propagation in the second half of the sutra as consisting of the material from chapter 18, "Zuiki kudoku hon," to the end of the sutra, covering sections 2 and 3 in the history of the formation of the text. Even this division between sections 2 and 3 generally accords with the division made by Chih-i between chapters 18 to 20 ("propagation after the Buddha's death") and chapters 22 to 28 ("transmission of the propagation"), with chapter 21 being skipped over.

Furthermore, section 2 in the history of the formation of the text covers the propagation part in the first half of the sutra and the introductory, correct tenets, and propagation parts of the second half as defined by Tao-sheng and Chih-i. The propagation part explains the method for disseminating the sutra in the future, and there is a propagation part for the first half as well as one for section 2 following its own "correct tenets," which form the central teaching that developed after section 1. Since the distinction is made only between the *merits* of propagation and the *transmission* of the propagation (according to Chih-i), we might force a comparison and think of them as being more or less common sections. If such a statement is too rash I will retract it, but what I would like to emphasize here is that no matter what complexities exist for the latter sections, the first section consisting of chapters 2 ("Hōben bon") through 9 ("Ninki hon") enjoys an integrity established by a consensus of all the Chinese commentators and modern researchers.

We can cite still another example of a commentator who held to the integrity of chapters 2 through 9. When the question arose among the disciples of the T'ang master Hsüan-tsang of whether or not all living beings possess the buddha nature, some insisted that there was a special group of people called *icchantika* who do not have the buddha nature. This idea of the Fa-hsiang (Hossō) School is contrary to the T'ien-t'ai view, but even the founder of that school, Tz'u-en (K'uei-chi, 632–682), who probably knew the Sanskrit version of the *Lotus Sutra,* agreed with Chih-i in setting up two divisions of the text: the correct tenets consisting of chapters 2 through 9, and the propagation part consisting of the rest of the sutra. To cite this example is to corroborate the appropriateness of considering the integrity of these chapters as a unit.

The idea of cause and effect, that is, of primary and secondary causes along with effects and retributions, permeates Buddhism, but its main intent is to assert the nonduality of cause and effect. In regard to the *Lotus Sutra,* Tao-sheng and Fa-yün provisionally distinguished between cause and effect, and Chih-i made a division between primary and secondary causes, but he always insisted on the nonduality of primary and secondary. However, when we think of this in ordinary terms, cause is prior and effect is subsequent, and this is obvious for the moment. As applied to the *Lotus Sutra,* we might think momentarily of the ideas of the first half as causes leading to the effect of practice in one's later years, and this means that section 1 as seen in the history of the formation of the text coincides with the section of correct tenets under the category of causes in the classification systems. Chih-i's "secondary gate" stands in contrast to the eternality and universality of the Buddha, who is a transhistorical reality of the "primary gate" of the latter half of the sutra, and is an expression from the standpoint of Śākyamuni, who manifested himself in the world. Insofar as the conclusion of this idea of the "second-ary gate" portends the universal and eternal aspects of the Buddha, the "secondary gate" forms the starting point for that teaching. In the eternality of the Buddha and the eternal Śākyamuni are the beliefs and ideas which, in a certain sense, may be called the life of the *Lotus Sutra*. At any rate, what I would like to emphasize here is that section 1 according to the modern view of the history of the for-mation of the text corresponds to the section of "correct tenets" according to the traditional analysis of the content and structure of the text.

## Summary

Both the traditional commentators and modern researchers base their conclusions on analyses of the structure of the text. Despite the many differences among all of them, there is a striking similarity in some of the major divisions observed in the text of the sutra. There is thus a common recognition that the sutra, considered in terms of its content as well as its historical development, consists of parts which are diverse and therefore distinguishable, but which are still capable of being related to each other as parts of a whole. From earlier to later, from secondary to primary, and from correct tenets to propagation, there is a constant process involving greater expansion of the structure of the text, its meaning, and its functions. Both the structure and the meaning of the text imply that the essential quality of the *Lotus Sutra* is that, having absorbed widely, it can be applied—infinitely, it would seem—to a great many aspects of culture.

TRANSLATED BY GEORGE J. TANABE, JR.

# The Ideas of the *Lotus Sutra*

TAMURA YOSHIRŌ

## Genesis of the *Lotus Sutra*

The *Lotus Sutra (Saddharma-puṇḍarīka-sūtra)*, one of the major Mahāyāna sutras, has been revered as a scripture for all people regardless of sect. To understand why this is so, it is necessary to go back to the origins of Buddhism itself. Around 500 B.C. the historical Buddha, Śākyamuni, founded Buddhism in India. After his death his teachings were compiled and several primitive sutras were formed by 250 B.C. However, disputes arose over which of the primitive sutras should be accorded the greatest importance, and this caused the opposing groups to split into schools and sects. By 100 B.C. there were as many as twenty schools and sects. The central figures in this sectarian Buddhism, also known as Abhidharma Buddhism, were professional priests. They undertook profound research and wrote many treatises interpreting Śākyamuni's teachings and the sutras, but they became such specialists that gradually they became dedicated to monasticism and removed themselves from the reality of everyday life. Then, around the beginning of the Christian Era, lay Buddhists active in the real world set about to reform Buddhism. This was the origin of Mahāyāna or "great vehicle" Buddhism.

Those who advocated the reform of Buddhism called their Buddhism the great vehicle leading to the truth and criticized existing Buddhism by calling it Hīnayāna, or Buddhism of the "small vehicle." It was believed that there were two types of Hīnayāna Buddhists: śrāvakas and pratyekabuddhas, comprising the so-called two vehicles of Buddhism. The term *śrāvaka* refers to one who attains enlightenment through hearing the voice of the Buddha, while a *pratyekabuddha* is one who attains enlightenment by his own effort in apprehending the impermanence of nature and human life. In contrast to these two vehicles, the Mahāyāna Buddhists held to the one vehicle of the bodhisattvas. A bodhisattva is a living being *(sattva)* who brings the truth of enlightenment *(bodhi)* to the world and strives to help others attain it in the real world. Actually, it refers to those Mahāyāna Buddhists who practice their religion diligently in the secular world.

What criticisms did the creators of Mahāyāna Buddhism voice against established Buddhism? They were concerned with two points: one had to do with the structure of the Buddhist order—that is, the community of monks—and the other had to do with doctrinal content. They felt that the structure of the order leaned toward monasticism, becoming isolated from the real world. In regard to doctrine, they believed that two-vehicle Buddhism misinterpreted the fundamental truth of *śūnyatā,* or emptiness, by conceiving of a return to nothingness and death as the final nirvana. Mahāyāna Buddhists, focusing their criticism on these two points, aspired to reform the Buddhist establishment. Their criticisms were particularly focused on those who interpreted *śūnyatā* in a nihilistic way, and their denunciations went so far as to suggest that those who had slid into such a view could not attain buddhahood.

The favored meeting grounds of the Mahāyāna Buddhists were stupas which enshrined relics of Śākyamuni and *caityas*—pagodas that were depositories for sutras—rather than monasteries or temples. In these places they strove to elucidate the true meaning of *śūnyatā* by drawing upon the core of reality in actual life. They incorporated this understanding in new compilations of sutras, and this was the origin of the Mahāyāna sutras.

The primitive portion of the *Perfection of Wisdom* sutras *(Prajñā-pāramitā-sūtra)* was first formulated about A.D. 50. The *Perfection of Wisdom* sutras strive to lay bare the fundamental truth of *śūnyatā* from the standpoint of Mahāyāna Buddhism. For example, the *Perfection of Wisdom Sutra in Twenty-Five Thousand Lines (Pañcavimśati-sāhasrikā-prajñāpāramitā-sūtra)* explains that emptiness is not reached by the negation of matter, for matter is emptiness and emptiness is matter. What this means is that emptiness is the real aspect of matter, or to put it differently, emptiness is what matter truly is. Therefore, matter comes into existence through emptiness. In short, emptiness is the basis of existence and is therefore the fundamental truth that brings matter into being. The Indian Mahāyāna scholar Nāgārjuna (ca. 150–250), who attempted to systematize the doctrine of emptiness, wrote, in his *Treatise on the Middle (Madhyamaka-śāstra),* "Where there is *śūnyatā,* there is matter. Where *śūnyatā* does not exist, nothing exists." Later in China the term which in Japanese is pronounced *shinkū-myōu*, "true emptiness is wonderful existence," was introduced.

The formation of the *Lotus Sutra* and the primitive portion of the *Flower Garland Sutra (Avataṃsaka-sūtra)* followed the *Perfection of Wisdom* sutras. The *Lotus Sutra* and *Flower Garland Sutra* elaborated the positive aspect of *śūnyatā* to ensure that emptiness would not be misunderstood as nothingness. Furthermore, they maintained that emptiness really meant selflessness—that is, individuals possess no independent or fixed nature. However, since we tend nevertheless to be preoccupied with the image of the self and cling to things, such graspings are the causes of illusion.

The attempt to elucidate the positive or correct meaning of emptiness is made by clearing away illusions. Both attachment to the self and attachment to things other than the self are exposed, leaving only a realization of the nonsubstantiality or emptiness of self and other. "Emptiness of self" means the relinquishment of attachment to the self and seeing things as they really are. "Emptiness of the other" means regaining the self that was lost through attachment to other things. These notions are found in two important Chinese translations of the *Lotus Sutra:* the *Sutra of the Lotus of the True Law (Cheng-fa-hua-ching),* translated by Dharmarakṣa in 286, and the *Sutra of the Lotus Flower of the Wonderful Law (Miao-fa lien-hua-ching),* translated by Kumārajīva in 406. The *Sutra of the Lotus of the True Law* interprets emptiness of self as "naturalness," and the *Sutra of the Lotus Flower of the Wonderful Law* explains it as "the real state" of all things. As for "emptiness of the other," the *Sutra of the Lotus of the True Law* interprets it as freedom or "unrestriction," while the *Sutra of the Lotus Flower of the Wonderful Law* explains it as "naturalness." The meaning of emptiness is to be found by letting things be natural and observing their real state; at the same time this produces a detachment toward things which is the freedom of the self. In short, emptiness is the fundamental principle that vitalizes things and the self. Thus the *Lotus Sutra* reflects a positive meaning of emptiness.

## Teachings of the *Lotus Sutra*

It is believed that the *Lotus Sutra* was completed in its present form around A.D. 50–150. However, chapter 12, "Devadatta," was probably added about the time of T'ien-t'ai Chih-i (538–597), the great patriarch of the T'ien-t'ai school of Buddhism. Thus the sutra originally contained twenty-seven chapters, exclusive of the "Devadatta" chapter. Once the *Lotus Sutra* was taken to China, complete or partial translations of it were undertaken repeatedly. It is said that there were six complete translations, and of these six, three are extant and three have been lost. The surviving three are the ten-fascicle, twenty-seven-chapter *Sutra of the Lotus of the True Law,* translated by Dharmarakṣa in 286; the seven-fascicle, twenty-seven-chapter (later eight-fascicle, twenty-eight-chapter) *Sutra of the Lotus Flower of the Wonderful Law,* translated by Kumārajīva in 406; and the seven-fascicle, twenty-seven-chapter *T'ien-p'in miao-fa lien-hua-ching,* translated by Jñānagupta and Dharmagupta in 601. This last is a revision of the translation made by Kumārajīva. The translation by Dharmarakṣa is very difficult to understand, and there are many places where it cannot be deciphered even now, but Kumārajīva's version is an excellent translation in elegant prose. Consequently, the *Sutra of the Lotus Flower of the Wonderful Law* has remained popular to this day. The conceptual features of the *Lotus Sutra* set forth in this version are elaborated in various directions from the positive meaning of the truth of emptiness that we have just discussed. In later generations, the *Lotus Sutra* was classified and characterized further on the basis of expanded ideas.

Kumārajīva worked on his Chinese version of the *Lotus Sutra* with his disciples and exchanged ideas with them as they translated. As they produced the translation they also wrote commentaries on the sutra in which they classified and characterized it. The *Commentary on the Lotus Sutra (Miao-fa lien-hua-ching-su),* written by one of Kumārajīva's disciples, Tao-sheng (d. 434), is the oldest extant commentary. In this commentary Tao-sheng makes a division between chapter 14, "Comfortable Conduct," and chapter 15, "Welling Up out of the Earth," and thus divides the sutra into two realms: the realm of cause and the realm of effect. This became the traditional division. Chih-i followed this division, but he defined the first half of the sutra as the realm of traces and the latter half as the realm of origin. He also observed that the first half, centered on chapter 2, "Expedient Devices," explains the wonderful law as the one vehicle, while the second half, centered on chapter 16, "Lifespan of the Tathāgata," elucidates the eternal life of Śākyamuni. These two concepts, the wonderful law as the one vehicle and the eternal life of Śākyamuni, are the central features of the *Lotus Sutra.* This division and characterization by Chih-i have been accepted to this day.

Because of their importance, these two major features deserve further comment. Śākyamuni, as a result of observing the real state of all existence, discovered that everything is permeated by the law *(dharma)* that governs it. In turn, there are individual laws that govern all things and phenomena, yet the various laws are not separate; they are one, united at the base, forming a unifying law. For example, the law of the mind and the law of the body are not two laws but are basically one. As we can all observe, one's mental attitude affects one's body and the state of one's body affects one's mind. This principle does not pertain just to the mind and the body: all things are linked at the base, forming one law. With regard to the laws that govern things, it is explained that the unifying law is the foundation of the various laws. The wonderful law as the one vehicle emphasized in chapter 2, "Expedient Devices," reveals this unifying law, which can be called the unifying truth of the universe. This truth is the positive expression of the truth (or law) of emptiness.

Thus the *Lotus Sutra* reveals the unifying truth, the wonderful law as the one vehicle, and at the same time teaches people to embrace faith in the wonderful law as the one vehicle and the unifying truth, unhindered by the various laws. Conversely speaking, the various laws are sustained by the wonderful law as the one vehicle. Thus, with reference to the laws of the mind and the body, the truly correct treatment for a sick body is achieved by comprehending the unifying law. The *Lotus Sutra* explains that, through faith in the wonderful law as the one vehicle, even those so-called two-vehicle Buddhists who misunderstood emptiness as nothingness and fell into nihilism can attain buddhahood, just like Mahāyāna bodhisattvas. The idea is that the three vehicles—śrāvaka, pratyekabuddha, and bodhisattva—are received equally and are united in the wonderful law as the one vehicle. In other words, the wonderful law as the one vehicle is the great unifying law of the universe that animates everyone and everything equally.

The idea of the whole universe being unified under the wonderful law as the one vehicle, which is portrayed in the *Lotus Sutra* as a vision, was developed further. Kumārajīva translated this concept as "the real state of all things." It can also be expressed as the real state of the universe. Drawing on the concept of the real state of the universe, Chih-i systematized the teaching of the "three thousand realms in one mind," and the Japanese priest Nichiren (1222–1282) depicted the ten realms of being in the form of a mandala. The teaching of the "three thousand realms in one mind" explains that the realm of the microcosm (one mind) and the realm of the macro-cosm (three thousand realms) are interdependent and one in their true state, forming a harmonious whole under the wonderful law as the one vehicle. The mandala of the ten realms of being illustrates diagramatically the existences of various beings in the universe divided into ten realms from hell to the world of the buddhas unified under the wonderful law as the one vehicle. One modern-day believer in the *Lotus Sutra,* Miyazawa Kenji (1896–1932), made the following appeal in his *Nōmin geijutsu gairon kōyō* (Introduction to the Farmer's Art):

> First of all,
> Let us all become sparkling, minute bits of dust
> And scatter in all directions in the sky.

He urged a commitment of self to the infinite universe through the *Lotus Sutra.*

The second half of the *Lotus Sutra,* which focuses on the eternal life of Śākyamuni as explained in chapter 16, "Lifespan of the Tathā-gata," states that Śākyamuni has actually been a buddha since the eternal past and emphasizes that the historical Śākyamuni was the physical manifestation of the eternal Śākyamuni in our world. In other words, Śākyamuni is originally eternal (the eternal original Buddha) and is based on the eternal truth *(dharma),* but he appeared in India to save sentient beings and then returned to the original world of eternal existence after performing that task. The historical Śākyamuni, who was born in India and died at the age of eighty, was not simply a being who was born and died, but a manifestation of the eternal Śākyamuni in this world.

Three explanations can be offered for this claim that Śākyamuni is the eternal Buddha. The first is that it was necessary to unify the vari-ous buddhas. The history of the worship of the Buddha indicates that the followers of Śākyamuni not only revered his relics but yearned for his presence after his disappearance from this world. Gradually they sought other buddhas as substitutes for Śākyamuni, and various bud-dhas came into being. The *Lotus Sutra* was intended to unify the vari-ous buddhas and various laws, and the sutra presents the eternal Śākyamuni as the unifying Buddha. It is explained in the *Lotus Sutra* that the various buddhas are emanations of the eternal Śākyamuni, and they are united in the eternal Buddha. Secondly, eternal exis-tence is seen wherever the unifying truth exists. In other words, the wonderful law as the one vehicle, the unifying truth of the universe, is not merely a law of nature but an eternal, personal, vital, and vibrant reality permeating all of life and living. Thirdly, the rhythm of eternal existence is perceived through the activity of practice in the real world. The historical Śākyamuni indicates this aspect precisely. In fact, the "Lifespan of the Tathāgata" chapter explains that the eternal Buddha, Śākyamuni himself, has been engaged in bodhisattva practices endlessly.

This third explanation can be viewed in the context of the history of the formation of the original text of the *Lotus Sutra*. When the circumstances of the compilation of the original *Lotus Sutra* are examined, an additional division can be put forward in contrast to the traditional division of the sutra into two realms. Although it overlaps the traditional second realm, the group of chapters from 10, "Preachers of the Dharma," through 22, "Entrustment," can be referred to as the third realm. Nichiren called this third realm *daisan hōmon*, meaning the third sphere of Śākyamuni's teaching. The teachings in this realm of the *Lotus Sutra* emphasize the need to endure the trials of life and to practice the true law. In short, they advocate human activity in the real world, or bodhisattva practices. The eternal Buddha is also considered anew in this context, and it is said that Śākyamuni himself endlessly undertook bodhisattva practices. This third realm emphasizing bodhisattva practices suggests the meaning and purpose of human existence in this world.

For instance, chapter 10, "Preachers of the Dharma," praises those who carry on the Buddha's work by receiving and transmitting even one sentence of the law as Tathāgata-apostles sent by the Buddha to save sentient beings. The latter part of the chapter exhorts the faithful to enter into the Tathāgata's abode, wear the Tathāgata's robe, sit on the Tathāgata's throne, and preach the law without fear. The Tathāgata's abode, robe, and throne correspond to mercy, forbearance, and emptiness. It means to be kind and compassionate to others, not to bear ill will against the world but to endure it, to rely on emptiness, and to be free from attachments. These are the criteria for bodhisattva practices in the real world, and in later times they came to be revered as the three criteria for propagation of the sutra.

Chapter 11, "Apparition of the Jeweled Stupa," relates that the stupa in which the Tathāgata Prabhūtaratna (Abundant Treasures) sat rose into the sky and Śākyamuni moved from the earth to the precious stupa in the sky, seating himself next to Prabhūtaratna. Almost simultaneously, buddhas who had emanated from Śākyamuni gathered from all directions, returning to Śākyamuni, and as they did so, all their worlds were united, becoming the world of the one Buddha. This has been interpreted to mean that the Tathāgata Prabhūtaratna was the past manifestation of Śākyamuni and that Śākyamuni's taking his seat beside him symbolizes that Śākyamuni has been a buddha eternally. In other words, Śākyamuni is the eternal Buddha, and the return of the buddhas and the unification of their worlds in the world of the one Buddha are expressions of Śākyamuni as the "unifying Buddha." Thus the "Apparition of the Jeweled Stupa" chapter has been interpreted as a preliminary statement of the theme of chapter 16, the eternal life of the Tathāgata. Both chapters, however, advocate bodhisattva practices and activities in this *sahā* world of the decay of the law, and expound entrusting the law to bodhisattvas. This being the case, the concepts of the precious stupa rising up, the gathering of buddhas who are emanations of the eternal Buddha, and the united world of the one Buddha should be understood as expressions from the standpoint of advocacy of bodhisattva practices.

Chapter 13, "Fortitude," also advocates the propagation of the Buddhist teaching in this evil world, emphasizing the practice of endurance and the martyrdom of bodhisattvas entrusted with that mission. "Welling Up out of the Earth," chapter 15, relates that a group of bodhisattvas, headed by the bodhisattvas Eminent Conduct, Boundless Conduct, Pure Conduct, and Steadfast Conduct, sprang up out of the earth. As the original disciples of the Buddha, and having succeeded him, they are entrusted with the mission of disseminating the law.

As mentioned earlier, "Lifespan of the Tathāgata," chapter 16, has been viewed traditionally as clarifying the eternal existence of Śākyamuni. In other words, since the statement in the preceding chapter that the numerous bodhisattvas who sprang up out of the earth were the original disciples of Śākyamuni led to questions about how it could be that there were so many disciples of Śākyamuni when it had been only a short time since he had attained enlightenment and become the Buddha, this chapter explains that Śākyamuni had actually become the Buddha in the past and infinite time had elapsed since then. It is further explained that Śākyamuni had gone through endless bodhisattva practices. Therefore, this chapter can also be considered in the context of the third realm which emphasizes bodhisattva practices.

Chapters 17 through 19 extol the merits of those who strive to do good works and dedicate themselves to the wonderful law as the one vehicle and to the eternal Śākyamuni. Chapter 20, "The Bodhisattva Never Disparaging," relates the tale of the bodhisattva Sadāparibhūta as a model of bodhisattva practice. Although he was persecuted in an earlier age of the decline of the law, Sadāparibhūta, believing in humankind's goodness, did not despise anyone, prayed for the attainment of buddhahood by all, and revered everyone he met. Honoring other human beings is thus shown to be an example of bodhisattva practice.

In chapter 21, "The Supernatural Powers of the Tathāgata," the Buddha, after mentioning the example of Sadāparibhūta, entrusts the law to the bodhisattva Eminent Conduct and other bodhisattvas who spring up out of the earth, imparting both words of praise and encouragement of their future practice and activities. In the following chapter, "Entrustment," the law is entrusted to all other bodhisattvas, and those entrusted with the law vow to accomplish the Buddha's mission. Thus the entrusting of the Buddha's mission to bodhisattvas is complete. The precious stupa in the sky returns to its original location, the assembled buddhas who emanated from Śākyamuni return to their own lands, and the bodhisattvas come back to the reality of this world. Here the curtain is drawn on the third realm.

On the basis of traditional analysis and an understanding of the historical evolution of the text, the central ideas of the *Lotus Sutra* can be said to encompass three elements: the law *(dharma),* the perfect being (buddha), and human beings (bodhisattvas); or truth, life, and practice. In other words, the unifying truth of the universe (the wonderful law as the one vehicle), eternal life (the eternal Śākyamuni), and human activities in the real world (bodhisattva practices) are the corresponding themes of the first realm of traces, the second realm of origin, and the third realm. These are the three great ideas of the *Lotus Sutra.* They also form the true essence of Mahāyāna Buddhism, and it is no exaggeration to say that the three treasures of Mahāyāna Buddhism were established by the *Lotus Sutra,* which is why since ancient times all Mahāyāna Buddhists have revered and extolled this sutra, regardless of sect.

## Faith in the *Lotus Sutra*

From India to Japan, the *Lotus Sutra* has been revered and extolled for its richness of secondary teachings in addition to its central ideas. The excellent translation by Kumārajīva also contributed to the popularity of this sutra in China and Japan. In India, people took notice of the idea of the wonderful law as the one vehicle, which characterizes the realm of traces in the *Lotus Sutra*. It appears that the Indian interest in a realm of universals led them to accept the idea of the wonderful law as the one vehicle as a testament of universal equality, and thus to revere the *Lotus Sutra*. A few early Indian writings can be cited in support of this view. In his *Treatise on the Great Perfection of Wisdom Sutra (Mahāprajñāpāramitā-upadeśa)*, Nāgārjuna commented that the *Lotus Sutra* is superior to the *Great Perfection of Wisdom Sutra* because it expounds the truth that even śrāvakas and pratyekabuddhas can attain buddahood equally through the one vehicle. Commentaries written during the fourth and fifth centuries, such as the *Treatise on Mahāyāna Buddhism* by Sālamati and the *Commentary on the Lotus Sutra (Saddharma-puṇḍarīka-śāstra)* by Vasubandhu (fourth or fifth century), focus on the same point. The latter work in particular emphasizes that equal truth (equal vehicles), equal worlds (equal societies), and equal existences (equal bodies) are expounded in the *Lotus Sutra*. The *Sutra of the Great Extinction (Mahāparinirvāṇa-sūtra)*, which was compiled in the fourth century, maintains that all sentient beings, having an innate buddha nature, can attain buddhahood equally; but the *Sutra of the Great Extinction* itself states that this idea came from the *Lotus Sutra*.

During the fifth or sixth century in China, with the translations of various sutras into Chinese by Kumārajīva and others, efforts were made to rank all the sutras according to the merits of their contents in order to assert the superiority of one or another sect. At this time, the *Lotus Sutra* was defined as the sutra that preaches the unifying truth. T'ien-t'ai Chih-i, accepting this definition, assigned the *Lotus Sutra* the highest position among all sutras and formulated his *Lotus* philosophy. Chih-i's immediate intent was to integrate the various ideas of Buddhism through the teachings of the *Lotus Sutra*, which elucidates the unifying truth, and to settle any arguments over the merits of various Buddhist theories and doctrines. The founding of a unified view of Buddhism led to the establishment of a unified view of the world and life that is plainly expressed in the teaching of the "three thousand realms in one mind" and in the idea that human beings are born with both good and evil natures.

Chih-i's understanding of the unifying truth of the *Lotus Sutra* as a synthesis of the microcosm (one mind) and the macrocosm (three thousand realms), good and evil, and ideals and reality is related to the general attitude in China that laid stress on the actual world. On this point, it differs in nuance from the reverence of the *Lotus Sutra* found in India, where the wonderful law as the one vehicle was viewed as the truth of an undifferentiated, universal equality. Chih-i's thinking on emptiness is a clear manifestation of this difference. Chih-i's logic of emptiness is based on the three concepts of emptiness, transience, and the middle. The first concept indicates the attainment of the state of emptiness by abandoning attachment to actuality (or transience, *chia* in Chinese). The second concept, which is the reverse of the first, means that one should not remain in the state of emptiness but should return once again to actuality and live correctly in the real world. In the first concept, transience is denied and emptiness is established, but in the second concept emptiness is denied and actuality is revived. The third concept concludes that emptiness must not be forgotten even after returning to actuality or transience; it is the middle path that unifies emptiness and transience. The second concept, returning from emptiness to actuality, reflects the Chinese stress on ordinary reality. These three concepts were expounded in the *Sutra on the Bodhisattva's Original Action (P'u-sa ying-lo pen-yeh-ching),* which was compiled in China in about the fifth century. Chih-i used ideas from the *Lotus Sutra* to add new flesh to and systematize these concepts.

Chih-i's thoughts on the *Lotus Sutra* resulted in the books referred to as the "Three Great Volumes on the *Lotus Sutra*" or the "Three Great Volumes of T'ien-t'ai": the *Textual Commentary on the Lotus Sutra (Miao-fa lien-hua-ching wen-chü,* 587), the *Profound Meaning of the Lotus Sutra (Miao-fa lien-hua-ching hsüan-i,* 593), and the *Great Concentration and Insight (Mo-ho chih-kuan,* 594). The *Textual Commentary on the Lotus Sutra* is an annotation of the sutra, the *Profound Meaning of the Lotus Sutra* explains the principles of the sutra, and the *Great Concentration and Insight* expounds the practices based on the sutra.

After Chih-i's time, the three great books became guides for all who revered the *Lotus Sutra.* They were studied extensively and expositions on them were written in China and Japan by commentators from various schools. However, Chih-i's were not the only commentaries on the *Lotus Sutra;* many were written both before and after his time. In addition to the *Commentary on the Lotus Sutra* by Tao-sheng, extant works include *Commentary on the Lotus Sutra (Miao-fa lien-hua-ching i-chi)* by Fa-yün (467–529) of Kuang-chai Temple; *Commentary on the Lotus Sutra (Miao-fa lien-hua-ching i-su), Treatise on the Profound Meaning of the Lotus Sutra (Fa-hua-ching*

*hsüan-lun), Synopsis of the Lotus Sutra (Fa-hua-ching t'ung-lüeh),*
and *Elucidation of the Meaning of the Lotus Sutra (Fa-hua-ching yu-i)* by Chi-tsang (549–623); and *Eulogy on the Profound Meaning of the Lotus Sutra (Miao-fa lien-hua-ching hsüan-tsan)* by K'uei Chi (632–682).

In 538 a Buddhist image and some sutras were brought to Japan by an envoy of King Songmong of the Korean kingdom of Paekche. This was the official introduction of Buddhism to Japan. Following this, the importation of Buddhist sutras and treatises and the exchange of Buddhist priests with Korea and China became extensive. Most of the Mahāyāna and Hīnayāna sutras reached Japan during the Nara period (645–794), and the doctrines of various schools were studied. These included the Sanron, Hossō, Jōjitsu, Kusha, Ritsu, and Kegon schools, which are known collectively as the Six Nara Sects; but the T'ien-t'ai Lotus teaching, esoteric Buddhism, the Pure Land invocation, and Zen were also introduced to Japan about that time, and they too were studied and revered.

Prince Shōtoku (574–622) was the first Japanese to undertake the writing of commentaries on the *Lotus Sutra.* As regent to Empress Suiko, the Prince devoted his energy to strengthening Japan. He adopted Buddhism as the mainstay of the nation, and he himself studied it. He attached special importance to the *Lotus Sutra,* the *Śrīmālā Sutra (Śrīmālādevī-siṁhanāda-sūtra),* and the *Vimalakīrti Sutra (Vimalakīrti-nirdeśa-sūtra),* giving lectures and writing commentaries on them. Shōtoku's commentaries on these three sutras are called *Sangyō gisho,* or *Commentaries on the Three Sutras,* and a copy of the *Commentary on the Lotus Sutra (Hokke gisho)* in the Prince's own handwriting is still extant. Many of the facts of Prince Shōtoku's life have been disputed and need further research, but he can be said to have been the first Japanese to have devoted himself to the *Lotus Sutra.* His interpretation of the *Lotus Sutra* shows elements unique to Japan and is good material for comparing Japanese and Chinese ways of thinking. For example, although he referred to the *Commentary on the Lotus Sutra* by Fa-yün of Kuang-chai Temple, Shōtoku altered its interpretation, rejecting some parts of it while adopting others in light of a view that can be regarded as a more Japanese approach to the affirmation of reality. Shōtoku was aware of his differences from the Chinese view and indicated his changes by writing, "My interpretation differs slightly," or "I do not adopt this here."

In Japan the *Lotus Sutra* produced a faith that placed great value not only on the ordinary world but on ordinary understanding as well. For instance, various stories and allegories of rich literary quality, such as the seven parables, were held in high esteem by the Japanese and were incorporated into literary works and depicted in pictorial art. Merits of faith that are emphasized in various parts of the *Lotus Sutra,* particularly in the chapters following chapter 23, were enthusiastically valued and were included in religious observances by ordinary people who sought benefits in this world.

Early in the Heian period (794–1185), the priest Saichō (767–822) systematized the *Lotus* doctrines anew and established the Tendai Lotus sect in Japan. His accomplishments equaled those of Chih-i in China. Saichō's influence extended into various fields in Japan, and his headquarters on Mt. Hiei gradually became a seminary for the Lotus priesthood. It was a Lotus academy that produced many talented men. Hōnen (1133–1212), Shinran (1173–1262), Dōgen (1200–1253), and Nichiren (1222–1282) all studied on Mt. Hiei at one time or another. Dōgen and Nichiren, in particular, espoused the *Lotus Sutra* as their spiritual support. Dōgen, the founder of the Sōtō Zen sect, quoted extensively from the *Lotus Sutra* in his great *Shōbō-genzō* (The Storehouse of the True Law.) It has been said that when he was seriously ill and close to death, Dōgen paced around his room chanting passages from chapter 21, "The Supernatural Powers of the Tathāgata": "In a garden or in a grove . . . on these [spots] the buddhas [enter] *parinirvāṇa.*" He wrote these passages on the pillars of his room as he finished chanting and named the room the "Lotus Sutra Hermitage."

Although it is well known that Nichiren established the Nichiren sect based on the *Lotus Sutra,* it should be noted that he was the first to emphasize the third realm, which stresses the need to practice the true law and endure life's trials. The repeated sufferings of Nichiren, such as his exile to Izu at age forty and his exile to Sado at age fifty, became turning points and helped him to understand the third realm of the *Lotus Sutra.* He compared himself to the bodhisattva martyrs mentioned in the sutra. In particular, he compared himself to the bodhisattva Eminent Conduct and other bodhisattvas who sprang up from the earth. Surviving writings from Nichiren's days of exile in Izu show that he started to quote from the third realm of the *Lotus Sutra* at that time, and this led to the development of ideas that are unique to Nichiren.

Nichiren's ideas about the *Lotus Sutra* were taken up by his followers and this brought about the birth of the organized Nichiren sect.

The influence of Nichiren's ideas on the general public during the
Muromachi period (1334–1568) may be seen in the fact that many of
Kyoto's *machishū,* or townsfolk, became followers of the Nichiren
sect. The *machishū,* who rose from Kyoto's autonomous guilds, fos-
tered what could be called the Lotus *machishū* culture. Some of the
Nichiren adherents were upperclass townsmen who acquired great
wealth and became leaders of the *machishū.* The Hon'ami family,
famous in the fields of the fine and decorative arts, and the Chaya
family, which was engaged in foreign trade, are representative of this
class.

When Nichiren temples in Kyoto were attacked by the monks from
Mt. Hiei during the seventh month of the fifth year of Temmon
(1536), the *machishū* took the lead in defending the temples. This
episode ended with the defeat of the followers of the Nichiren sect.
Twenty-one Nichiren temples were destroyed by fire, and the priests
took refuge at their subtemples or other temples in Sakai and Osaka
with which they had connections. It was estimated that tens of thousands of Nichiren Buddhists lost their lives, and the Nichiren Lotus
faith in Kyoto stood on the brink of ruin. However, when permission
to rebuild the temples of those priests who had taken refuge in Sakai
was granted in the eleventh year of Temmon (1542), the Lotus
*machishū* played a central role in rebuilding Kyoto, and commerce,
industry, the arts, and literature once again thrived under their aegis.

What, then, were the bonds between the *machishū* of Kyoto and
the Nichiren sect? It could be that the spirit of positive accommoda-
tion with and vigorous cultivation of reality seen in Nichiren's idea of
the *Lotus Sutra* concurred with the interest of the *machishū* in working for profit.

Thus the culture of the Lotus *machishū* which originated in the
Muromachi period quickly revived itself after a temporary interrup-
tion and was succeeded by the arts and literature of the Momoyama
(1568–1615) and Edo (1615–1868) periods. It is interesting to note
that through the late Edo period many of the most famous artists and
literati were supporters of the Nichiren Lotus sect. In the field of
painting there were such people as Kanō Motonobu (1476–1559),
Hasegawa Tōhaku (1539–1610), Kanō Tan'yū (1602–1674), Hishi-
kawa Moronobu (ca. 1618–1694), Hanabusa Itchō (1652–1724), Utagawa Toyoharu (1735–1814), Katsushika Hokusai (1760–1849), An-
dō Hiroshige (1797–1858), and Utagawa Kuniyoshi (1797–1861). In
the field of decorative art there were Hon'ami Kōetsu (1558–1637)
and Ogata Kōrin (1658–1716). Among writers Chikamatsu Mon-

zaemon (1653–1724), Ihara Saikaku (1642–1693), Ōta Nampo (1749–1823), and Jippensha Ikku (1765–1831) can be cited. In addition there were actors, such as Nakamura Utaemon III (1778–1838) and Nakamura Baigyoku II (1842–1921), and the *haiku* poets Matsunaga Teitoku (1571–1653) and Takarai Kikaku (1661–1707). In other areas, the *go* master Hon'inbō Nikkai (1555–1618) was a priest in a Nichiren temple, while Ōhashi Sōkei (1555–1634), a *shōgi* master who played against Hon'inbō, was also a believer in and a supporter of the Nichiren sect. Gensei (1623–1668), a Nichiren priest from Kyoto, made a name for himself in the literary world.

One is intrigued by the large number of Nichiren Buddhists who were prominent leaders in the world of arts and letters down to the end of the Edo period. Of course, their works did not necessarily reflect their faith in Nichiren Buddhism, but some extant works do appear to be the fruits of that faith. The link between Nichiren Buddhism and the artistic culture of the Momoyama and Edo periods appears to be the townsman class *(chōnin)*, which supported both. It is akin to the link between the *machishū* culture of the Muromachi period and the Nichiren Lotus faith, a relationship that was continued by the townsman class of the Momoyama and Edo periods. It should also be pointed out that most of the popular new sects in Japan down to the present day have been dominated by the Nichiren faith. Bearing this in mind, faith in the Nichiren sect and veneration of the *Lotus Sutra* should be regarded as important foundations of Japanese culture and religion.

## Conclusion

In order for the *Lotus Sutra* to be applied to actual life, its ideas had to be derived from the parables and stories that made the sutra so popular. These ideas were articulated in the interpretations of Chinese and Japanese commentators, many of whom were drawn to the sutra by its own merits and not simply through sectarian affiliation. Enhanced by these interpretations, the sutra took on greater meaning, for without the understanding of a positive view of emptiness, a unifying truth that embraces all life, an eternal Buddha who reigns throughout time, and the bodhisattva practices that must be carried out in society, the *Lotus Sutra* could not have had the wide influence and applications that it did.

# The *Lotus Sutra* and Saichō's Interpretation of the Realization of Buddhahood with This Very Body

PAUL GRONER

The ultimate goal of Buddhist practice is the attainment of buddhahood or supreme enlightenment. However, the definition of buddhahood, the amount of time required to realize it, and the number of people who can hope to attain it have often been topics of bitter controversy among Buddhist schools. At certain points in Buddhist history, these issues have been the subject of intense scrutiny, resulting in substantial revisions in the definition of buddhahood and the path to it. During the ninth century, Japanese monks interpreted Indian and Chinese positions on buddhahood and arrived at their own unique and innovative approach to these issues.

At the beginning of the ninth century, many Japanese monks would have accepted the position of the Chinese Fa-hsiang (Hossō) school that buddhahood was the result of three incalculable eons of practice and was a goal which only a few had the potential of ever realizing. Buddhahood was primarily a subject of scholarly speculation rather than a goal attainable through religious practice. Even though some schools of Chinese Buddhism which theoretically allowed for the rapid realization of enlightenment had been introduced to Japan, they had little impact on actual practice among Japanese monks. For example, although Tao-hsüan (702–760) had brought Hua-yen (Kegon) and Northern school Ch'an (Zen) teachings with him from China in 734, the Northern school Ch'an transmission seems to have had little or no effect on Japanese monks, and Hua-yen was studied as an academic discipline, not as a practical means to enlightenment. Some Japanese monks retreated to the mountains during the Nara period in order to meditate and perform religious austerities, but they generally expected their practices to improve their memories or to lead to mastery of special powers, not to the realization of enlightenment.[1] The Hossō teaching that only a few people could attain buddhahood not only discouraged people from hoping for enlightenment; it also was in close agreement with the court's policy that Buddhism was primarily for the protection of the state and its high officials and was not to be propagated among commoners.

By the end of the ninth century, this situation had radically changed due to the establishment of two new schools, Tendai and Shingon. Large numbers of monks and lay believers had come to accept the position that buddhahood could be attained during a person's lifetime through intense practice. Moreover, monks from these traditions, especially the Tendai school, argued that buddhahood was a real possibility for everyone, including commoners, not just a chosen few in the nobility. In order to make the rapid realization of enlightenment possible, new religious practices were introduced, developed, and interpreted.

This chapter concerns the introduction of one of the key concepts employed by both Tendai and Shingon monks in the redefinition of buddhahood and the path to it, namely, the teaching concerning "the realization of buddhahood with this very body" (sokushin jōbutsu).[2] Although the Shingon view of sokushin jōbutsu has been discussed in several studies in English, the Tendai position on this subject still has not been adequately examined.[3] The discussion here is divided into three sections: (1) an examination of the issues involved in determining whether the topic first arose in Tendai or Shingon circles, (2) the passage in the Lotus Sutra which serves as the scriptural source for the Tendai position, and (3) a survey of Saichō's views on it.

## The Emergence of Japanese Theories of the Rapid Realization of Buddhahood

The possibility of realizing buddhahood in this existence was first emphasized in Japan by the founders of the two schools which later dominated much of Heian period Buddhism, Saichō (767–822), founder of the Tendai School, and Kūkai (774–835), founder of the Shingon school. Scholars are not in agreement about which of these two men first began to emphasize the rapid realization of enlightenment. Those who have argued that Saichō was first base their position on a passage from Saichō's biography, the Eizan daishiden, compiled several years after Saichō's death. According to it, Saichō talked about a "direct path" (jikidō) to enlightenment in a series of ten lectures on the *Lotus Sutra* at Mount Takao in 802.[4] Saichō was thus thinking about the rapid realization of enlightenment even before traveling to China. Unfortunately, the text contains virtually no information about Saichō's thought in the lectures and has been criticized as reflecting Tendai views at the time of Saichō's death, rather than as being an accurate record of Saichō's position in 802. However, since the series of ten lectures would have included a lecture on the *Sutra of Innumerable Meanings (Wu-liang i-ching)*, the text which includes the term "direct path," Saichō may well have begun to argue in 802 that Tendai was superior to other traditions because it enabled the practitioner to quickly realize enlightenment.[5]

The development of Saichō's thought on rapid realization over the next thirteen years is not clear because no written record of his views survives. However, from 816 until his death in 822, Saichō wrote a number of works attacking Hossō doctrines and practices and advocating Tendai teachings. As he developed his ideas, he sometimes took technical terms which had not been significant in the Chinese tradition and gave them new meanings. His interpretation of the Mahāyāna precepts is one example of this activity. In his discussions of rapid realization, Saichō introduced and developed terms which had not played a very significant role in Chinese Buddhism in order to express his own views. Among them were "direct path" and the "realization of buddhahood with this very body." Rapid realization was compared to the superhuman powers which enabled Buddhas to travel wherever they wished in an instant.[6] Although Saichō referred in vague ways to *sokushin jōbutsu* in many of his works, he did not discuss it at any length until he compiled the *Hokke shūku* in 821, one year before he died.[7]

At the same time that Saichō was using the rapid realization of enlightenment as a criterion to justify the superiority of his teachings over those of the Nara schools, Kūkai was developing similar arguments. In fact, fuller records survive for Kūkai's early views on rapid realization; of particular importance are the *Goshōrai mokuroku*, written in 806 and the *Benkemmitsu nikyōron*, probably compiled in 815.[8]

In the *Benkemmitsu nikyōron*, Kūkai cites a passage from the *P'u-t'i i-hsin lun* (Aspiration to Enlightenment, *T* 32, no. 1665) which includes the term *sokushin jōbutsu* but does not develop the theme.[9] Not until he wrote such works as the *Sokushin jōbutsugi* was this subject developed. The issue of whether Saichō or Kūkai took the lead in developing the theme of *sokushin jōbutsu* depends on the dating of Kūkai's *Sokushin jōbutsugi* (*T* 77, no. 2428) and several related works. The key to this problem lies in some letters written by Kūkai to the Hossō scholar Tokuitsu and in a work by Tokuitsu, the *Shingonshū miketsumon* (*T* 77, no. 2458).

A letter from Kūkai to Tokuitsu sent on the fifth day of the fourth month of Kōnin 6 (815) provides one of the few fixed dates in the discussion. In the letter, Kūkai states that he will send some texts on esoteric Buddhism to Tokuitsu.[10] Tokuitsu's *Shingonshū miketsumon*, a collection of criticisms of esoteric teachings, was probably written after Tokuitsu had studied texts he had received from Kūkai. Since the *Shingonshū miketsumon* includes a refutation of Shingon views on *sokushin jōbutsu*, it is probably the earliest surviving text indicating that Kūkai was interested in this issue.[11] If the text was written shortly after Kūkai sent his letter to Tokuitsu, it would indicate that Kūkai had already begun to develop his views on this topic by 815 or 816.[12] The *Sokushin jōbutsugi*, Kūkai's fullest statement on this doctrine, was probably written around 822–826, after Saichō's death, and might have been intended as a reply to some of Tokuitsu's criticisms.[13] This scenario would place serious discussion of *sokushin jōbutsu* as originating with Kūkai; Saichō's treatment of the *sokushin jōbutsu* would have been a response to Kūkai's discussions, but still probably would have occurred before the *Sokushin jōbutsugi*.

Other scholars, especially those who have done research on Tendai issues, favor a date of 822 or later for Tokuitsu's *Shingonshū miketsumon*.[14] Although Saichō replied in detail to Tokuitsu's arguments concerning Tendai, no evidence that he replied directly to the *Shingonshū miketsumon* survives. In addition, Kūkai's only direct response to Tokuitsu's criticisms is found in the *Himitsu mandarakyō fuhōden*, a work on esoteric Buddhist lineages written after 821. Since Kūkai probably would have responded to Tokuitsu's criticisms soon after he saw them, a later date for Tokuitsu's *Shingonshū miketsumon* is indicated. This scenario would have allowed time for Saichō to call attention to the theme of *sokushin jōbutsu* in the *Hokke shūku*, and for both Tokuitsu and Kūkai to respond to Saichō's position by writing works of their own. However, internal evidence in the *Shingonshū miketsumon* suggests that Tokuitsu might have compiled the text and then added to it later after he received Kūkai's response.[15]

The issue of whether Saichō or Kūkai first called attention to the term *sokushin jōbutsu* cannot be definitively decided for several reasons. First, although recent studies have shed light on the composition of the *Shingonshū miketsumon,* no conclusive evidence has yet emerged which enables scholars to decisively place it in a specific year from 815 and 824. Second, both Saichō and Kūkai probably began to talk about the concept several years before they actually wrote about it, and no record of those conversations survives. Thus the actual chronology for the emergence of the concept of *sokushin jōbutsu* remains unclear. Both men were probably aware of what the other was saying and doing and responded to their competitor's activities.[16]

An investigation of the sources for each man's views also fails to yield decisive evidence. Saichō and Kūkai used completely different sources for their discussions of *sokushin jōbutsu.* In Kūkai's authoritative treatment, the *Sokushin jōbutsugi,* a variety of esoteric sources are cited as scriptural authority for the teaching. Of these sources, the *P'u-t'i i-hsin lun* attributed to Nāgārjuna, was the most important because it actually contained the term *sokushin jōbutsu.* Kūkai quoted the following passage which contained the term in both his *Sokushin jōbutsugi* and *Benkemmitsu nikyōron*: "It is through the teachings of Mantrayāna that we can attain enlightenment in this very existence; this teaching explains the way of *samādhi* which is either neglected or totally ignored by other teachings."[17]

Saichō was aware of the existence of the *P'u-t'i i-hsin lun,*[18] but never mentioned it in his discussion of *sokushin jōbutsu.* Instead, Saichō relied entirely on the *Lotus Sutra* (*T* 9, no. 262) and a related sutra, the *Kuan P'u-hsien p'u-sa hsing fa-ching* (*T* 9, no. 277) for scriptural support of his position on *sokushin jōbutsu.* If Saichō had lived long enough to learn about Kūkai's views on *sokushin jōbutsu* in detail, he might have cited esoteric sources to support his positions on the rapid realization of buddhahood since he had often argued that Tendai and esoteric Buddhism both had the same purport. However, near the end of his life, Saichō concentrated increasingly on Tendai doctrine and the *Lotus Sutra* and occasionally criticized Shingon positions. In *Hokke shūku,* Saichō argued that the scriptures used by other schools did not provide for "entry into the ranks of the buddhas with this very body" *(sokushin nyū),* a statement which would seem to include the Shingon school.[19] But since Saichō had argued that esoteric teachings and the Tendai perfect teachings had the same import *(emmitsu itchi),* he presumably would not have been opposed to the use of esoteric practices in the realization of *sokushin jōbutsu.*[20]

The earliest use of the term *sokushin jōbutsu* in a T'ien-t'ai text is found in the *Fa-hua wen-chü chi* (*T* 34, no. 1719), Chan-jan's sub-commentary on Chih-i's line-by-line commentary on the *Lotus Sutra*, the *Fa-hua wen-chü* (*T* 34, no. 1718).[21] Since the term appears in Chan-jan's discussion of the dragon king's daughter's realization of buddhahood, the section of the *Lotus* which Saichō chose as the basis of his discussion of *sokushin jōbutsu*, Chan-jan's use of the term undoubtedly played a vital role in shaping Saichō's views on the subject. Both Chih-i and Chan-jan mentioned a text entitled [*P'u-sa-ch'u*] *t'ai-ching* (*T* 12, no. 384) in their discussions of the dragon king's daughter. In the *T'ai-ching*, the transformation of women into men and their subsequent realization of buddhahood, a common theme in early Mahāyāna sutras, is described. Like many of the Mahāyāna texts in which buddhahood and women are mentioned, the *T'ai-ching* argues against clinging to discriminations between concepts such as male and female. According to Chih-i:

> The *T'ai-ching* states that "the women in the realms of Māra, Śakra and Brahmā all neither abandoned (their old) bodies nor received (new) bodies. They all realized buddhahood with their current bodies *(genshin).*" Thus these verses state that the dharma nature is like a great ocean. No right or wrong is preached (within it). Ordinary people and sages are equal, without superiority or inferiority.[22]

Chan-jan, in commenting on this passage, used the term *sokushin jōbutsu* to describe the realization of both the dragon king's daughter and the women in the *T'ai-ching*.[23] Saichō's use of the term clearly was derived from Chan-jan's subcommentary,[24] and his discussion of *sokushin jōbutsu* is primarily based on the story of the dragon king's daughter in the "Devadatta" chapter of the *Lotus*. Thus the contents and history of that chapter must be briefly considered.

## The "Devadatta" Chapter of the *Lotus Sutra*

Both the contents and the textual history of the "Devadatta" chapter are controversial. The story of the dragon king's daughter, described in the next paragraph, occupies the second half of the "Devadatta" chapter.[25]

Mañjuśrī had just returned to Mt. Gṛdhrakūta from a highly successful visit to the dragon (Nāga) palace of King Sāgara, where he had preached only the *Lotus Sutra*. Upon his return, the bodhisattva Praj-ñākūṭa asked about who had been converted through the teachings and whether anyone in the dragon kingdom had been able to quickly gain enlightenment by putting the scripture into practice. Mañjuśrī replied that the eight-year-old daughter of the dragon king had been able to do so. Prajñākūṭa noted that since Śākyamuni had devoted himself to religious austerities for eons in order to become a buddha, it seemed doubtful that a mere girl could realize it so quickly. The dragon king's daughter then appeared before them. Śāriputra, the representative of the Hīnayāna point of view, suggested that a woman's body is impure and not a fit receptacle for buddhahood; moreover, women could not attain five high states: (1) Brahmā, (2) Śakra, (3) Māra, (4) sage-king and (5) buddha. Thereupon, the dragon king's daughter handed a valuable gem to the Buddha, who accepted it. She then asked whether the gem had been given and received swiftly. Śāriputra answered that the transaction had indeed been swift. The dragon king's daughter then announced that she would become a buddha before their eyes even more rapidly. Instantaneously she turned into a man, went to a realm called "Spotless" in the south, and sat on a jeweled throne as a buddha. Many of the assembled crowd, as well as those in this *sahā* world, upon seeing the dragon king's daughter realize buddhahood, attained a state of nonretrogression or received predictions that they would realize buddhahood in the future.

The chapter was the last addition to the *Lotus Sutra* and probably circulated in both India and China as an independent text for a short time.[26] The chapter was included in Dharmarakṣa's translation in 286.[27] However, in the early fifth century when Kumārajīva translated his version of the *Lotus Sutra*, which was to become the standard text in East Asia, he used a Sanskritic text which did not include the "Devadatta" chapter. A copy of the "Devadatta" chapter was brought from Kao-ch'ang in Central Asia by Fa-hsien and translated by Fa-hsien and Fa-i around 490 and was added to the Kumārajīva translation.[28] In 601, a complete translation of the *Lotus* was made by Jñānagupta and Dharmagupta as the *T'ien-p'in miao-fa lien-hua-ching* (*T* 9, no. 264). The version of the *Lotus* which circulates today as Kumārajīva's translation (*T* 9, no. 262) includes the 490 translation of the "Devadatta" chapter as well as parts of the *T'ien-p'in miao-fa lien-hua-ching* which were not originally translated by Kumārajīva.

Because East Asian commentators on the *Lotus* used Kumārajīva's translation rather than that by Dharmarakṣa, early Chinese and Japanese commentaries did not include sections on the "Devadatta" chapter. Thus it was not discussed in the commentaries by Fa-yün (467–529; *T* 33, no. 1715), Tao-sheng (355–434; *ZZ* 2.23.4), or Shōtoku Taishi (574–622; *T* 56, no. 2187).

Chih-i (538–597), the de facto founder of the T'ien-t'ai school, was probably the first Chinese writer to comment on it. Chih-i claimed that Kumārajīva had translated the "Devadatta" chapter, but that an official in the palace kept the chapter so that the *Lotus Sūtra* had circulated without it. A century later, during the Liang dynasty (502–557), several monks had added Kumārajīva's translation of the chapter back into the text.[29] Several decades later, the San-lun patriarch Chi-tsang (549–623) criticized Chih-i's explanation, arguing that Kumārajīva had never translated it.[30] Chi-tsang claimed that the "Devadatta" chapter which was added to Kumārajīva's version had been translated by Paramārtha (499–569), not Kumārajīva. The uncertain status of the chapter was discussed in a number of later Chinese and Japanese works. It was eventually used by Japanese Hossō critics of *sokushin jōbutsu* to call the scriptural basis of *sokushin jōbutsu* into question. Since the chapter had been translated earlier by Dharmarakṣa, Hossō monks could not argue that it was an apocryphal text *(gikyō)*, but they could argue that Kumārajīva might have had a special reason for not translating the chapter, perhaps because he feared that later monks might misinterpret it. In addition, Prince Shōtoku, the reputed author of the first commentary on the *Lotus* compiled by a Japanese, did not comment on the "Devadatta" chapter, probably because his commentary was based on the text by Fa-yün. Because Prince Shōtoku played a vital role in the introduction and establishment of Buddhism in Japan and was regarded as a culture hero, later generations identified him with a number of Buddhist figures, including the T'ien-t'ai patriarch Hui-ssu and the bodhisattva Kannon (Avalokiteśvara). Hossō monks noted that if these identifications were correct, then the incarnation of Hui-ssu or Kannon had purposely not mentioned the chapter.[31]

Despite the problems with the textual history of the "Devadatta" chapter, it suited Saichō's needs in several ways. Since it had not been commented upon by many previous scholars, Saichō did not have to worry about being criticized for differing from earlier commentaries; he could develop his themes in his own way.[32] In addition, in those commentaries which did include sections on the dragon king's daughter, the author had not dealt with the path to enlightenment;

this theme had generally been reserved for other sections of texts.[33] Finally, the story of the dragon king's daughter differed from many other stories in the *Lotus Sutra* in that instead of merely predicting the eventual enlightenment of a person of little experience, it showed her gaining it immediately.

## Saichō's Interpretation of *Sokushin Jōbutsu*

Saichō's discussions of the rapid realization of buddhahood are found in his polemical writings criticizing the Hossō school and defending Tendai teachings. He argued that Tendai teachings were superior because they led to buddhahood more rapidly than Hossō practices. Tendai practices could benefit everyone, but Hossō practices would not result in buddhahood for anybody in Japan because nobody could follow them. Saichō argued that the perfect religious faculties *(enki)* of the Japanese had already matured so that they need not bother with lesser teachings.

Saichō introduced and developed the term *sokushin jōbutsu* in his last written work, *Hokke shūku*, as a part of his program to demonstrate the superiority of the *Lotus Sutra* and the Tendai interpretation of it. The power of the *Lotus Sutra* to lead the practitioner to realization with his current body is introduced as the eighth of ten reasons why the *Lotus Sutra* is superior to other texts. The following passage demonstrates how Saichō employed the description of the dragon king's daughter to prove that the *Lotus Sutra* applied to all sentient beings and would quickly bring them salvation.

> This passage (about the dragon king's daughter) concerns those beings who can realize buddhahood only with difficulty and reveals the power of the *Lotus Sutra* to help them. She is an animal, (one of lower levels of the) six destinies [realms], obviously the result of bad karma. She is female and clearly has faculties which are not good. She is young and thus has not been practicing religious austerities for a long time. And yet, the wondrous power of the *Lotus Sutra* endows her with the two adornments of wisdom and merit. Thus we know that the power of the *Lotus Sutra* reveals it to be the jewel among the scriptures and a rarity in the world.[34]

Saichō argued that the story of the dragon king's daughter was significant for all sentient beings, not just for one individual. Her story revealed that the power of the *Lotus Sutra* could be effective for virtually any sentient being. Even if a person could not emulate the dragon king's daughter's rapid realization of buddhahood, merely recognizing and appreciating her achievement was sufficient to lead a person to a significant advance in practice as demonstrated by the achievements of those beings who witnessed the dragon king's daughter's realization. Since not all sentient beings possessed the same religious faculties, Saichō admitted that those with lesser abilities might require additional time to realize buddhahood, but they would still realize buddhahood much more rapidly than the Hossō practitioner who was said to require three incalculable eons. If those with superior faculties did not realize enlightenment in this life, they surely would realize buddhahood within three lifetimes.

> The dragon king's daughter who converted others (to the ultimate teaching) had not undergone a long period of religious austerities; nor had the sentient beings who were converted undergone a long period of austerities. Through the wondrous power of the sutra, they all realized buddhahood with their bodies just as they are *(sokushin jōbutsu)*. Those with the highest grade of superior faculties realize buddhahood in one lifetime; those with the medium grade of superior faculties require two lifetimes to realize buddhahood. And those with the lowest grade of superior faculties will realize buddhahood within three lifetimes. They will meet the bodhisattva Samantabhadra, enter the ranks of the bodhisattvas, and acquire the *dhāraṇī* which will enable them to master nonsubstantiality.[35]

In the *Shugo kokkaishō* (Essays on Protecting the Nation), a text compiled in 818, several years before the passage above was written, Saichō discussed the classification of practitioners into three categories which required from one to three lifetimes to realize buddhahood and identified it as a Hua-yen (Kegon) teaching.[36] Since Saichō had studied Hua-yen doctrine as a youth, its influence in his writings is not surprising. However, in several works written at the very end of his life, Saichō harshly criticized Kegon teachings, arguing that they were provisional, discussed only the causes of enlightenment *(inbun)* but did not explain enlightenment itself *(kabun)*, and required many eons to complete.[37] Moreover, Saichō did not cite the *Hua-yen-ching* in the *Hokke shūku* as a source for teaching that those people with advanced religious faculties would realize buddhahood within three lifetimes *(sanshō jōbutsu)*, but instead chose to cite the closing sutra for the *Lotus, Kuan P'u-hsien-ching* (Sutra of Meditation on the

Bodhisattva Samantabhadra), to support the teaching that a person could realize buddhahood within three lifetimes.[38] Saichō had rejected the teachings which had attracted him earlier in his life in favor of concentrating on the *Lotus* and Tendai teachings.

Saichō advanced his ideas primarily to counter Hossō views that the realization of buddhahood was only for a limited group of sentient beings and would require eons. Saichō died before he could elaborate on the actual contents of the concept of the "realization of buddhahood in this very body." However, he did place the concept of *sokushin jōbutsu* in the broader context of the Tendai path to enlightenment when he noted that it referred to partial, not complete enlightenment. But even this reference to *sokushin jōbutsu* as partial enlightenment was brief and made in the context of a discussion of the possibility of enlightenment within three lifetimes.[39]

The difference between partial and full realization can be explained through an examination of the Tendai path to enlightenment. Chih-i discussed various forms of the path to buddhahood throughout his life. Although he considered descriptions of the path from a variety of Hīnayāna and Mahāyāna sources, only the path for followers of the T'ien-t'ai perfect teaching played a significant role in discussions of *sokushin jōbutsu*. Since Saichō had argued that all Japanese had perfect religious faculties, Japanese Tendai scholars had little need to consider other versions of the path.[40] Two descriptions of the path play a significant role in understanding Saichō's view of the path for followers of the perfect teaching. The first, based on the apocryphal *P'u-sa ying-lo pen-yeh-ching* (T 24, no. 1485), was divided into fifty-two stages and was considered to be especially representative of the unique teaching *(bekkyō)*, but was also used in descriptions of the path for the perfect teaching. In addition, five preliminary stages for disciples *(gobon deshii)* which were derived from a passage in the *Lotus Sutra* were sometimes placed before the fifty-two stages, making a total of fifty-seven stages for followers of the perfect teaching.[41]

The second description of the path for the perfect teaching consisted of six levels of identity *(roku soku)*; it was used to describe the path only for followers of the perfect teaching. The six levels of identity play an important role in discussions of *sokushin jōbutsu*. Unlike the first system, the six levels of identity had no single canonical source. Although Chih-i referred to a variety of sutras and *śāstras* in his discussion of individual parts of the six levels, the system itself was probably based on his own experience. Chih-i's position on doctrine and religious practice evolved throughout his life and his views of the six levels of identity vary according to which work is consulted.[42] The following discussion reflects the systematic view of the six levels of identity which was probably followed in Saichō's time. It is taken from the *Tendai Hokkeshū gishū,* a handbook on Tendai by Saichō's disciple Gishin (781–833), which was completed several years after Saichō's death.

> Question: For what sort of person is (the perfect teaching) preached?
> Answer: For someone with the very highest of religious faculties.
> Question: What stages (on the path) does a follower (of the perfect teaching) go through?
> Answer: The six levels of identity.
> Question: Why are they called the six levels of identity?
> Answer: Because there are six (levels), the beginning and end are not confused. Because they are (levels of realization of an essential) identity, the identification of the beginning and the ultimate stages (is maintained). Because they are identical in principle, they are called (levels of) identity. Because there are differences in the phenomenal realm, the (following) six levels are established. . . .
> Question: What is the significance of the hierarchical classification of six levels of identity?
> Answer: Since sentient beings originally have the three virtues *(santoku)* as their (true) nature, the (first stage) is called the identity in principle *(risoku)*. When they come to know of this (true nature) through (Buddhist) teachings, they have entered (the second level of) verbal identity *(myōji soku)*. As they practice religious austerities on the basis of their knowledge, they are in (the third level of) identity of practice *(kangyō soku)*. Gradually the practitioner masters insight and calm abiding meditations until (his activities) come to resemble the functioning of the ultimate *(shin'yū)*. This is the (fourth level of) identity of resemblance *(sōji soku)*. When the three virtues have partially appeared and the practitioner has partially realized the Buddha's dharma *(Buppō)*, he has attained the (fifth level of) partial identity *(bunshō soku)*. Finally, when his wisdom is perfect, (the defilements) fully eliminated and the three virtues completely manifested, he is in the (sixth level of) ultimate identity *(kukyō soku)*.[43]

The six levels of identity are matched with the fifty-seven stages of the perfect teaching as follows:

| Six Levels of Identity | Fifty-seven Stages |
|---|---|
| 1. Identity in principle | No corresponding stage |
| 2. Verbal identity | No corresponding stage |
| 3. Identity of practice | 1–5: Five (preliminary) stages of disciples *(gohon deshii)* |
| 4. Identity of resemblance | 6–15: Ten degrees of faith *(jisshin)* |
| 5. Partial identity or partial realization | 16–25: Ten abodes *(jūjū)* |
| | 26–35: Ten degrees of practice *(jūgyō)* |
| | 36–45: Ten degrees of dedication of merits *(jūekō)* |
| | 46–55: Ten lands *(jūji)* |
| | 56: Virtual enlightenment *(tōgaku)* |
| 6. Ultimate identity | 57: Supreme enlightenment *(myōkaku)* |

The fifth level of identity, partial realization, was identified by Saichō with *sokushin jōbutsu*. It was particularly important to Tendai practitioners because it represented the beginning of the elimination of ignorance and the development of the enlightened mind *(hosshin)*. The first abode *(shojū)* was the lowest of the forty-one stages to be included in partial realization. The attainment of the first abode marked a key transition in the practitioner of the perfect teachings, signifying that his understanding of Buddhism was qualitatively different than it had been at earlier stages. In the ten degrees of faith, which directly preceded the first abode, a person strove to eliminate defilements, but from the first abode onward he began to eliminate the ignorance which was the basis of the defilements and to develop the untainted wisdom *(murochi)* which was the essence of enlightenment.

The importance of the first abode was also marked by calling the practitioner a "sage" *(shō)* from that point onward. In the previous stages he had been called an ordinary person or "worldling" *(bonbu)*.[44] Thus, with the attainment of the first abode, the mind of the Buddha begins to be manifest. The practitioner still had to increase his wisdom and apply it to various forms of spiritual ignorance, but he had made a qualitative leap with the attainment of the first abode. Gishin describes the first abode and its relation to subsequent stages as follows:

Question: Since (the practitioner) has realized supreme enlighten-
    ment when he attains the first abode and the enlightened
    mind emerges, what need is there for the remaining stages
    (after the first abode)?
Answer: The realization of a part of supreme enlightenment is
    called the realization of supreme enlightenment; but the
    advent of the enlightened mind is not the same as the full and
    final realization of supreme enlightenment.
Question: How is this to be understood?
Answer: Through the metaphor of a lamp.
Question: What is the metaphor?
Answer: If a lamp is lit in a dark room, the light spreads through-
    out the room. If two, three, or even forty-two lamps are lit,
    the room becomes progressively brighter. If a person under-
    stands this metaphor, then he can also understand the mean-
    ing of statements such as "the realization of one stage is the
    realization of all stages. . . . "
Question: How long does it take for a bodhisattva of this (perfect)
    teaching to realize buddhahood?
Answer: He can attain the first abode, the stage at which the
    enlightened mind emerges, in a single lifetime.[45]

Attainment of the first abode was also significant because it guar-
anteed that the practitioner had mastered the three truths so that he
would not retrogress in the path in three crucial respects: degree of
attainment, practice, and thought. Between the first and seventh
degrees of faith, he eliminated the defilements which arose due to
wrong views and thoughts *(kenjiwaku)* through the truth of emptiness *(kūtai)*; since these were the defilements which bound him to
the round of birth and death, their destruction enabled him to reach
"a degree of attainment from which he would not backslide" *(ifutai)*.
Between the eighth and tenth degrees of faith, he destroyed the multitudinous defilements *(jinjawaku)* which prevented him from effectively preaching to others; because these were caused by clinging to
emptiness, he used the truth of provisional existence *(ketai)* to van-
quish them. His practice became so firm that he would not backslide

from practices which benefit others *(gyōfutai)*. Finally, with the realization of the first abode, the practitioner's meditation and understanding were so firmly established that he would not backslide by thinking *(nenfutai)* of anything not conducive to his ultimate enlightenment. The rest of his practice which focused on eradicating ignorance *(mumyōwaku)* was based on the middle truth *(chūtai)*.[46] Since the three types of defilements all can be eliminated through the three truths, an advanced practitioner can skip stages and thereby quickly realize enlightenment. Moreover, since each of the three truths contains the other two, the perfect practice of any one of them would lead to the realization of the other two.

The distinction between the worldling and the sage was especially important for the concept of "the realization of buddhahood with this very body." The body and life span of a worldling were alloted *(bundan shōji)* in accordance with his past good and bad karma as well as the obstructions from his defilements. In contrast, the body and life span of a sage were based on untainted good karma *(muro zengō)* and the obstructions caused by his remaining ignorance. The physical quality of the sage's body and his lifespan could change *(hennyaku shōji)* depending on his intentions and attainment on the path to buddhahood. The type of karma which influenced the practitioner's physical body changed with the attainment of the first abode; the defilements had been destroyed and only ignorance remained to be eliminated. Thus the term *sokushin jōbutsu,* the realization of buddhahood with this body, suggested that a practitioner's body, just as it is, could be transformed into the body of an advanced bodhisattva or a buddha. It was not necessary to die and be reborn with a better body before attaining such higher states. The attainment of partial realization *(bunshō soku)* by reaching the first abode or a higher stage entailed not only major mental changes, but also important physical ones.[47]

A practitioner did not have to wait until he had attained the first abode to experience dramatic physical changes, according to Saichō. Immediately before the section on *sokushin jōbutsu* in the *Hokke shūku,* Saichō argued that the *Lotus Sutra* would enable the worldling to purify his "six sense faculties so that any sense faculty could perform the function of any another faculty with this very body" *(sokushin rokkon goyū)*. This stage was equivalent to the realization of the fourth identity.[48]

Saichō's description of the path followed traditional T'ien-t'ai presentations of the fifty-seven stages and the six levels of identity in most ways. His major departure was his emphasis on determining the amount of time which the realization of buddhahood would require, a concern which was due to his preoccupation with defending Tendai teachings against Hossō attacks. Chinese T'ien-t'ai treatments of the path, while presenting the theoretical rationale which permitted the rapid realization of buddhahood, had not been preoccupied with determining the length of time required to complete the path. Chih-i had ample opportunity to observe the dangers of overemphasizing sudden enlightenment, but Saichō had not detected such abuses in Japan; instead he was striving to establish Tendai in an environment dominated by gradualist presentations of the path.[49]


## Conclusion

The rapid realization of enlightenment was one of the dominant themes in the early Heian period. Both Saichō and Kūkai were fascinated by the concept and developed their views on the subject at the same time, sometimes even using the same terminology, as in the case of *sokushin jōbutsu*. While the two men influenced each other, it is extremely difficult to arrive at a definite conclusion concerning which man first introduced the concept of *sokushin jōbutsu*.

Saichō's use of the term *sokushin jōbutsu* was typical of many expressions he employed. After finding a term which had not been extensively used in Chinese Buddhism, Saichō would apply it in order to develop his ideas on a subject. His selection of the story of the realization of buddhahood by the dragon king's daughter fits this pattern. When Saichō introduced the concept of *sokushin jōbutsu,* he was primarily interested in arguing that the rapid realization of buddhahood was possible through the power of the *Lotus Sutra* and that Tendai practices were superior to those of the Hossō school. This approach is demonstrated by his choices of certain interpretations of the story of the dragon king's daughter for refutation in the *Hokke shūku*. He defended the story from claims that it was merely an expedient teaching without much significance for the ultimate Buddhist teaching.

Saichō also used the story to argue that buddhahood could actually be realized by Japanese practitioners. By bringing buddhahood to the level of the person who had partial realization and defining how a person who had attained this stage would not retrogress and would have certain physical qualities, Saichō claimed that buddhahood could be readily attained.

Saichō's death shortly after he had written about *sokushin jōbutsu* left Tendai monks with a fascinating, but sketchily defined concept. When Kūkai wrote about esoteric Buddhism using the same term in a more systematic fashion, Tendai monks felt compelled to develop their own distinctive positions on the subject by clearly defining the practices which would lead to it, the physical and mental attributes which would result from it, and finally the matter of whether the practices of a single lifetime were sufficient for a person to realize buddhahood.[50]

## NOTES

1. For a study of monks who meditated in mountains during the Nara period, see Sonoda Kōyū, "Kodai Bukkyō ni okeru sanrin shugyō to sono igi," *Nantō Bukkyō* 4 (1967): 45–60.

2. The term *sokushin jōbutsu* was translated as "attaining enlightenment in this very existence" by Yoshito Hakeda in *Kūkai: Major Works* (New York: Columbia University Press, 1972). I have used the translation "realization of buddhahood with this very body" because the word "realization" reflects the sense of discovering the buddha nature, a theme in much of the Tendai literature concerning *sokushin jōbutsu*. The phrase "with this very body" has been chosen because it suggests the concern with the physical qualities of buddhahood, a major interest of subsequent Tendai monks.

3. Representative studies in English on Shingon teachings include Hakeda, *Kūkai*; Minoru Kiyota, *Shingon Buddhism: Theory and Practice* (Los Angeles: Buddhist Books International, 1972); and Hisao Inagaki, "Kūkai's *Sokushin jōbutsu-gi*," *Asia Major* 17, no. 2 (1972): 190–215.

4. Ninchū, *Eizan Daishiden, Dengyō Daishi zenshū* (Tokyo: Nihon Bussho kankōkai, 1975), 5:9. Hereafter cited as *DZ*.

5. Even Shingon scholars are divided on the authenticity of this passage. Tomabechi Seiichi criticizes the *Eizan Daishiden* passage in "Sokushin jōbutsu no kentō: Saichō Kūkai no kyōhanron ni oite," *Mikkyōgaku kenkyū* 16 (1984): 155. Katsumata Shunkyō recognizes it as being authentic. See his *Mikkyō no Nihonteki tenkai* (Tokyo: Shunjūsha, 1920), 134.

Although Saichō is the first Tendai monk to give the term *jikidō* a major role in the classification of doctrines and practices, the term can be found in the *Wu-liang i-ching* (*T* 9.387b; tr. Katō Bunnō et al., *The Threefold Lotus Sutra*, 19) and in Chih-i's works. See, for example, *Fa-hua hsüan-i* in Nihon Bussho kankōkai, ed., *Tendai Daishi zenshū* (Tokyo: Nihon Bussho kankōkai, 1979), 3:547.

6. For a discussion of these terms, see Paul Groner, *Saichō: The Establishment of the Japanese Tendai School*, 184–190. The Chinese origins and the development of later Japanese Tendai comparisons of rapid realization with a buddha's superhuman powers are discussed by Ōkubo Ryōshun in "Jinzūjō: toku ni Nihon Tendai ni okeru ichi mondai," *Waseda daigaku daigakuin bungaku kenkyūka kiyō, Betsusatsu* 13 (1986): 45–58; and "Jinzūjō ni tsuite: Enmitsu nikyō ni okeru *Daibon hannya Daichidoron* no juyō o chūshin ni," *Tendai gakuhō* 28 (1986): 160–163. Kūkai also used terms such as *jinzūjō*.

7. The earliest use of the concept of *sokushin jōbutsu* with a reference to the dragon king's daughter in Saichō's writings occurs around 819 in *Ketsugonjatsuron, DZ,* 2:715. Earlier references to the rapid realization of buddhahood in Saichō's works vaguely suggest that buddhahood might be realized with this very body. For a survey of such passages, see Asai Endō, *Jōko Nihon Tendai hommon shisōshi* (Kyoto: Heirakuji shoten, 1973), 180–183.

8. For edited translations, see Hakeda, *Kūkai,* 140–157.

9. *Benkemmitsu nikyōron* in *Kōbō Daishi chosaku zenshū* (Tokyo: Sankibō Busshorin, 1971), 1:24. Katsumata Shunkyō in *Mikkyō no Nihonteki tenkai,* 141–148, has compiled a number of quotations which suggest that Kūkai was interested in *sokushin jōbutsu* from the time he returned to Japan from China.

10. *Kōya zappitsushū* in Takagi Shingen, *Kōbō Daishi no shokan* (Kyoto: Hōzōan, 1981), 40–44. Kūkai's overtures to Tokuitsu in Tōgoku may have been an important factor in Saichō's decision to travel to that area and proselytize the following year. Another letter which may have preceded the one mentioned above is found in the *Shūryōshū* in *Kōbō Daishi chosaku zenshū* (Tokyo: Sankibō Busshorin, 1973), 3:386–391.

11. The *Shingonshū miketsumon* (*T* 77.863c) also includes a sentence criticizing Tendai views on *sokushin jōbutsu,* but the topic is introduced and dropped so abruptly that it may have been added to the text later after Tokuitsu had read Saichō's *Hokke shūku.* See Sueki Fumihiko, "*Shingonshū miketsumon* no shomondai," *Bukkyō bunka* 16 (1985): 67.

12. Katsumata suggests a date around 815 for Tokuitsu's *Shingonshū miketsumon;* see *Mikkyō no Nihonteki tenkai,* 145–146. Tomabechi has argued for an even earlier date for the *Miketsumon,* placing it before one of Kūkai's letters; see "*Shingonshū miketsumon* to Kōbō Daishi," *Chizan gakuhō* 33 (1984). While I have not been able to obtain a copy of this article, it is summarized in Sueki, "*Shingonshū miketsumon,*" 59.

13. Katsumata in *Mikkyō no Nihonteki tenkai,* 152, mentions one theory dating the composition of *Sokushin jōbutsu gi* around 819, but eventually suggests a date several years later because many of the teachings presented by Kūkai are significantly more advanced than they were in earlier texts (ibid., 152). Kanaoka Shūyū in *Kūkai jiten* (Tokyo: Tōkyōdō shuppan, 1979), 140, places the date of compilation between 815 and 824 but does not consider Katsumata's argument that the high level of development of Kūkai's teaching on the six elements would indicate that the composition must have fallen near the end of this period.

14. Shioiri Ryōchū, *Dengyō Daishi,* 336–337; Shimaji Daitō, "Tokuitsu no kyōgaku ni tsuite," in Tamura Kōyū, ed., *Tokuitsu ronsō* (Tokyo: Kokusho kankōkai, 1986), 80.

15. For Kūkai's response to Tokuitsu, see *Himitsu mandarakyō fuhōden, Kōbō Daishi chosaku zenshū,* 2:93. Sueki advances the theory in "*Shingonshū miketsumon,*" 65–66, that Tokuitsu's work was written in several stages.

16. Asai Endō in *Jōko Nihon Tendai,* 189–191, is undecided about whether the term was first emphasized in Tendai or Shingon circles. Tomabechi Seiichi in "Sokushin jōbutsu no kentō," 160–162, argues that Kūkai wrote about rapid realization earlier than Saichō and believes that Saichō recognized the importance of the theme of *sokushin jōbutsu* first. However, both scholars have noted the difficulty of coming to a definitive chronology for the early development of the term.

17. *T* 32.572c. Quoted in *Kōbō Daishi chosaku zenshū*, 1:24, 44. See also Hakeda, *Kūkai*, 227.

18. *Hokke shūku*, DZ, 3:78–79.

19. *DZ*, 3:277.

20. Tomabechi in "Sokushin jōbutsu no kentō," 161, has argued that Saichō felt no need to discuss esoteric passages because Kūkai had already done so. Saichō therefore concentrated on *Lotus Sutra* passages in order to support his contention that the perfect teachings were essentially the same as esoteric teachings. Tomabechi's argument ignores the general tendency in all of Saichō's later works to focus on *Lotus Sutra* and Tendai texts.

In addition, although Saichō never overtly cites esoteric texts in his discussion of *sokushin jōbutsu*, the terms "verbal mystery" *(kumitsu)* and "physical mystery" *(shimmitsu)* are used to describe the dragon king's daughter's prediction of her impending buddhahood and her subsequent physical transformation. See *DZ*, 3:264. Additional evidence that Saicho might have intended to integrate esoteric Buddhist themes into his interpretation of *sokushin jōbutsu* is found in his citation of a passage from the *Kuan P'u-hsien p'u-sa hsing fa-ching* which identified Śākyamuni and Vairocana (*T* 9.392c; Katō, *The Threefold Lotus Sutra*, 362; cited by Saichō in *DZ*, 1:215 and 3:266). This passage had played a key role in earlier arguments that esoteric and perfect teachings were identical in purport. See Groner, *Saichō*, 260–263, for a discussion of this theme. However, Saichō died before he could discuss the implications that esoteric Buddhism had for *sokushin jōbutsu*.

21. Chan-jan, *Fa-hua wen-chü chi*, *T* 34:314b. The *Fa-hua wen-chü chi* was first brought to Japan by Saichō (*Taishūroku, DZ*, 4:351).

22. Chih-i, *Fa-hua wen-chü*, *T* 34.117a. The passage in the *T'ai-ching* to which Chih-i referred is found in *T* 12.1034a–35c. The term *sokushin jōbutsu* is mentioned in *T* 12.1034c. The frequency of passages concerning the enlightenment of women in early Mahāyāna texts is probably due to the important role which women played in the rise of Mahāyāna. In most of the early Mahāyāna scriptures, women were said to receive a male body when they realized buddhahood. However, in some texts the argument was made that phenomena was devoid of substantial characteristics such as male and female (*T'ai-ching*, *T* 12.1034c). For a survey of early Mahāyāna texts discussing the enlightenment of women, see Hirakawa Akira, *Shoki Daijō Bukkyō no kenkyū* (Tokyo: Shunjūsha, 1969), 262–282; and Nancy Schuster, "Changing the Female Body: Wise Women and the Bodhisattva Career in Some Mahāratnakūṭasūtras," *Journal of the International Association of Buddhist Studies* 4, no. 1 (1981): 24–69. Schuster translates and analyzes a number of texts similar to the *T'ai-ching*.

23. Chan-jan, *Fa-hua wen-chü chi*, *T* 34.314b.

24. The *T'ai-ching* is not cited in discussions of the dragon king's daughter in the *Lotus* commentaries by Chi-tsang or Tz'u-en. See Chiba Shōkan, "Dengyō Daishi no sokushin jōbutsugi," 180.

25. *Miao-fa lien-hua-ching*, *T* 9.35a–c; Leon Hurvitz, trans., *Scripture of the Lotus Blossom of the Fine Dharma*, 198–201.

26. For a detailed list of extant Sanskrit versions and an analysis of the compilation of the chapter, see Tsukamoto Keishō, "Daibahon no seiritsu to haikei."

27. Hirakawa Akira, *Indo Bukkyōshi* (Tokyo: Shunjūsha 1974), 1:362.

28. *Ch'u san-tsang chi chi*, *T* 55.13b; Ōchō Enichi, *Hokke shisō*, 239–241.

29. Chih-i, *Fa-hua wen-chü*, *T* 34.114c.

30. Chi-tsang, *Fa-hua i-su*, *T* 34.452a–b.

31. The status of the chapter is discussed in a variety of sources, including Chan-jan, *Fa-hua wen-chü chi*, *T* 34.312b–c; Shōshin, *Mongu shiki, Dainihon Bukkyō zensho* (hereafter cited as *DNBZ*) (Tokyo: Bussho kankōkai, 1912–1922), 22:118; Jōkei (1155–1213) of the Hossō School, *Hokke kaijishō*, *DNBZ*, 19:322; and Shūshō (1202–1278) of the Kegon School, *Hoke-kyō jōgūōgi shoshō*, *DNBZ*, 14:132.

32. Saichō often chose to develop his own terminology or themes in his writing, ignoring the complex doctrinal system which had been developed in Chih-i's writings. Although the reasons for this tendency are not always clear, Saichō's early study of Hua-yen teachings many have left him better versed in that system. Or perhaps he realized that in some cases, such as his views on the precepts, T'ien-t'ai writings could be cited to refute him. Whatever the reason, Saichō's development of new terminology gave his writings an immediacy which made them persuasive. For example, his treatment of the dragon king's daughter, discussed below, is done as a simple line-by-line commentary without reference to other T'ien-t'ai writings.

33. The *Lotus Sutra* includes no discussion of the path to enlightenment, but does have several terms which can be interpreted as references to stages. As a result, discussions of the path are found in various sections of the commentaries on the text. However, such discussions, even in a single commentary, are not necessarily consistent. For discussions of the path in Chinese commentaries on the *Lotus*, see Maruyama Takao's articles, "*Hokke genron* ni okeru ryakui jōbutsu," *Indogaku Bukkyōgaku kenkyū* 29, no. 2 (1981): 78–83; and "Chūgoku Hokke kyōgaku ni okeru ryakui jōbutsu," *Indogaku Bukkyōgaku kenkyū* 30, no. 2 (1982): 542–549.

34. *DZ*, 3:261. The six destinies (or realms of existence) are those of gods, humans, titans *(asuras)*, animals, hungry ghosts, and hell-dwellers. The first of the two adornments consists of the first five of the six perfections; the second adornment corresponds to the sixth perfection, wisdom. They are called adornments because the accomplishment of the perfections is manifest in physical qualities.

35. *DZ*, 3:266–267. Since for Saichō even a person who required three lifetimes to realize buddhahood had perfect faculties, this categorization could not be used to justify the study of Hossō or other "inferior" teachings. Samantabhadra appears to those who think of the *Lotus* and grants the practitioner three *dhāraṇīs*. According to the *Lotus Sutra*, the first *dhāraṇī* mentioned enables a person to transform his cravings into the wisdom to master nonsubstantiality (*T* 9.61b; Hurvitz, *Lotus*, 333).

Asai Endō in *Jōko Nihon Tendai*, 186, has argued that Saichō adopted the position that *sokushin jōbutsu* could occur over one, two, or three lifetimes to account for the transformation of the body of the dragon king's daughter into a male body. However, this explanation ignores the statements in Chan-jan's *Fa-hua wen-chü chi* that the dragon king's daughter neither abandoned her current body nor received a new one.

36. *Shugo kokkaishō*, *DZ*, 2:275–276.

37. *Ketsugonjitsuron*, *DZ*, 2:713; *Hokke shūku*, *DZ*, 3:241, 244. For a description of the Hua-yen position on the realization of buddhahood within three lifetimes, see Ishii Kyōdō, *Kegon kyōgaku seiritsu shi* (Kyoto: Heirakuji shoten, 1979), 423–425; and Yoshizu Yoshihide, *Kegon Zen no shisōshiteki kenkyū* (Tokyo: Daitō shuppansha, 1985), 95–96. Ishii notes that the Hua-yen position was probably originally based on passages in Tendai texts such as Chih-i's *Fa-hua wen-chü* (*T* 34.2c). Saichō's decision to ignore the Hua-yen sources which he had cited in earlier works

may have been due to his realization that the teaching could be supported with Tendai texts. The changes in Saichō's attitudes toward Hua-yen doctrines are analyzed in Hayashi Senshō, "Dengyō kyōgaku ni okeru Kegon kyōgaku ni tsuite," *Ōsaki gakuhō* 93 (1938): 63–86; and Yoshizu Yoshihide, "Kegon kyōgaku e no Saichō no taiō ni tsuite," *Kegongaku kenkyū* 1 (1987): 33–64. Saichō also criticized the Hua-yen position on sudden enlightenment, saying that it was sudden enlightenment after eons of practice (Groner, *Saichō*, 189). Although there would seem to be similarities between the Hua-yen interpretation of *shinman jōbutsu* (realization of buddhahood with the completion of the ten degrees of faith) and Saichō's interest in the pivotal role of the first abode, the connection is not supported in Saichō's discussion of *sokushin jōbutsu*, and significant differences in the two concepts do exist.

38. *Kuan P'u-hsien-ching*, *T* 9.389c; Katō, *The Threefold Lotus Sutra*, 348.

39. *DZ*, 3:266.

40. For a discussion of perfect faculties, see Groner, *Saichō*, 180–183.

41. A list and description of the fifty-seven stages can be found in Hurvitz, "Chih-i", *Melanges chinois et bouddhiques* 12 (1962): 268–271, 363–368. Descriptions of the path for the Hīnayāna, pervasive and unique teachings are also found in Hurvitz. For a useful chart showing how the various descriptions of the path are related, see David W. Chappell, ed., *T'ien-t'ai Buddhism: An Outline of the Fourfold Teachings*, 33–34. Concise descriptions of the path are found in the passages on each of the four teachings in this text.

42. For discussions of the evolution of Chih-i's views on the six levels of identity, see Satō Tetsuei, *Zoku Tendai Daishi no kenkyū* (Kyoto: Hyakkaen, 1981), 428–435; and Katō Tsutomu, "Rokusoku no seiritsu katei ni tsuite," *Tendai gakuhō* 23 (1981): 120–123. For discussions in English of the six levels of identity, see Neal Donner, "Sudden and Gradual Intimately Conjoined: Chih-i's T'ien-t'ai View," in Peter Gregory, ed., *Sudden and Gradual: Approaches to Enlightenment in Chinese Thought*, Studies in East Asian Buddhism, no. 5 (Honolulu: University of Hawaii Press, 1988); and Chappell, *T'ien-t'ai Buddhism*, 160–161.

43. *Tendai Hokkeshū gishū*, *T* 74.267. The three virtues *(santoku)* are three innate qualities—(1) dharmakāya, (2) wisdom, and (3) emancipation or freedom from suffering—which allow all sentient beings to have the potential of realizing buddhahood.

44. In much of Mahāyāna, a person is said to become a sage only when he enters the first land, a stage much higher than the first abode. The Tendai school maintains the position that the first abode in the perfect teaching is equivalent to the first land in the unique *(bekkyō)* teaching. Moreover, when viewed from the perspective of the perfect teaching, all the stages after the first abode in the unique teaching are fictions; no one actually ever realized them since they were merely teaching devices. Instead a follower of the unique teaching would switch to the stages of the perfect path.

45. *Tendai Hokkeshū gishū*, *T* 74.267–268. The lamp metaphor suggests that the last forty-two stages are different in degree only, not in quality. Consequently, a practitioner could probably skip many of them.

46. *Hokke shūku, DZ*, 3:265.

47. The issue of exactly when the physical changes associated with Buddhist practice occurred is extremely complex. Not only do the positions taken by various schools in East Asia differ, but the position taken by a school will vary according to

the religious faculties of the practitioner and the type of teachings he follows. For a survey of the positions held by East Asian schools, see *Mochizuki Bukkyō daijiten* (Tokyo: Sekai seiten kankō kyōkai, 1958), 1:121c–123c.

48. *DZ,* 3:258–260.

49. Asai Endō in *Jōko Nihon Tendai,* 184–185, argues that Saichō faithfully followed Chih-i's view of the path. For a discussion of Chih-i's view of the dangers of the sudden path, see Dan Stevenson, "The Pathless Path: Practical Considerations Behind Chih-i's Systematization of the Six Identities," paper delivered at the 1988 annual meeting of the American Academy of Religion. Chih-i's lack of interest in the time required to realize buddhahood is discussed in Hibi Nobutada, "Chūgoku Tendai ni okeru jōbutsu e no katei," in Watanabe Hōyō, ed., *Hokke Bukkyō no Butsudaron to shujōron* (Kyoto: Heirakuji shoten, 1985), 195–213.

50. These themes will be developed by the author in a subsequent essay.

# Pictorial Art of the
## *Lotus Sutra* in Japan

MIYA TSUGIO

Faith in the *Lotus Sutra* was widely established in Japan by the early seventh century. As the text grew in popularity, artworks inspired by the *Lotus Sutra* flourished in various media including painting, sculpture, calligraphy, architecture, and the applied arts. Because the sheer amount of *Lotus*-related art is considerable, a systematic study might well begin with a typology of just one area. In this chapter we shall focus on pictorial art, made up chiefly but not exclusively of paintings.

Pictorial representations based on the *Lotus Sutra* can be broadly subdivided into two groups:

1. Those used predominately as *honzon,* the central image of worship in religious services, rituals, and devotions.
2. Those intended to explain the meaning of the sutra.

The first kind is also termed *raihaizō,* or "images used for worship," and the second belongs more specifically to the category called *kyō-i-e,* or "illustrations of the significant ideas of a sutra." These two categories indicate the functional nature of the paintings, which served to promote both faith in and understanding of the *Lotus Sutra.* These categories, of course, are not mutually exclusive, and the suggested typology is certainly not meant to separate faith from understanding but rather to indicate an emphasis upon the one as it complements the other.

## Pictorial Art of the *Lotus Sutra* Used for Worship

The works in this first category were used as central images in services such as the Eight Lectures on the *Lotus Sutra (Hokke hakkō).* They were also used in esoteric Buddhist rituals such as the *Hoke-kyō-hō* or as the object of worship for personal prayers and devotion. One of the oldest examples is the cast bronze plaque at Hasedera of "Śākyamuni Preaching the *Lotus Sutra*," which, although not a painting, has a strong pictorial quality. This plaque was sponsored by the priest Dōmyō of Gufukuji and others in 686 for the longevity and prosperity of Emperor Temmu. It is based on the "Apparition of the Jeweled Stupa" chapter, which describes the following events: (1) Prabhū-taratna, a buddha of the past, causes his stupa to emerge from the earth in order to prove that the *Lotus Sutra* Śākyamuni expounds is true; (2) Śākyamuni calls forth the buddhas from the ten directions of the universe who are his alter egos; (3) Śākyamuni then opens the doors of the treasure stupa hovering in the sky and takes his seat beside Prabhūtaratna. These three incidents symbolize the truth, universality, and eternal nature of the teachings of the *Lotus Sutra*. The plaque represents this story with a hierarchical grouping of deities, organized symmetrically to the left and right of the centrally placed stupa in which Śākyamuni and Prabhūtaratna sit. This arrangement reinforces the message of the superiority of the *Lotus Sutra* by the subordination of all forms to the buddhas within the stupa, but does not narrate the details of the story as presented in the sutra. Because the composition is balanced and orderly, the dramatic, even fantastic, atmosphere of the story is not fully exploited. However, in view of the fact that the plaque was primarily intended to serve the well-being of an emperor rather than the propagation of the sutra, the austerity of the composition can be regarded as appropriate.

Many images intended for worship used the stupa of Prabhū-taratna as the focal point of the composition. In so doing they emphasized the preeminence of the sutra as a whole rather than any single lesson or doctrine within it. A relief carving, entitled "*Lotus mandala*," in the collection of Yokokura-dera in Gifu prefecture, is one such example. This wood carving systematically distributes eighteen deities, such as the buddhas of the four directions, the four deva kings, and various bodhisattvas, in four registers with Śākyamuni and Prabhūtaratna seated within the stupa at the center of the second and third registers; the bodhisattvas Mañjuśrī, seated on a lion, and Samantabhadra, mounted on an elephant, are placed to the right and left of the stupa (in the third register). The artist took certain liberties with the text by portraying popular bodhisattvas such as Mañjuśrī and Samantabhadra, who, while associated with the *Lotus Sutra*, are not specifically mentioned in the "Apparition of the Jeweled

Stupa" chapter. The point was not to explicate the contents of a particular chapter but rather to assert the superiority of the text as a whole. Although this carving was produced in the mid-Heian period, it retains the hierarchical and rigid composition seen in the plaque at Hasedera.

The term "mandala" is often used loosely in Japan for any composition that arranges figures in symmetrical rows, such as those described above, or for groupings which echo the typical arrangement seen in true Mandalas of the esoteric schools. The term is also applied to paintings that summarize the contents of texts, a practice I will describe in a moment. (In this essay I shall capitalize Mandala when referring to works directly connected with the esoteric teachings in order to distinguish them from works which by tradition have had the term mandala affixed to them.)

Esoteric *Lotus* Mandalas produced as the main image for the esoteric rite *Hoke-kyō-hō* were based on texts such as Pu-k'ung's translations, *Ch'eng-chiu miao-fa lien-hua-ching wang yu-ch'ieh kuan-chih i-kuei* (J. *Jōju myōhō renge-kyō ō yuga kanchi giki*) and *Fa-hua man-t'u-lo wei-i hsing-se fa ching* (J. *Hokke mandara igi gyōshiki hōgyō*), which were transmitted from T'ang China to Japan by Ennin (also known as Jikaku Daishi, 792–862). According to an entry for the nineteenth day of the first month of 840 in *Jikaku Daishi zaitō sōshin roku*, a record of objects obtained in China, Ennin sent a booklet of *Lotus* Mandalas to Enryakuji. Moreover, a booklet of *Lotus* Mandalas is also noted in the *Nittō shingu shōgyō mokuroku*, the inventory of texts which Ennin brought back from China and submitted to the emperor in 847.

The esoteric *Lotus* Mandala divides the "platform," or the surface of the painting, into three concentric "halls," or squares. An eight-petaled lotus is placed in the middle of the central square. At its center is drawn the two buddhas within the stupa. The eight great bodhisattvas (Mañjuśrī, Maitreya, Avalokiteśvara, Samantabhadra, Bhaiśajyarāja, Gadgadasvara, Nityodyukta, and Aksayamati) are depicted on each petal of the lotus, and the four great disciples (Kāśyapa, Subhūti, Śāriputra, and Maudgalyāyana) are placed at the four corners of the central square. Sixteen bodhisattvas are placed in the second layer. In the third layer, the four deva kings, eight classes of beings *(hachibushū)*, and four great vidyārāja *(myōō)* are drawn. Thus the *Lotus* Mandala demonstrates the diagrammatic composition characteristic of esoteric works.

The typical esoteric Mandala formula was sometimes altered to reflect a peculiarly Japanese approach. A *Lotus* Mandala from the

Kamakura period at Oribe Jinja in Nara prefecture, for example, includes the ten *rākṣasī* or female demons *(jūrasetsunyo)*, who appear in the "Dhāraṇī" chapter, in a row underneath the configuration of the Mandala. This addition creates a new composition which vividly attests to the Japanese faith in the ten female demons.

The subject of the foregoing esoteric and exoteric works can be defined as representations of the theme of the assembly in the heavens. Other images used for worship focused on the theme of Śākyamuni preaching to the assembly at Vulture Peak. The "Hokke-dō Kompon mandala" is the oldest work of this type. Originally in the Hokke-dō at Tōdaiji, it was purchased by the Boston Museum of Fine Arts in the Meiji period. Although the lower part of the painting is damaged, the upper portion displays Śākyamuni surrounded by disciples and various bodhisattvas within a setting of mountains and forests. Śākyamuni's eternal expounding of the law to the assembly on Vulture Peak, and, by extension, to all people, is the intended message of the painting. Therefore, like the assembly in the skies, the assembly at Vulture Peak concentrates on the importance of the sutra itself rather than on any particular doctrine. This painting was probably produced for the *Lotus* convocation *(Hokke-e)* that was performed at the Hokke-dō in 746. The condition of the lower part of the work makes it impossible to know whether originally there may have been narrative illustrations of the content of the sutra beneath the preaching scene, as some scholars have suggested. However, if there were, this painting would have embodied both functions of worship and explanation.

That paintings existed which attempted to fulfill both roles is apparent when one examines the hanging scroll at Kaijūsenji in Kyoto prefecture, commonly referred to as a *Lotus Sutra* mandala. The delicate beauty of the brushwork and sense of color reflect the refined sensibilities of the Fujiwara aristocracy and thus suggest a date of the latter half of the twelfth century. This work combines the theme of Śākyamuni preaching at Vulture Peak with scenes from selected chapters of the sutra in such a way as to give nearly equal balance to both. The following scenes are depicted in a dreamlike manner:

1. Beneath a theriomorphic Vulture Peak, Śākyamuni, near the picture's center, expounds the law to the assembly.
2. At the upper right, the jeweled stupa appears in the sky.
3. To the right of center, bodhisattvas emerge from underground.

4. At the lower left, the buddhas from the ten directions sit beneath jeweled trees.
5. At the lower right are scenes of hell.

Scenes 2 and 4 are based on the "Apparition of the Jeweled Stupa" chapter and scene 3 is based on the "Welling Up out of the Earth" chapter. Hells are mentioned in several chapters, but the specific reference is unclear. Although scenes based on several chapters are employed, all but the hell scenes emphasize groups of deities rather than narrative episodes. The preaching scene, by its prominent placement and size, clearly is intended as the dominant motif, but the very presence of figures based on specific chapters weakens the sense of this work as an image used solely for worship, and reveals the difficulty in separating the functions of adoration and instruction in religious art.

Paintings of assemblies of various deities from the sutra parallel those of the assembly at Vulture Peak or in the heavens. These works place a large representation of Śākyamuni at their center flanked by bodhisattva attendants, drawn smaller than the Buddha, and by a group of even smaller deities ranged to the extreme right and left of the bodhisattvas. Variation appears only in the choice of attendants. The "Sangatsu-kyō mandala" (mandala of the sutra of the third month, named after the *Lotus* convocation held in the third month), in the Shana-in in Shiga prefecture belongs to this group. This work of the Kamakura period uses as attendants the bodhisattvas Samantabhadra and Mañjuśrī, the ten disciples, the ten female demons, and two of the four deva kings (Dhṛtarāṣṭra and Vaiśravaṇa), who, as the "Dhāraṇī" chapter explains, protect the believers of the *Lotus Sutra*.

Representations of assemblies of deities from the *Lotus Sutra* did not always center on Śākyamuni and could focus on other popular deities. The bodhisattva Samantabhadra, whose role is described in the twenty-eighth chapter and in the closing sutra, *Kanfugengyō,* and the ten female demons, from the "Dhāraṇī" chapter, were widely revered as protectors of believers in the *Lotus Sutra,* and paintings that combined both images were frequently produced from the end of the Heian through the Kamakura periods. The forming of these images probably developed among the aristocracy as early as the mid-Heian period, although the first documentary evidence does not appear until the mid-twelfth century, when an entry for the ninth day in the tenth month of 1155 in the *Hyōhanki,* the diary of Taira

Nobunori, the minister of military affairs, notes that Fujiwara
Tadamichi held a religious ceremony at Hōjōji in which the figures of
Samantabhadra and the ten female demons were used as the central
image of worship.

Extant paintings of Fugen and the ten female demons begin with
the late Heian painting at Rozanji, which places Samantabhadra,
mounted on a six-tusked elephant, in the center of a hanging scroll
and encircles him with the figures of Vaiśravaṇa, Dhṛtarāṣṭra, Bhaiṣajyarāja, Pradānaśūra, and the ten female demons. There are many
more examples from the Kamakura period. If categorized according
to their configurations, four varieties emerge: those that place the
deities on the ground, those that have the deities floating on clouds,
those in which the ten female demons are dressed in Chinese robes,
and those in which the demons are in Japanese costumes. However, it
is not certain which arrangement was the earliest.

The idea of women becoming buddhas is explained in the "Devadatta" and "The Bodhisattva Medicine King" chapters; consequently, faith in the *Lotus Sutra* among Heian women of the
aristocratic class was particularly fervent. The paintings of Samantabhadra and the ten female demons may have been sponsored by
women as an outgrowth of their particular interest in the sutra. Such
a hypothesis is also suggested by the highly refined, aristocratic sense
of form which characterizes the depictions from both the Heian and
the Kamakura periods.

Samantabhadra's popularity is evidenced too by the fairly large
number of extant paintings that feature him, either alone or with a
few attendants, but always mounted on a six-tusked elephant amid
clouds. Works of the late Heian period are the oldest extant examples, and those at Tokyo National Museum and Bujōji in Tottori prefecture are particularly famous. The iconography accords with the
descriptions in the "Encouragements of the Bodhisattva Samantabhadra" chapter and stresses his protective role. Consequently
these paintings were used not only as the central image for religious
services and rites but also as objects for personal devotion.

The pictorial art that served as the main images in religious services
share certain general features. The format and size, for example,
often reflect the public nature of their function, and many employ a
hanging scroll format in sizes that range from about 100 × 60 cm to
the very large work at Shana-in measuring 237.6 × 134.2 cm. The
subject matter is usually an assembly scene, whether it be the heavenly assembly at Prabhūtaratna's stupa, the preaching assembly at

Vulture Peak, or the assembly of deities described in various chapters of the sutra. With few exceptions, a detailed depiction of the setting of the assembly is omitted. Rather, all the works emphasize the deities, with the central figures, chiefly Śākyamuni or Śākyamuni and Prabhūtaratna, dominating all other figures by virtue of their placement, frontal posture, and large size. The subsidiary roles of the attendants are made clear by their smaller size and by the frequent employment of a three-quarter view which faces them toward the central deities. In short, the hierarchical and symmetrical arrangement of the figures, the lack of detailed depictions of the locale, and the lack of narrative episodes all combine to emphasize the eternal and unchanging nature both of the Buddha and of the *Lotus Sutra*.

The images of Samantabhadra also reflect this orientation, although he is frequently placed at an oblique angle to the viewer to create a sense of movement in keeping with the text's promise that he will descend to help any believer. Such images clearly emphasize the power of the deities and thereby the potency of the text. They awaken in the viewer a sense of awe and humility befitting their use in religious services.

## Pictorial Art of the *Lotus Sutra* Used for Didactic Purposes

Although all religious art is, in some sense, didactic, in this essay the didactic category refers to works which were produced specifically for instructional purposes. In Japanese, such works are called *kyō-i-e* (illustrations of the significant ideas of the sutra). *Kyō-i-e* for the *Lotus Sutra* include pictures that explain the entire sutra (along with the opening and closing sutras) as well as particular chapters. These works are often more narrative in their content and more informal in their style than the art used as the main images in religious services.

Paintings that illustrate the meaning of the *Lotus Sutra* are also broadly referred to as *Lotus Sutra hensō*. *Hensō* literally means "transformed appearance" and refers to the transformation of the doctrines and ideas of a sutra into pictures. In Japan, however, the term *hensō* was sometimes replaced by the term "mandala," and was used particularly for large-scale paintings. Thus many of the paintings under discussion are traditionally called *Lotus Sutra* mandalas, but, unlike the *Lotus Sutra* Mandala mentioned in the preceding section, these works have no connection to esoteric Buddhist ideas or rituals.

This interchanging of terms makes for some confusion. When, for example, the phrase "Hoke-kyō mandala" appears in historical records, it is frequently difficult to judge whether the term refers to an esoteric *Lotus* Mandala or a picture of the *hensō* and therefore didactic type. However, early references to works which appear to have been *hensō* include the following:

1. Pictures of "the significant ideas of the twenty-eight chapters of the *Lotus* and the opening and closing sutras" were depicted on each pillar in the three-story pagoda of Hōjōji, which was reconstructed by Regent Fujiwara Morozane in 1079. (This is recorded in fascicle 13, "Hōjōji to kuyō gammon," in *Honchō zoku monzui.*)
2. The "Apparition of the Jeweled Stupa" and "The Life Span of the Tathāgata" chapters were illustrated on the wall behind the statue of the Buddha in the Shaka Hall of Ninnaji that was dedicated in 1135. (This is noted in *Ninnaji shoin geki.*)
3. In 1173, pictures of "the twenty-eight chapters of the *Lotus*" were depicted on the sliding screens of Saishō-in constructed by Empress Kenshunmon-in (Jishi), consort of Retired Emperor Goshirakawa. (This is noted in entries for the ninth, twelfth, thirteenth, and twentieth days of the seventh month of the third year of Jōan [1173] in *Koki.*)
4. The "significant ideas of the twenty-eight chapters of the *Lotus Sutra*" were painted in colors on the three doors and four walls of Kashōji in Ōshu. Kashōji was a temple begun by Motohira and completed by his son Hidehira. (This is mentioned in an entry for the seventeenth day of the ninth month in the fifth year of Bunji [1189] in *Azuma kagami.*)

Since these records refer to paintings of "the significant ideas of the twenty-eight chapters of the *Lotus Sutra*," the subject matter of the paintings is clearly indicated. However, it is not possible to determine whether the *Lotus* paintings in the temples constructed by the Heian nobles were actively used as *e-toki* (paintings explained by a narrator) or whether they were merely interior decorations. Possibly they can be regarded as both illustrative and decorative. Certainly many of the following extant examples of paintings of the significant ideas of the *Lotus Sutra,* though intended to instruct, also enliven the interiors of temples.

There are two broad divisions in the didactic illustrations of the

*Lotus Sutra:* large works, most often in the hanging scroll format, intended for use in the public spaces of temples and halls; and smaller-scale works, often handscrolls, that were frequently sponsored by individuals and were used in more intimate or private settings.

A *hensō* of the *Lotus Sutra,* the "Kinji hōtō mandala" in ten scrolls at Tanzan Jingu, produced in the late twelfth century during the transitional period between the end of the Fujiwara and the beginning of the Kamakura periods, demonstrates how exhaustive the treatment of the sutra can be. In this work, the texts of each of the eight fascicles, the opening sutra, and the closing sutra are copied in the configuration of a nine-story pagoda in gold dust on indigo paper. The pagoda is placed at the center of each scroll and illustrations of the sutra's contents, drawn in gold and silver, are arranged around it. Chinese and Korean examples of sutras copied in the shape of a pagoda exist, but only the Japanese examples include pictorializations of the contents of the text.

The illustrations which surround the character-pagoda are all taken from the *Lotus Sutra* and include parables, tales of the previous lives of the Buddha and bodhisattvas, acts of merit, and miracles. About 215 of these narrative episodes appear on the set of scrolls. Moreover, short excerpts from the text of the sutra are included, written within rectangular tabs, which help the viewer understand the contents of each scene. Therefore, this *hensō* combines three meritorious activities: constructing a pagoda, copying the sutra, and expounding or explaining the sutra.

*Lotus hensō* with character-pagodas were also produced in the Kamakura period, as is seen in the eight scrolls of the "Kinji hōtō mandala" now owned by Ryūhonji, but which originally may have come from Hōryūji. Although this work of the mid-thirteenth century does not include the opening and closing sutras, the compositional form is similar to that of the scrolls at Tanzan Jingu. However, the pictorial surface does not reflect the "horror vacuui" that is expressed in the Tanzan example. Since the composition is more spacious, the Ryūhonji scrolls contain fewer pictorial episodes, a total of about 120. On each scroll certain enlarged and detailed scenes, which correspond to the selection of scenes used for the frontispieces in scrolls of the *Lotus Sutra* from the Heian period, make it clear which episodes were regarded as most important.

Other large-scale *Lotus Sutra hensō* from the Kamakura period include the wall paintings in the pagoda at Saimyōji in Shiga prefec-

ture and the set of seven-scroll hanging scrolls, originally from Kan-
nonshōji in Shiga prefecture, now owned by Nara National Museum.
The Saimyōji paintings can be dated to the time of the construction
of the pagoda in the mid-thirteenth century. The paintings are placed
on the walls on both sides of the doors located at the center of each of
the four walls of the pagoda. Thus there are eight individual painting
surfaces, each containing illustrations to one of the eight fascicles of
the *Lotus Sutra*. Essential passages from the fascicle are written at the
top center of each panel, and within each panel the various scenes are
accompanied by narrow tabs containing the chapter titles. The
Saimyōji wall paintings contain about sixty narrative or episodic
scenes. Most likely those Heian works referred to in records as paintings of the "significant ideas of the twenty-eight chapters of the
*Lotus Sutra*" were similar to the Saimyōji wall paintings, which can
therefore can be seen as inheriting the Heian tradition of *Lotus Sutra*
painting.

The scrolls at Nara National Museum, on the other hand, are based
on the *Lotus Sutra* in seven fascicles, with each scroll representing one fascicle. Generally, each scroll has four preaching
scenes, dominated by Śākyamuni preaching at Vulture Peak at the
top of the scroll, and four narrative episodes. The narrative themes
adopt traditional subject matters similar to those of the Saimyōji
paintings, but are distinct in their continued emphasis on assembly
scenes characteristic of images used for worship. However, the lively
presentation of episodes such as the burning house from the "Parable" chapter make the instructional aspect undeniable, and stylisti-
cally the paintings suggest a date of the second half of the thirteenth
century.

The illustrations in the didactic works discussed above closely
adhere to the sutra text, and are indebted to Heian models in terms
of their style or selection of subject matter. Two works from the end
of the Kamakura period and the opening years of the Muromachi
period expand their instructional roles by including stories that
explain deities or ideas that are not specifically detailed in the text of
the sutra itself. The first example of this, the *Lotus Sutra* mandala in
twenty-two scrolls at Hompōji in Toyama prefecture, illustrates one or
two chapters of the *Lotus* on each scroll. This is the largest and most
comprehensive set of extant *Lotus Sutra henso*. According to inscriptions found on nearly each scroll, the priest Jōshin solicited funds for
the paintings in the spring of 1326 and they were completed in the
winter of 1328. The painter was a certain Kammyō about which noth-

Frontispiece to fascicle one of the *Lotus Sutra*. Handscroll. Gold and silver ink on dark blue paper. 26.3 × 22 cm. Hyakusaiji, Shiga Prefecture. Twelfth century.

Frontispiece to "Expedient Devices," from the Heike Nōkyō. Ink, colors, and gold and silver on paper. Height circa 25 cm. Itsukushima Jinja, Hiroshima Prefecture. 1164. National Treasure.

*Lotus Sutra* on fan-shaped paper. Ink and colors on paper. 23.3 × 48.8 (top) cm. Shitennōji, Osaka. Twelfth century. National Treasure.

Detail of fascicle one of the *Lotus Sutra*. One of eight wall paintings. Ink and colors on wood. Each panel 170.2 × 93 cm. Saimyōji, Shiga Prefecture. Thirteenth century.

*Lotus Sutra Mandala.* Hanging scroll. Colors on silk. 101.5 × 81.8 cm. Taisanji, Hyōgo Prefecture. Fourteenth century. Important Cultural Property.

Fascicle one of the *Lotus Sutra Mandala (Kinji Hōtō Mandala)*. One of eight hanging scrolls. Gold and silver ink on dark blue paper. 111.5 × 58.7 cm. Ryūhonji, Kyoto. Thirteenth century.

Fascicles three and four of the *Lotus Sutra Mandala*. One of four hanging scrolls. Ink and colors on paper. 180 × 86 cm. Honkōji, Shizuoka Prefecture. 1335. Important Cultural Property.

*Lotus Sutra Mandala.* ''Fortitude'' and ''Comfortable Conduct'' chapters. One of twenty-one hanging scrolls. Ink and colors on silk. 187 × 127.3 cm. Hompōji, Toyama prefecture. 1326–1328. Important Cultural Property.

ing is known. Based on an examination of the colophons written on narrow vertical tabs within each painting, one can generally say that illustrations representing the underlying doctrines in each chapter are placed in the center of the scroll or in a large, prominent space; an assembly scene is frequently placed at the top of each scroll; and the parables or explanatory episodes are placed near the lower edge of the scroll (with the exception of the parable of the burning house from the "Parable" chapter). Moreover, there is a tendency to treat the parables in a less serious manner, while auditors in the assemblies appear with formal attitudes of obeisance. Finally, prominent scenes are composed in such a way as to distinguish them from less important ones. These methods make this *hensō* unique in its conscientious portrayal of both the stories and the doctrinal arguments of the sutra.

The *Lotus* mandala in four scrolls at Honkōji in Shizuoka prefecture depicts two of the eight fascicles of the *Lotus* on each scroll. They were executed in 1335 according to the inscription on the back of the paintings. The subject of each scene is identified in narrow vertical tabs. These inscriptions make it apparent that the scenes tend to be arranged from the top to the bottom of the scroll in accordance with their textual order. The four scrolls include so many episodes, however, that the work sometimes lacks compositional coherence and clarity.

The Hompōji and Honkōji works differ from the earlier *hensō* in several aspects. First, they attempt such comprehensiveness that unless the viewer is thoroughly conversant with the text, it is difficult to understand all the details of the various scenes without the brief, explanatory colophons. In contrast, the Saimyōji wall paintings depict traditional choices of subject matter and thus the viewer could easily understand their content. It is likely, therefore, that both the Hompōji and Honkōji sets were produced with the expectation that an *e-toki* or narrator would explain the details to the ordinary temple visitor. Currently, at both temples, oral narrations of the content of the paintings are conducted.

Second, as noted above, the Hompōji and Honkōji works include material from sources other than the *Lotus Sutra*. The Honkōji set, for example, depicts the miracle of Rāhula being thrown into a fire pit (which does not harm him) and the story of Sessan Dōji, a *jataka* tale in which Śākyamuni appears as a young boy who throws himself off a cliff in order to hear a verse of scripture from a bodhisattva disguised as a demon. The Hompōji scrolls also include episodes that are not described in the sutra, such as the story of Maudgalyāyana's exorcism of the dragon king, which is inserted in the scroll devoted to the "Belief and Understanding" chapter, and the esoteric practices of Rāhula, which are added to the scroll dealing with the "Prophecies Conferred on Learners and Adepts" chapter. The six realms of transmigration are also frequently illustrated. These additions reflect a more complex expository nature than that of earlier paintings and highlight the necessary role that a narrator must have played in their elucidation. Consequently the Hompōji and Honkōji scrolls can be regarded as works embodying a new conception of *Lotus Sutra* illustrations in which related themes from other sources were interwoven into the pictorial text of the *Lotus* itself.

Paintings intended for use in a public setting sometimes employed a more intimate format. The *Hoke-kyō emaki,* which intersperse paintings with a translation of the sutra into Japanese, is one such example. In addition to the formal translation that precedes each section of painting, there are brief excerpts and descriptions, possibly intended to aid a narrator, integrated into the paintings. At present the Hatakeyama Kinenkan Museum, the Kōsetsu Museum, and the Ueno family in Hyōgo prefecture own fragments from this set. Although the pictures and text are now disordered, they illustrate two complete passages from the "The Supernatural Powers of the Tathāgata" and "Entrustment" chapters, and originally formed a single scroll within a set of seven scrolls based on the *Lotus Sutra* in seven fascicles. The style suggests a date of the mid-thirteenth century, and the features of the scrolls are similar to those seen in the previously mentioned "Kinji hōtō mandala" and the frontispieces of the Heian period. The work, therefore, is within the traditional lineage of *Lotus Sutra hensō* and demonstrates the perseverance of the classical illustrations of the *Lotus Sutra.*

The didactic paintings thus far described share some of the formal qualities that were also found in the images used for worship. They frequently employed the large hanging scroll format and were intended for use within temples. However, because they narrate the stories of the text, they also adapt some of the techniques used in secular handscrolls of the Heian and Kamakura periods. The same figure, for example, is depicted repeatedly, but in front of a changing background to indicate a passage of time. The figures display emotions through their posture, gesture, and facial expressions. Narratives scenes are placed within detailed settings, and clouds, architectural elements, or landscapes separate the individual scenes, thereby helping to organize the composition. Thus while the painting, viewed as a whole, may seem complex and formal, the particular episodes are individualized and lively.

In addition to the works listed above, examples of *Lotus Sutra hensō* in Japan include illustrated frontispieces to copies of the sutra text and sutra cases of sprinkled gold lacquer. Whereas the didactic paintings described above were intended for public use and often sponsored by the clergy, the frontispieces and sutra cases were frequently sponsored by individuals and reflect a more personalized understanding of the *Lotus Sutra*.

The earliest reference to frontispiece paintings *(mikaeshi-e)* for the *Lotus Sutra* appears in the *Kanjūji bunsho,* which notes that Master of the Buddhist Law Ningyō designed frontispieces for a set of scrolls which was comprised of the *Hannya shingyō, Amida-kyō,* the opening and closing sutras, and a *Lotus Sutra* copied in gold characters, and which was dedicated by Emperor Daigo in 925 for his deceased mother. In an entry for the nineteenth day of the twelfth month of 954, the *Murakami Tennō gyōki* notes that there were "cover" (i.e., frontispiece) paintings executed by the renowned court painter Asukabe Tsunenori on a set of sutras that were sponsored by Emperor Murakami in that same year. The set included the same selection of sutras used in 925 with a *Lotus Sutra* in gold characters copied by Emperor Murakami himself. The content of the frontispiece paintings by Tsunenori is not clear. However, *Eiga monogatari* gives us a glimpse of the varieties of *Lotus* illustrations in the sutra scrolls of the period. According to the chapter entitled "A Drop of Moisture from a Stalk," thirty court women who served Empress Kenshi (the second daughter of Michinaga and consort to Emperor Sanjō) copied the *Lotus Sutra* in the format of one chapter per scroll in order to pray for the extinction of their sins. The dedicatory service was carried out on the tenth day of the ninth month in 1021 at the Amida Hall of Hōjōji with Priest Yoshō as lecturer. The frontispiece paintings of these sutra scrolls are described in the *Eiga monogatari* as follows:

[The frontispieces] provided textual illustrations—the "Gushing Forth" chapter, for instance, depicted the emergence of multitudes of bodhisattvas from the earth, and the "Eternal Life" chapter showed the Buddha's eternal abode on Vulture Peak. It was all quite beyond words. The "Devadatta" chapter was illustrated with a drawing of the dragon king's abode. Viewing the sutra was like seeing collections of elegant verses.[1]

In the chapter entitled "An Imperial Visit to the Horse Races" in *Eiga monogatari,* Michinaga's third daughter, Inshi, who was consort to Emperor Goichijō, had a miniature, jeweled stupa made as an icon for her personal devotions. It was dedicated at a service in 1024, at which the Tendai archbishop Ingen officiated. The *Lotus Sutra* used on that occasion was copied on colored paper embellished with underdrawings and included illustrations of the ideas of the sutra on the cover.[2] Thus, in the cases described above, illustrations of the sutra's contents were depicted on the frontispieces sponsored by Heian aristocrats, and were executed by priest-painters, court painters, or even the aristocrats themselves.

Among references to sutra boxes, the third fascicle of *Ochikubo monogatari* mentions a sutra box that was used at a performance of the Eight Lectures on the *Lotus Sutra* sponsored by Captain of the Guards Michiyori and his wife, Ochikubo, to celebrate the longevity of his father, Middle Counsellor Tadayori. It was described as "a lacquered box with illustrations in sprinkled gold of the most important parts of the sutra."[3] Thus we can ascertain that the significant ideas of the *Lotus Sutra* were also included as subject matter in the applied arts from at least the end of the tenth century, when *Ochikubo monogatari* was written.

There are a number of extant works that correspond to the accounts in the early records. Among the applied arts, for example, the sutra box in sprinkled gold lacquer (called "Sutra Box of the Buddha's Merits") dating from the early eleventh century in the Fujita Museum recalls the one described in *Ochikubo monogatari.* The Fujita sutra box depicts the story of the dragon king's daughter becoming a buddha and the story of Asita from the "Devadatta" chapter on the sides of the cover. On the sides of the box itself are illustrations of boys building stupas made of sand from the "Expedient Devices" chapter, rain falling on the herbs and trees from the "Medicinal Herbs" chapter, the suffering of Sadāparibhūta Bodhisattva from the "The Bodhisattva Never Disparaging" chapter, and the merits of Avalokiteśvara from the "Universal Gate of Avalokiteśvara Bodhisattva" chapter. These have a recognizably narrative sense and demonstrate that such illustrative paintings were already used by the early eleventh century.

Texts of the *Lotus Sutra* accompanied by illustrated frontispieces were produced in great numbers from the eleventh to the early thirteenth centuries. Among the extant examples are *saiji-kyō,* which contain the complete text of the sutra within a single scroll, and the *ippon kyō,* which devote one scroll to each chapter. Most numerous of all are sets of eight scrolls, one scroll per fascicle *(ikkan kyō),* copied in gold characters on dark blue paper. The illustrations to these sets display an orderliness and regularity that suggest a widespread and consistent agreement as to the appropriate choice of illustrations.

Generally, the frontispiece paintings to the eight scroll sets were drawn in gold and silver. In many of them, Śākyamuni is depicted in his preaching form seated on a lotus dais beneath jeweled trees at Vulture Peak and flanked by bodhisattvas and disciples. Many also include illustrations from the text which are placed around the preaching scene. Compara ively early works, such as those dated to the beginning of the eleventh century, often have a surface that is filled with illustrations of the text. But the subject matter becomes conventionalized by the latter half of the twelfth century. Below is a listing of the standard illustrations in these orthodox sets.

> Frontispieces to the opening sutra contain a scene of travelers crossing a river in a boat, signifying the passage across the river of life and death to the shore of nirvana.
>
> Frontispieces to the first fascicle of the *Lotus Sutra* depict worshippers in front of stupas and buddhas, the six realms of transmigration, and the preaching scene at Vulture Peak, which shows musical instruments in the heavens and scattered flowers signifying the good omens described in the introductory chapter. Most numerous of all are scenes of young boys making stupas out of sand as described in the "Expedient Devices" chapter.
>
> Almost without exception, frontispieces to the second fascicle illustrate the story of the burning house and the three carts from the "Parable" chapter. Some also illustrate the parable of the prodigal son from the "Belief and Understanding" chapter.
>
> Frontispieces to the third fascicle often use a scene of farmers plowing their fields in a rainstorm to allude to the comparison of the Buddha's grace to a rain cloud that benefits all plants without distinction as described in the "Medicinal herbs" chapter. Many also depict people from a land of famine being treated to a king's banquet, an episode found in the "Bestowal of Prophecy" chapter. A few examples illustrate the conjured city from the "Parable of the Conjured City" chapter.
>
> Frontispieces to the fourth fascicle overwhelmingly include the parable about digging for water on a high plateau from the "Preachers of the Dharma" chapter, and the appearance of Prabhūtaratna's stupa, as explained in the "Apparition of the Jeweled Stupa" chapter. Representations of episodes from the "Receipt of Prophecy by Five Hundred

Disciples" and the "Prophecies Conferred on Learners and Adepts" chapters are very rare.

Frontispieces to the fifth fascicle feature scenes of the dragon king's daughter rising from the sea to offer of a jewel to the Buddha, and the story of the king in search of the law. The king is depicted as a young servant who gathers firewood and water for Asita. Both of these stories are from the "Devadatta" chapter. There are also examples of the bodhisattvas emerging from underground as explained in the "Welling Up out of the Earth" chapter.

Frontispieces to the sixth fascicle illustrate the story of the wise physician with a scene of the preparation of medicine from the "The Life Span of the Tathāgata" chapter. Figures expounding the sutra convey the idea of the great merits reaped by anyone who hears the expounding of the sutra as explained in the "The Merits of Appropriate Joy" chapter.

Almost all frontispieces to the seventh fascicle depict Sadāparibhūta Bodhisattva in the guise of a priest fleeing from his attackers as described in the "Bodhisattva Never Disparaging" chapter. They also demonstrate Śākyamuni transmitting the law, as explained in the "Entrustment" chapter, by depicting him as he steps down from his dais to place his hand on the foreheads of the bodhisattvas. Stalks of lotus flowers are often drawn in front of the Buddha to represent the imminent arrival of Gadgadasvara Bodhisattva as explained in the "The Bodhisattva Fine Sound" chapter. Scenes of multiple stupas or the sacrifice of the arms of Bhaiṣajyarāja Bodhisattva, as explained in the "The Supernatural Powers of the Tathāgata" and "The Bodhisattva Medicine King" chapters, are represented infrequently.

Most often, frontispieces to the eighth fascicle of the *Lotus Sutra* represent Avalokiteśvara's power to save believers from all kinds of misfortune, as detailed in "The Universal Gate of Avalokiteśvara Bodhisattva" chapter, with scenes of men falling from a mountain peak or being caught in stormy seas. They also include illustrations of the magical power of two young princes who can emit water and fire from their heads and feet as explained in the "King of Fine Adornment" chapter.

Almost without exception, the frontispieces to the closing sutra depict Samantabhadra mounted on a six-tusked elephant as he descends upon clouds to appear before a secluded priest seated in a cave reading the sutra.

The consistent choice of subject matter and its conventionalized portrayal reveal the Heian aristocrat's understanding as to what were the most significant aspects of the text. These subjects were illustrated widely and were immediately recognizable, and this helped to reinforce their understanding. Moreover, the subjects of the illustrations also became the topics for poetry. In the Heian period, *waka* based on each of the twenty-eight chapters of the *Lotus (ippon kyō waka)* and ballads *(imayō)* based on the sutra were composed. Their themes, particularly in the *imayō*, correspond to the subjects of the *Lotus* illustrations. I have published an article which points out that the subject of the paintings and the content of the *imayō* agree to such an extent that their relationship recalls that of the inscriptions and pictures on *shigajiku* (poem-picture scrolls) of the Muromachi period.[4]

The existence of large numbers of sutra scrolls with conventionalized and orthodox frontispiece illustrations does not mean, however, that there was no room for variation, interpretation, and greater personalization of the illustrations. The *Eiga monogatari* passage cited above notes a variety of embellishments, and a small group of extant hand-copied sutras, which I shall call decorated sutras, display far more individuality than the large corpus of orthodox works described above. Both groups, the sutra scrolls with orthodox illustrations and those with decorative treatments, were sponsored by the upper classes, but the former had their roots in Chinese traditions while the latter reflect a uniquely Japanese approach.

The extant decorated sutras are overwhelmingly *Lotus Sutras,* a fact which is a remarkable testament to the esteem in which it was held. The decorative devices used in the design of these scrolls include variously colored paper, gold or silver foil sprinkled on top of the dyed paper, hand-drawn designs of various motifs such as floral patterns or birds, hidden characters in reedlike script *(ashide),* and poem-pictures *(uta-e).* Moreover, figures drawn in the style of courtly stories can be seen as underdrawings on the paper used to copy the sutra. The splendor is not limited to these devices. There are also examples in which characters of the text were written not only in ink, gold, or silver, but in various colors. Others employ decorative devices such as those seen in the *rendai-kyō,* in which each character of the text is placed on a lotus flower; the *hōtō-kyō,* in which each character is enclosed within a pagoda or jeweled stupa; and the *ichiji ichibutsu-kyō,* in which a buddha is drawn alongside each character. In addition, many of the decorated scrolls have covers and frontispieces with illustrations taken from the contents of the sutra. Even the metal fittings of the outer cover, the scroll axes, and the cords used to tie the scrolls demonstrate beautiful craftsmanship. The decorated sutras are visual and aesthetic expressions of the essence of faith.

Among the extant examples of magnificently decorated *Lotus*

*Sutra* of the *ippon kyō* type, two are particularly famous. The first is the *Kunōji Sutra,* named after the temple to which it originally belonged. It was copied in 1141 by Retired Emperor Toba, Empress Bifukumon-in, and other aristocrats as a joint effort to gain merit. The second is the set of sutras known as the *Heike Nōkyō* that Taira Kiyomori dedicated at Itsukushima Jinja out of gratitude for his family's prosperity. They include, besides the *Lotus Sutra,* the opening and closing sutras, the *Hannya shingyō,* and *Amida-kyō.*

In contrast to the orthodox frontispieces which fulfill their didactic role by faithfully adhering to the contents of the sutra, these two sets, and others like them, have pictures on the outer covers and frontispieces that present symbolic pictorializations of the *Lotus Sutra* itself. In other words, they depict subjects such as stalks of lotus growing in a lotus pond, the sun or moon rising from behind the hills in a field, or courtiers sitting beside a lotus pond. Even in pictures directly related to the ideas of the sutra, the paintings emphasize common activities of the aristocrats such as men and women copying sutras, courtiers huddling under an umbrella in a field, aristocrats reading a sutra in front of an image of the Buddha, or a secluded person quietly reading a sutra in a hut in the wilds. If these pictures were detached from the text and viewed independently, they could be regarded merely as genre scenes because the allusions to the text are subtle, not obvious.

Even when decorated frontispieces incorporate traditional religious subject matters, they differ sufficiently from the orthodox tradition to be regarded as unique. For example, the frontispiece to the "Preachers of the Dharma" chapter of the *Heike Nōkyō* simply depicts the ten kinds of offerings. The frontispiece to the "Life Span of the Tathāgata" chapter has deities and men playing in a field, and the frontispiece to "The Universal Gate of Avalokiteśvara Bodhisattva" chapter illustrates the Valahassa *Jataka* story in which merchants escape from a country of demons by clinging to a white horse which represents a transformation of Avalokiteśvara. The unique characteristics of the decorative frontispiece paintings derive from the same aesthetic sensibilities found in the *Lotus*-based *waka* which express religious sentiments symbolically in a very allusive manner. The *waka* and decorative scrolls form a striking contrast to the more straightforward explanatory style of *imayō* and the orthodox scrolls in blue and gold.

The *Lotus Sutra* permeated the everyday life of the aristocrats to such an extent that one can regard the idealized or symbolic expressions of the sutra's ideas in the decorative frontispieces as reflections of the Heian aristocracy's thorough grasp of the essential meaning of the *Lotus Sutra*. The depiction of the aristocrats within the decorative frontispieces, for example, attests to the incorporation of the world of the *Lotus Sutra* into their own lives. In fact, on the days on which the "Devadatta" chapter was the lecture topic in the Eight Lectures on the *Lotus Sutra*, the aristocrats participated in processions in which they played the role of the king who carried firewood and sought water for Asita.

The most extreme example of the interpenetration of this world and the world of the *Lotus* can be found in the fan-shaped booklets of the *Lotus Sutra* at Shitennōji. In this work from the late Heian period, the *Lotus Sutra* and the opening and closing sutras are copied onto fan-shaped paper embellished with gold and silver flakes of foil, marbelized patterns, and block-printed underdrawings. These sheets were then folded in half and made into a set of ten books. At present Shitennōji owns five books (fascicles one, six, seven, and the opening and the closing sutras) while Tokyo National Museum possesses one book (fascicle eight). What is significant in these booklets is the underdrawings which depict the everyday life of both commoners and aristocrats and have no direct connection to the contents of the sutra. They include love scenes, children at play, and all kinds of ordinary activities. One theory proposes that they illustrate some appropriate (but unknown) fictional tale. Another theory suggests that the use of printing for parts of the underdrawings indicates that these were ordinary, decorated fans which were converted into sutras. However, for reasons suggested above, I believe the underdrawings express the very ideal of life within the world of the *Lotus Sutra* as embraced by the aristocrats at that time. In a sense, the decorated scrolls make no distinction between their roles as objects of worship or of teaching, and they reflect instead the superimposition of the *Lotus Sutra* in every aspect of life no matter what the activity.

In the foregoing discussion of the pictorial art of the *Lotus Sutra*, I have concentrated chiefly on examples from the Heian and Kamakura periods because they are unsurpassed as works of art. The art of these periods served the aristocratic class and the large, powerful temples, and reflect their aesthetic sense and taste. This is particularly apparent in the art based on the *Lotus Sutra*, for it is clear that many of the artworks were produced or sponsored by devotees of the *Lotus Sutra*, not just by disinterested professional artists. Whether the works were intended for worship or for instruction, the variety of presentations and the new developments—such as the addition of well-known stories not explicitly mentioned in the sutra, the incorporation of the common activities of the aristocratic class, and the development of new iconography such as the combination of Samantabhadra with the ten female demons in Japanese costumes—are visual evidence of the profound role the *Lotus Sutra* played in the artistic life of the Japanese.

TRANSLATED BY WILLA JANE TANABE

## NOTES

1. William H. and Helen Craig McCullough, trans., *A Tale of Flowering Fortunes,* vol. 2 (Palo Alto: Stanford University Press, 1980), 531–532.

2. Ibid., 641.

3. Wilfred Whitehouse and Eizo Yanagisawa, trans., *Ochikubo Monogatari,* rev. ed. (Tokyo: Hokuseido Press, 1965), 209.

4. Miya Tsugio, "Hoke-kyō no e to imayō no uta."

# Poetry and Meaning:
# Medieval Poets and the *Lotus Sutra*

YAMADA SHŌZEN

## The Development of Buddhist Poetry

The *Goshūishū,* compiled in 1088, was the first imperial anthology to contain poems under the heading "Buddhist Poetry" *(shakkyōka).* These Buddhist poems did not merit a separate chapter of their own, however, and were placed in the last chapter along with two other kinds of poetry: "poems on the deities of heaven and earth" *(jingika),* or Shinto poems, and "seventeen-syllable verse" *(haikai).* In all, some nineteen Buddhist poems were included, amounting to a very small proportion of the total number of poems in the *Goshūishū.*

Buddhist poetry was established as an independent classification in the *Senzaishū,* compiled in 1183. The entire nineteenth chapter of this anthology is entitled "Shakkyōka" and contains fifty-four poems. The twentieth chapter is devoted to "Shinto poetry" and includes thirty-three poems. Thus Buddhist and Shinto poems were regarded as separate types, and the fact that there were more Buddhist poems suggests that they were more highly esteemed. All the imperial anthologies compiled after the *Senzaishū* contain separate chapters of Buddhist poetry, indicating that literature and Buddhism were closely linked thereafter. As we shall see, the connections between literature and Buddhism were developed particularly through the thirty-one-syllable poetic form called *waka.*

In general, Buddhist poetry is comprised of three types: (1) poems based on sutras *(kyōshika),* (2) poems about religious rites and lecture services, and (3) miscellaneous poems which do not fit the previous categories. Sutra poems are those in which the poet has extracted phrases from a scripture such as the *Lotus Sutra* and, using them as themes or titles, composed verses about the meaning, beliefs, or ideas contained in the phrases. Poems on religious rites and services were written on the occasion of lecture services such as the Eight Lectures on the *Lotus Sutra (Hokke hakkō)*; the lecture on nirvana *(nehan kō)*; or rites such as the transfer of merit at memorial services, the dedication of temples, the burial of sutras, or funeral services. The third group of poems are those connected with other Buddhist beliefs and activities, including, for example, poems in praise of the bodhisattva Kannon, pilgrimages to Mount Kōya, and holy men.

Having distinguished these three types of Buddhist poems on the basis of their content, we can determine the degree to which sutra poems appear in the imperial anthologies in relation to the other types of Buddhist poems. The accompanying table shows the ratio of sutra poems in the sixteen imperial anthologies that contain sections of Buddhist poetry.

As the table demonstrates, sutra poetry forms the nucleus of Buddhist poetry. The heart of Buddhism is, after all, the sutras, and Buddhist poetry evolved from that heart. The poetry on Buddhist rituals and lecture services is peripheral by comparison. The poems of the third type are the most extraneous, being, as they are, nearly indistinguishable from ordinary poems. Quantitatively, they appear in greater numbers than do the poems of rituals and services, but qualitatively their religious sensibility is shallow. It is necessary to remember that such qualitative aspects are not reflected in the table.

**TABLE 1**

| Imperial Anthology | Compilation Date | No. of Buddhist Poems | No. of Sutra Poems | Ratio |
|---|---|---|---|---|
| Goshūishū | 1088 | 19 | 8 | 42.1% |
| Senzaishū | 1188 | 54 | 35 | 64.8% |
| Shinkokinshū | 1206 | 63 | 38 | 60.3% |
| Shinchokusenshū | ca. 1234 | 56 | 33 | 58.9% |
| Shokugosenshū | 1251 | 52 | 28 | 53.8% |
| Shokukokinshū | 1265 | 73 | 38 | 52.1% |
| Shokushūishū | ca. 1278 | 66 | 43 | 65.2% |
| Shingosenshū | 1303 | 106 | 56 | 52.8% |
| Gyokuyōshū | 1313-1314 | 110 | 51 | 46.4% |
| Shokusenzaishū | ca. 1320 | 106 | 46 | 43.4% |
| Shokugoshūishū | 1325-1326 | 42 | 21 | 50.0% |
| Fūgashū | 1344-1346 | 63 | 34 | 54.0% |
| Shinsenzaishū | 1359 | 118 | 41 | 34.7% |
| Shinshūishū | 1364 | 78 | 33 | 42.3% |
| Shingoshūishū | 1383 | 35 | 19 | 54.3% |
| Shinzokukokinshū | 1439 | 66 | 29 | 43.9% |
| Totals | | 1107 | 553 | 50.0% |

## The Development of Sutra Poetry

When did sutra poetry, the chief type of Buddhist poetry, originate? In the third volume of the *Manyōshū* there is the following poem by Prince Ichihara:

| | |
|---|---|
| Inadaki ni | Peerless is the gem |
| Kisumeru tama wa | That I wear on my locks; |
| Futatsu nashi | Such are you to me |
| Ka ni mo kaku ni mo | That my heart moves at your will.[1] |
| Kimi ga ma ni ma ni | |

This poem is probably based in part on a section of the "Comfortable Conduct" chapter in the *Lotus Sutra* which tells the parable of the Great Wheel-Turning King who rewards his brave soldiers with various prizes determined according to their merits:

The bright pearl in his topknot is the only thing he will not give them. What is the reason? Only on top of the king's head is such a gem to be found. If he gives it away, the king's retainers assuredly will be greatly alarmed.[2]

While the first three lines of the poem could be based on this parable, the last two lines seem to be the main point of the poem. Thus the poem may represent nothing more than a borrowing from the sutra story in order to express one's willingness to entrust everything —even one's greatest treasure—to one's beloved. From a strictly religious viewpoint, then, it is impossible to call this a sutra poem.

On the other hand, two poems in the sixteenth chapter of the *Manyōshū* come closer to being sutra poems. They are said to have been inscribed on the face of a *koto* found within the Buddha Hall at Kawahara-dera.

| | |
|---|---|
| Ikishini no | Loathing both seas of life and death, |
| Futatsu no umi o | How deeply I long |
| Itowashimi | For the upland of nirvana, |
| Shioi no yama o | Untouched by tides of change![3] |
| Shinobi tsuru ka mo. | |

| | |
|---|---|
| Yo no naka no | Living constantly |
| Shigeki kari io ni | In the temporary abode |
| Sumi sumite | Of this busy world, |
| Itaramu kuni no | I do not know the path |
| Tazuki shirazu mo. | To the realm I seek. |

In *Manyō dai shōki* (compiled in 1690), the sixth volume of his study on the *Manyōshū,* Priest Keichū suggests that the phrase *ikishini no futatsu no umi* is based on the lines from the *Kegon Sutra,* vol. 62, that read, "How can we cross over the seas of both life and death and enter into the ocean of the Buddha's wisdom?" The phrasing is close enough to make this a reasonable possibility. These two poems are about the only possible examples of sutra poetry found in the *Manyōshū,* but even they are barely recognizable as such. Thus sutra poetry had not fully appeared at the time of the poets whose works were compiled in the *Manyōshū.*

There are two poems attributed to Priest Gyōgi (668–749) in the *Shūishū.* It is clear that the first is based on the "Devadatta" chapter of the *Lotus Sutra* and was written to praise the sutra. The second one is based on the *Shinchi kangyō* or *Daichi doron* and will not be discussed here.

| | |
|---|---|
| Hoke kyō o | For collecting firewood, |
| Waga eshi koto wa | Gathering herbs, |
| Takigi kori | And carrying water, |
| Na tsuke mizu kumi | My reward is |
| Tsukaete zo eshi. | The *Lotus Sutra.* |

This poem is based directly on a story about the Buddha, who, in a previous life as a king, renounced his kingdom and then served a sage by providing him with firewood, water, and herbs in order to obtain the *Lotus* teaching from the wise man. This kind of poem, however, is an anomaly for its time and cannot be found in other collections. It is not until the mid-Heian period—that is, not until the time of the compilation of the *Goshūishū* in 1088—that we see the appearance of full-fledged sutra poetry. Fujiwara Kintō, Ise no Tayū, Akazome'emon, and the mother of Prince Yasusuke are examples of well-known poets who cite sutra titles or phrases in the headnotes to their poems in the *Goshūishū.*

All these poets lived about the same time as Princess Senshi (964–1035), author of *Hosshin wakashū* (A Collection of Poems on the Aspiration for Enlightenment, compiled in 1012), which can certainly be called a collection of sutra poetry. It is thought that the appropriation of sutras for the titles and themes of poems rapidly gained popularity about the time of the reign of Emperor Ichijō (986–1011). Although Imperial Princess Senshi served as a shrine maiden at Kamo Shrine, she was also a pious Buddhist. According to the preface of the work, Senshi knew that poetry was effective in the praise of scriptures since it was used to praise deities in the *Lotus Sutra*. However, because she herself was a woman who, having been born in Japan, did not know Sanskrit or Chinese, she decided to praise the buddhas and bodhisattvas through the thirty-one-syllable *waka*. Fifty-five poems in the *Hosshin wakashū* use lines from sutras as their titles, and of these the largest group is the thirty-one poems based on the *Lotus Sutra*. These thirty-one poems include one poem on each of the twenty-eight chapters of the *Lotus Sutra*, one poem each on the opening and closing sutras, and one additional poem based on the lines "we beg to take this merit" (Hurvitz, 143) from the "Parable of the Conjured City" chapter. Next are ten poems on the ten vows of Fugen (Samantabhadra) from the *Kegon Sutra*, four poems from *Shigu zeigen*, two poems from the *Ninnō-kyō*, and eight other poems, one each from various sutras including the *Heart Sutra*. That the poems related to the *Lotus Sutra* amount to over half of the total clearly reveals how deeply the influence of the Tendai sect, which regarded the *Lotus Sutra* as its fundamental scripture, had permeated aristocratic society of the time. *Hosshin wakashū* marks an important stage in the development of sutra poetry.

## Background of the Development of Sutra Poetry

Although it may seem that *Hosshin wakashū* appeared suddenly, a detailed investigation reveals that there are precedents leading to the collection of such sutra poetry. A passage in volume eleven of the mid-Heian work *Honchō monzui* (Elegant Literature of Japan) refers to "a preface to poems composed in praise of the twenty-eight chapters of the *Lotus Sutra*." According to this passage, during the national mourning at the death of Higashi Sanjō-in (Fujiwara Senshi, empress of En'yū and Michinaga's sister, who died on the twelfth day of the twelfth month of 1001), Michinaga invited poets such as Fujiwara Kintō, Fujiwara Arinobu, Minamoto Toshikata, Fujiwara Yukinari, and others to compose poems using the chapters of the *Lotus Sutra* as titles. Although other poets such as Priest Gyōgi or Priest Henshō had composed numerous poems on the *Lotus Sutra*, they had not used the titles or passages of the text as poem titles, and the poets under Michinaga must have been conscious that they were doing it for the first time.

According to *Gonki*, the diary of Fujiwara Yukinari, this poetry meeting took place from the eighth to ninth months of 1002, ten years before the completion of *Hosshin wakashū*. The poems on the twenty-eight chapters of the *Lotus Sutra* regarded as those written by Kintō on that occasion are contained in Kintō's anthology, *Kintō shū*. The poems written by the other poets are scattered throughout imperial anthologies. In the preface to the *Hosshin wakashū*, Princess Senshi notes that because she is a woman she decided to praise the sutra by composing *waka*. In view of this, it may be that Michinaga and the others conceived of using the Japanese form of poetry, that is, *waka*, with sutra lines as titles because Higashi Sanjō-in was a woman. If they had been composing for a man, the poems would probably have been written in Chinese.

According to the section on Buddhist ceremonies in volume ten of *Honchō monzui*, compositions in Chinese praising the dharma or the Buddha and using phrases from the *Lotus Sutra* as titles were frequently composed at lecture services such as the *kangaku-e* or *kuge-e*. Prose and poetry in Chinese remain from authors such as Yoshishige Yasutane, Ki no Tadana, Takashina no Sekizen, and Ōe Mochitoki. They composed poems on lines from the sutra such as "recite Namo Buddhāya but once" (Hurvitz, 40); "heaping up earth, make Buddha shrines" (Hurvitz, 38), from the "Expedient Devices" chapter; "on mountains and in forests composing their thoughts," from the "Introduction" chapter (Hurvitz, 9); "the World Honored One in his great Loving Kindness," from the "Belief and Understanding" chapter (Hurvitz, 98); and "his life span cannot be measured," from the "Discrimination of Merits" chapter (Hurvitz, 246). At the *kangaku-e* twenty priests from Mt. Hiei and twenty students from the literature and history division of the university of the time met two times a year, in spring and autumn, to hear lectures on the *Lotus Sutra* and compose poems in Chinese praising the dharma and the Buddha. The *kuge-e* was held at Rokuharamitsuji, where eminent priests from both Nara and Kyoto annually delivered the Eight Lectures on the *Lotus Sutra* for the sake of the ordinary people. On these occasions it was also common for the priests to compose poems in Chinese. This kind of lecture service *(kō-e)* had arisen from about the time of Emperor Murakami (r. 946–996). In short, composing Chinese poetry using sutra lines as titles had been popular among the Chinese-style poets for more than fifty years before *Hosshin wakashū* was compiled.

We cannot overlook the composition of poetry in Chinese when we consider the development of sutra poetry in Japanese. Indeed Chinese-style poetry can be thought of as the mother of sutra poetry in Japanese. It is a well-known fact that in aristocratic society of the time men customarily used Chinese while women wrote in *kana*. Of course, the sutras were written in Chinese. Moreover, the study of various sutras, among which the *Lotus Sutra* was preeminent, proceeded first among men, the standard bearers of culture, rather than women. This is the most important reason why Chinese-style sutra poetry was established before the Japanese style of sutra poetry. As it spread throughout society, the new religious trend of writing poetry on sutra titles and themes came to include women as well. The practice of Chinese-style poetry on sutras thus provided a natural impetus for the development of sutra poetry in *waka* form.

## The Early Period of Poetry Based on the *Lotus Sutra*

I have pointed out that sutra poetry by Kintō, Ise no Tayū, Akazome'emon, and the mother of Prince Yasusuke are contained in the *Goshūishū,* and we must now look at just what kind of works these are, having been composed shortly after the inception of sutra poetry.

On the "Parable" chapter:

| | |
|---|---|
| Kado de ni wa | Although we heard |
| Mitsu no kuruma to | There were three carts |
| Kikashikado | At the gate, |
| Hate wa omoi no | It turned out to be |
| Hoka ni zo arikeru. | Something beyond our imagination. |

(Paraphrase: Although the children left the burning house because they had heard that three carts were to be given to them, in the end they were given an inconceivably splendid cart drawn by a large white bullock.)

On "The Universal Gate of the Bodhisattva Avalokiteśvara" chapter:

| | |
|---|---|
| Yo no sukuu | Who will not enter |
| Uchi ni wa dare ga | The world of salvation |
| Irazaramu | Through the wide gate |
| Amaneki kado o | No one can close? |
| Hito shisasaneba. | |

(Paraphrase: Through the pledge of Kannon Bosatsu who tries to save all people, everyone will be rescued and no one will be able to close the gate of compassion that is opened so widely.)

These two verses are from a set of poems on the twenty-eight chapters of the *Lotus Sutra* contained in Kintō's collection, *Dainagon Kintō shū*. Kintō uses only the chapter titles and does not employ phrases from the chapters as poem titles. However, he incorporates the contents of certain sections in his composition. The first poem, for example, is about the parable of the burning house and the three carts. In order to save his children who will not flee a burning mansion, a father promises to give them pleasure carts drawn by a sheep, a bullock, and a deer to lure them out of the house. Once the children have escaped, he gives them an even more superior cart drawn by a great white bullock. We are to understand the poem in the same way that we understand the parable—the Buddha will also lead people who live in a dangerous and illusory world to a safe place through the great vehicle of the *Lotus Sutra*. The second poem adheres strictly to the main point of the chapter upon which it is based. The phrase "the world of salvation" refers to the pledge of Kannon Bosatsu to save all who cling to the power of his compassion, and the poem also incorporates part of the title which can be translated as the wide gateway or gate *(amaneki kado)*.

These two poems are not characterized by profound study of the sutra or by a particular religious bent. They amount to an intellectual understanding and explanation of the text, and do not reach a level of intense faith. Kintō's poems on the twenty-eight chapters of the *Lotus Sutra* are, on the whole, limited to this kind of superficial, intellectual explanation.

The two examples below are from the poems on the twenty-eight chapters by Akazome'emon. For the sake of comparison, I have chosen the poems on the same chapters that Kintō wrote about.

On the "Parable" chapter:

| | |
|---|---|
| Moyuru kaji no | Just as we emerged |
| Ie o idete zo | From the flaming house of fire, |
| Satorinuru | We realized that |
| Mitsu no kuruma wa | The three carts |
| Hitotsu narikeri. | Are one. |

(Paraphrase: The rich man's children—that is, all of us—leave the burning house of illusions and for the first time attain enlightenment. When we do so the three carts which represent the Hīnayāna teachings are unified in the one great white bullock cart which is the one great vehicle of the *Lotus Sutra*.)

On "The Universal Gate of the Bodhisattva Avalokiteśvara" chapter:

| | |
|---|---|
| Mi o sutete | Though he preached |
| Amaneku hō o | The universal law |
| Toku uchi ni | Of self-abandonment: |
| Mada watasarenu | Sadly I myself |
| Waga mi kanashi na. | Have yet to be saved. |

(Paraphrase: Kannon Bosatsu explains that those who throw away their self-interest will be saved, but to my regret and sorrow, I have not yet been enlightened.)

Both of these poems are from the poems on the twenty-eight chapters in *Akazome'emonshū*. In the second example, Akazome'emon applies the phrase "Sadly I myself have yet to be saved" to herself. This chapter is one of those that explains that women can become buddhas, and it is likely that she was especially impressed with it. Akazome'emon based the first example on the story of the burning house and the three carts in the "Parable" chapter, but it appears that here, as in many of her other poems on the *Lotus Sutra,* she was especially impressed with the idea of the one vehicle of the *Lotus.* In these respects, we see that Akazome'emon approached the sutra in a more active and personal way than Kintō did. This personal quality, however, still does not add much substance or depth to the study and understanding of the *Lotus Sutra* itself.

This same tendency can also be seen in *Hosshin wakashū.* The appearance of whole strings of sutra poems gives the impression that substantive investigation of the sutra was carried out, but when we read these poems carefully one by one, we find that there is considerable effort reflected in the pursuit of surface meanings of the sutra phrases, and that this does not amount to a systematic, comprehensive understanding of the *Lotus Sutra.* However, it is extremely significant that women at this time had already achieved this level of comprehension.

## The Development of Poetry on the Twenty-eight Chapters of the *Lotus Sutra*

Following the works of Kintō and Akazome'emon in the *Shikashū taisei* (Compendium of Private Anthologies), we find poems based on the twenty-eight chapters of the *Lotus Sutra* in the *Nyūdō Sadaijinshū* (Collection of the Lay Brother and Minister of the Left), an anthology of poems by Fujiwara Yorimune (935–1065), although only twenty-two of the original twenty-eight poems remain. In *Jōjin Ajari hahashū* (The Collection of Jōjin Ajari's Mother), there is a group of twelve poems, one on each of the eight fascicles of the *Lotus Sutra* and one each on the *Muryōgi-kyō, Kanfugengyō, Muryōju-kyō,* and *Amida-kyō*. Although the poems were based on fascicles rather than chapters, the poetry is essentially of the same type. The mother of priest Jōjin, a Tendai priest who traveled to China, handles the correspondences between poem and text very well.

Nine poems on the *Lotus Sutra* appear in the section on Buddhist poetry in the *Sanboku ki kashū* (Poems of Useless Wood) by Minamoto Toshiyori (1055–1129). Far more numerous, however, are poems on texts such as the *Muryōju-kyō, Kammuryōju-kyō, Kubon ōjō-kyō, Ryūju junirai bun, Ōjō ronge, Jūjū bibasha-ronge,* and *Ōjōyōshū*. Toshiyori's case is exceptional and runs counter to the prevailing trend, since his collection includes very few poems on the *Lotus Sutra,* suggesting that his personal beliefs strongly inclined to Pure Land teachings.

In Fujiwara Tadamichi's (1097–1164) work, *Tadamichishū* (Tadamichi's Collection), poems on the twenty-eight chapters are included in their proper order along with one poem each on the opening and closing sutras, making a total of thirty. He also included explanatory marginal notes for each verse. The reason for this is made clear at the end where he writes that the poems were composed in order to teach the very heart of the *Lotus Sutra* to Retired Emperor Konoe. Tadamichi carefully read the sutra, chose the central phrases of each chapter, and composed poems that made the central ideas easy to understand. Compared to the works of Kintō and Akazome'emon, Tadamichi's poems display a more studious approach. Tadamichi served as regent and prime minister, and his daughter, Kujō-in (Teishi), became empress to Konoe. It is interesting to note that Tadamichi's *Lotus Sutra* poems were composed for instruction at the very center of the court.

In the private anthologies after *Tadamichishū,* poems on the twenty-eight chapters are found in *Hindōshi* (Poems on the Way of Poverty), the collection of Fujiwara Norinaga (1109–1162?). Although they are not entered in order, twenty-seven poems on the *Lotus Sutra* are included. Norinaga was a trusted attendant to Retired Emperor Sutoku and therefore was overthrown in the Hōgen wars, but he was an earnest Buddhist particularly devoted to esoteric or Shingon Buddhism. Many of his extant poems can be viewed in that light, but he does not impose a particularly esoteric viewpoint on his *Lotus* poems.

The *Tsukimōde wakashū* (Poems on Monthly Visits to Temples) was compiled by Kamo Shigeyasu in 1182. Shigeyasu, a Shinto priest at Kamo Shrine, solicited the so-called one hundred poems of the Juei era from poets of his time. Other private anthologies also were compiled through solicitations and these include works such as Fujiwara Suketaka's *Zenrin oyōshū* (Collection of Clotted Leaves at a Temple), Taira Tsunemasa's *Tsunemasa Asonshū* (The Collection of Lord Tsunemasa), Taira Tadanori's *Tadanori hyakushū* (One Hundred Poems of Tadanori), and Fujiwara Chikamori's *Fujiwara Chikamorishū* (The Collection of Fujiwara Chikamori). All of these contain sections on Buddhist poetry which include poems based on the *Lotus Sutra:* in Suketaka's collection there are five, in Tsunemasa's there are four, in Tadanori's there are four, and in Chikamori's there are two. Of the thirty-six poets enlisted for the "one hundred poems of the Juei era," some, such as Taira Tsunemori and Taira Chikamune, did not include poems on the *Lotus Sutra* in their own anthologies, but on the whole the poets composed poems on the twenty-eight chapters. Although not all of the one hundred poems by the thirty-six poets are extant today, we can say on the basis of those that do survive that at the end of the Heian period it was customary for poets to write on the twenty-eight chapters of the *Lotus Sutra*.

Of course, it does not suffice to trace the development of poetry based on the *Lotus Sutra* only in the private anthologies, for the imperial anthologies must also be investigated. When these are taken into account, it is clear that subsequent to the establishment of sutra poetry, poems based on the *Lotus Sutra* far exceed those based on other scriptures. As the very core of Buddhist poetry, poetry on the *Lotus Sutra* extended to all poetic circles, and the practice of composing poems on the sutra's twenty-eight chapters was a well-established convention inherited by the poets in the era of the *Shinkokinshū*.

## Saigyō's Poems on the Twenty-eight Chapters of the *Lotus Sutra*

I would like to answer the question of how poetry on the *Lotus Sutra* developed in the period of the *Shinkokinshū*, which was commissioned in 1201 and completed in 1206, by comparing three poets: Fujiwara Shunzei (also called Toshinari, 1114–1204), Jien (1155–

1225), and Saigyō (1118–1190). These poets are the most representative of this period.

In Saigyō's work *Monjoshū*, poems on the twenty-eight chapters of the *Lotus Sutra* are arranged in order. He uses phrases from each of the twenty-eight chapters as titles to the poems and allots two poems each for the "Parable of the Conjured City" and "The Universal Gate of the Bodhisattva Avalokiteśvara" chapters, so that there are thirty poems in all. He also includes a poem for each of the sutras that usually accompanied the *Lotus Sutra*: the *Muryōgi-kyō*, *Kanfugen-gyō*, *Hannya shingyō*, and *Amida-kyō*, making a total of thirty-four sutra poems. In his major anthology, *Sankashū*, there are seventeen other poems on the *Lotus Sutra*. In comparison with other poets, then, not only did Saigyō write a considerable amount of *Lotus* poetry, but many of them remain.

Saigyō's poems on the twenty-eight chapters have special characteristics not seen in the works before him. Some of these features can be seen in the following selections from his works.

"Preachers of the Dharma" chapter:

If a man devotes to [the *Lotus Sutra*] a single moment of rejoicing, on him, too, I confer the prophecy of Anuttarasamyaksaṃbodhi (Hurvitz, 174).

| | |
|---|---|
| Natsu kusa no | Even the white dew |
| Hitoba ni sugaru | Clinging to every blade |
| Shiratsuya mo | Of summer grass |
| Hana no ue ni wa | Does not accumulate |
| Tamarazarikeri. | On this flower. |

In the opening paragraph of the "Preachers of the Dharma" chapter the Buddha addresses the bodhisattva Yakuō and promises that "if after the Thus Come One has passed into extinction there is a man who, having heard of the Scripture of the Blossom of the Fine Dharma a single gāthā or a single phrase, devotes to it a single moment of rejoicing, on him too, I confer the prophecy of Anuttarasamyaksaṃbodhi [perfect enlightenment]" (Hurvitz, 174). The meaning of the poem is not one which everyone can easily grasp, and it is difficult to understand how the meaning of the phrase in the poem's title and the meaning of the poem connect with one another. Why doesn't the dew accumulate on the flower? How is the poem explained by the promise that one who hears a *gāthā* and believes or rejoices with all his heart will receive a prophecy?

This problem can be solved only by the discovery that Saigyō based this poem on his studies of the *Dainichi-kyō sho,* a commentary on the *Dainichi-kyō (Mahāvairocana Sutra)* written by I-hsing, a T'ang priest. Kūkai regarded this text as important and must have scrutinized it repeatedly, as is evidenced by the fact that he wrote *Daishō monshidai,* a descriptive index of its contents. A passage in the *Nyū mandara guen shingon* (mantra for entering the mandala) of the fourth fascicle of *Dainichi-kyō sho* explains that there are two kinds of prophecy: unconditional prophecy called *muyōki,* and conditional prophecy called *yūyōki.* An unconditional prophecy conferred by the Buddha reveals who, when, in what realm, and which buddha the recipient will be. A conditional prophecy is less specific and merely states that a person will become a buddha in some realm at some time in the future. As an example of unconditional prophecy, I-hsing paraphrased the passage above from the "Preachers of the Dharma" chapter, and explained that it was like the Buddha saying that after his death anyone hearing even a *gāthā* of the *Lotus Sutra* would be given a prophecy of unsurpassed enlightenment. The conditional prophecy, he wrote, could be seen in the idea that if everyone has the buddha nature and can give rise to the root of goodness continually, they will certainly achieve unsurpassed enlightenment.

Thus Saigyō wrote the poem from the standpoint of the *Dainichi-kyō sho* and explains the "Preachers of the Dharma" chapter in terms of the discussion of unconditional prophecy and perfect enlightenment presented in that text. The word "flower" in the poem, of course, means the flower of the *Lotus Sutra,* and the dew is the standard metaphor for conditioned things—that is, every transient thing which comes to be and passes away. That the dew does not accumulate on the flower means that the prophecies in the *Lotus Sutra* are unconditional prophecies of perfect enlightenment. Unlike the ordinary grass of summer, the smooth perfection of the lotus blossom does not allow the transient dew to cling with the vagaries of conditional prophecies.

Saigyō's study of the voluminous *Dainichi-kyō sho* is also reflected in other poems in the *Monjoshū,* particularly in his six poems on the six elements (earth, water, fire, wind, space, and consciousness), which all cite the *Dainichi-kyō sho.*[4] His incorporation of the *Dainichi-kyō sho* in his poetry on the *Lotus Sutra* clearly reveals that not only was he a Shingon priest, but he had thoroughly studied those texts that formed the fundamental doctrines of esoteric Buddhism. Saigyō's method of overlapping the *Lotus Sutra* with another text is significant and is not a method employed in earlier poems on the twenty-eight chapters.

"The Universal Gate of the Bodhisattva Avalokiteśvara" chapter:

(The sun of wisdom) that can subdue winds and flames of misfortune / And everywhere give bright light to the World . . . (Hurvitz, 318).

| | |
|---|---|
| Fukaki ne no | Had I not been told |
| Soko ni komoreru | Never would I have known |
| Hana ari to | That hidden deep |
| Ii hirakazuba | Within the root |
| Shirade yamamashi. | Lies a flower. |

I will abbreviate the details of my reasoning, but this poem, I believe, is based on Kūkai's *Hoke-kyō kaidai,* in which he says Myōhōrenge (Exquisite Lotus Blossom) is the secret name of the bodhisattva Kanjizai, or Avalokiteśvara, popularly referred to as Kannon. Kūkai explains that in this world of the five defilements, Myōhōrenge appears as Kanjizai in order to protect practitioners from various illusions and the impurity caused by their own passions, and to lead them to the realization that all sentient beings possess the essence of the Tathāgata and that their true self-nature is pure and bright. In other words, hidden in our own self is the pure flower of the essence of the Tathāgata, just as flowers are hidden in deeply buried roots.

"Parable of the Conjured City" chapter:

The sixteenth is I myself, Śākyamuni-buddha, who in the Sahā land has achieved Anuttarasamyaksaṃbodhi (Hurvitz, 147).

| | |
|---|---|
| Omoi are ya | Imagine! |
| Mochi ni hito yo no | The full moon, doubled |
| Kage o soete | By the light of that night, |
| Washi no miyama ni | Setting behind |
| Tsuki no irikeru. | Vulture Peak. |

The light of the full moon, symbol of enlightenment, is augmented by the luminescence of the Buddha's full enlightenment at Vulture Peak, behind which it is setting. In a brief line following this poem, Saigyō makes it clear that this poem was composed by layering the idea of the sixteen great bodhisattvas explained in *Bodaishin ron* (On the Aspiration for Enlightenment) with the idea of the sixteen bodhisattvas explained in the "Parable of the Conjured City" chapter.

As the foregoing examples demonstrate, Saigyō composed his poems by combining passages from the *Lotus Sutra* with ideas from esoteric Shingon teachings derived from texts such as the *Bodaishin ron, Hoke-kyō kaidai,* and *Dainichi-kyō sho.* The meaning of the *Lotus Sutra* was thus expanded to embrace esoteric Buddhist doctrines. Most importantly, Saigyō's method transformed poetry on the *Lotus Sutra* from a certain superficiality to a level in which the poems take on philosophical meaning and depth. Because of the emergence of a superior poet like Saigyō, *Lotus* poetry evolved in new directions in the early medieval period.

## Jien's Poetry on the *Lotus Sutra*

Jien was a representative poet of his age, as is attested by the fact that he had ninety-two poems included in the *Shinkokinshū,* second only to Saigyō, who had ninety-four. He was also a high priest who served as a Tendai *zasu,* or chief abbot. The rank of *zasu* is not only the highest office within the Tendai sect; it was recognized beyond the Tendai sect as the apex of authority and leadership for the entire Japanese Buddhist world of that time. Jien's eminence is apparent from the fact that he was recommended to that position four times.

Jien, of course, also wrote poems on the twenty-eight chapters of the *Lotus Sutra.* In his collection of poetry called *Shūgyokushū* (A Gleaning of Treasures) is a section titled "Ei hyaku shū waka" (One Hundred Poetic Compositions) based on one hundred lines extracted from various chapters of the *Lotus Sutra.* While there are other examples of his *Lotus* poetry, these one hundred poems will serve to illustrate his special characteristics as a poet.

The first observation that can be made of Jien's work is that he viewed the *Lotus Sutra* as the sole, unsurpassed vehicle of enlightenment and salvation.

"Expedient Devices" chapter:

There is the dharma of only One Vehicle (Hurvitz, 34).

| | |
|---|---|
| Izukata mo | Though I search |
| Nokosazu yukite | Every field |
| Tazunu to mo | Overlooking nothing, |
| Hana wa minori no | All the flowers are but |
| Hana bakari koso. | The flower of the law. |

In this poem, "the flower of the law" obviously refers to the Lotus Blossom of the Fine Dharma, that is, the *Lotus Sutra*.

"Parable" chapter:

One great Carriage . . . (Hurvitz, 60).

| | |
|---|---|
| Ushiyasa wa | I know |
| Kakaru kuruma o | This is a splendid cart, |
| Ari to shite | And yet |
| Noraba ya to dani | I never thought of |
| Omowazarikeru. | Riding it. |

In the well-known parable of the burning house from this chapter, the father saves his children from the flaming house by offering a "splendid cart," that is, the *Lotus Sutra*.

"Preachers of the Dharma" chapter:

The Dharma Blossom is foremost (Hurvitz, 178).

| | |
|---|---|
| Haru no yama | Abandoning distant views |
| Aki no nohara o | Of spring mountains |
| Nagame sutete | And autumn fields, |
| Niwa ni hachisu no | I see only the lotus blossom |
| Hana o miru kana. | In my own garden. |

In the context of the "Preachers of the Dharma" chapter, it is clear that when Jien speaks of giving up views of the spring mountains covered with flowering trees and the autumn fields where the maple leaves fall, he is speaking of abandoning the various Hīnayāna teachings, for there is nothing better than to look at the lotus flower, which is the *Lotus Sutra* in his own garden of the Tendai sect.

"The Bodhisattva Medicine King" chapter:

. . . Is first . . . (Hurvitz, 298).

| | |
|---|---|
| Hachisu koso | The lotus is the best |
| Kiyoki hana ni wa | Of pure blossoms, |
| Suguretare | Just as the moon |
| Hoshi no naka ni wa | Shines brightest |
| Tsuki zo sayakeri | Among the stars. |

The phrase "is first" that prefaces the poem comes from a sentence that reads: "Further, just as among a multitude of stars the moon, child of the gods, is first, this Scripture of the Dharma Blossom, also in the same way, is the brightest among a thousand myriads of billions of kinds of scriptural dharmas" (Hurvitz, 298).

All the lines extracted by Jien to preface his poems that we have seen thus far reflect the idea that the *Lotus Sutra* is uniquely foremost, and obviously express his own bias. The Tendai sect to which he belonged regarded the *Lotus Sutra* as the most important text, and Jien's attitude may thus be regarded as natural. However, if we compare his approach with Saigyō's method of drawing on Shingon scriptures, we can clearly see the difference in their respective viewpoints. The meanings of the texts—and in their priestly contexts those meanings were appropriated along sectarian lines—could not be divorced from the practice of poetry.

Jien's view of the supremacy of the one vehicle of the *Lotus Sutra* is reflected in other poems as well, as the following example demonstrates.

"Expedient Devices" chapter:

The suchness of their nature . . . (Hurvitz, 22–23).

| Tsu no kuni no | Even the truth of Naniwa |
| Naniwa no koto mo | In the province of Tsu |
| Makoto wa | Can be apprehended |
| Tayori no kado no | From the path leading |
| Michi yori zo shiru | To the steadfast gate. |

The landscape at Naniwa changes with the four seasons, but we can know its true nature, just as we can know the true form of all things, through the teachings of the "Expedient Devices" chapter, which is the gate of entry into the *Lotus Sutra*. Jien is confident that the *Lotus Sutra* provides the key that will unlock the truth in all things.

While Jien's doctrinal preferences clearly determine his message, as we have seen, his *Lotus* poetry cannot be understood solely in terms of the sutra. We must also examine his relationship to other poets. The second characteristic of Jien as a poet is that he was well versed in the tradition of *waka*, and he incorporated that tradition in his poetry, harmonizing it with his religious world-view. The next two poems provided the imagery used in Jien's poem on Naniwa. Saigyō's poem on Naniwa in the *Shinkokinshū* reads:

| Tsu no kuni no | Spring at Naniwa |
| Naniwa no haru wa | In the province of Tsu |

Yume nareya                         Is now but a dream:
Ashi no kareha ni                   The wind sweeps over
Kaze wataru nari.                   The withered reeds.

Saigyō's poem was itself patterned after one written by the priest
Nōin in the *Goshūishū*:

Kokoro aramu                        How I wish to show
Hito ni miseba ya                   Someone of feeling
Tsu no kuni no                      The sight of spring
Naniwa watari no                    Sweeping through Naniwa
Haru no keshiki o                   In the province of Tsu.

By alluding to these two poems, Jien skillfully places his poem within
the framework set by the earlier works and yet manages to adjust the
theme to fit his own religious system. While Saigyō and Nōin dwell
on the changing feelings that passing seasons bring, Jien, the high
priest of Tendai, sees that underlying those transformations is the
constant truth of the *Lotus Sutra*.

There are other poems by Jien that draw upon the poetic tradition.
The following is another example:

"Entrustment" chapter:

As the Buddha commands . . . (Hurvitz, 292).

Mi tabi nadete                      Because he touched their heads thrice
Chigishi kimi no                    And commanded them to their vows,
Mikotonori nareba                   They did "show and teach,"
Kyō made dare mo                    and "afford benefits and joy"
Sono shikyō riki.                   Even until today.

In the "Entrustment" chapter, the Buddha patted the bodhisattvas'
foreheads three times and entrusted them with the task of propagating the teachings of the *Lotus Sutra* to all people. He asked them to
vow to "show and teach" mankind and "to afford them benefits and
joy." The phrase "to show and teach, to afford benefits and joy" *(shikyō riki)* is an essential message of the *Lotus Sutra*. Moreover, it is an
exact quotation from the sutra, read in the Chinese style of pronunciation. In a poem by Dengyō Daishi (Saichō), we find a precedent for
using a phrase meant to be read in Chinese-style pronunciation
within a *waka:*

| Anokutara | O buddhas |
|---|---|
| Sammyakusambodai | Of perfect enlightenment! |
| No buttachi | Grant your divine protection |
| Waga tatsu soma ni | To this timbered mountain. |
| Myōga arasetamae. | |

The first two lines of the poem are the Sino-Japanese transliteration of *anuttara samyaksambodhi*, the Sanskrit term meaning "perfect, unsurpassed enlightenment." While there are precedents for this practice of directly incorporating phrases from sutras in Japanese poems, it was still unusual and an exception to the rule of using Japanese diction. Yet there is a freshness to Jien's poem derived from the unexpected use of the phrase. The phrase *shikyō riki* frequently appears in the *Lotus Sutra* and can be found in the "Parable of the Conjured City," "Receipt of Prophecy by Five Hundred Disciples," "The Merits of Appropriate Joy," "The Former Affairs of the King Fine Adornment," and "The Encouragements of the Bodhisattva Samantabhadra" chapters. I would surmise that Jien's intention in using this phrase was to try to restore it to wider use.

By examining Jien's poetry on the *Lotus Sutra*, we have seen three important characteristics: an emphasis on the *Lotus Sutra* as the one, unsurpassed vehicle for salvation; a skillful harmony between religious content and poetic tradition; and a resulting depth of religious feeling. Further investigation would of course lead to observation of additional characteristics, but these three are the main points which will suffice for now.

## Fujiwara Shunzei's Poetry on the *Lotus Sutra*

It is unnecessary to say that Shunzei, compiler of the *Senzaishū* and father of the renowned poet Fujiwara Teika (also known as Sadaie, 1162–1249), was an active master in medieval poetic circles. His personal collection of poetry, *Chōshū eisō*, contains a set of twenty-eight poems on the *Lotus Sutra* arranged in order. He composed additional poems on the *Lotus Sutra*, but we will not consider them in trying to ascertain the characteristics of his *Lotus* poetry. We know from the account in the opening paragraph that Shunzei's set of poems was composed in response to a request by Taikenmon-in (1101–1145) around the time of the Kōji era (1142–1144). At that time Shunzei was only twenty-nine or thirty years old, and since he enjoyed a long life, dying at ninety, this set of *Lotus* poems can be said to be from his youthful period. What method did he use in composing these poems?

"Medicinal Herbs" chapter:

Since I have neither "that" nor "this", / Nor any thought of love or hatred (Hurvitz, 106).

| | |
|---|---|
| Haru same wa | The spring rain |
| Ki no mo ka no mo no | Soaks this and that, |
| Kusa mo ki mo | The grasses and trees, |
| wakazu midori ni | Dyeing them all green |
| Somuru narikeri. | Without distinction. |

The spring rain falls indiscriminately here and there, on grasses and trees, causing them all to flourish, just as the Buddha's compassion falls widely over all people and causes them to flourish. The parable of the three kinds of herbs and two kinds of trees, one of the seven great parables in the sutra, appears in the "Medicinal Herbs" chapter. It likens the Buddha's compassion to the spring rain which falls equally everywhere, though the grasses, trees, and herbs grow differently according to the differences in their natures. So too, the Buddha's compassion benefits everyone, for he gives it freely without distinction, but, depending upon the differences in the individual recipients, there will be distinctions in how they receive it. The phrase in the title comes from a passage which in its entirety reads:

I, in viewing all,
Regard all without exception as equal,
Since I have neither "that" nor "this,"
Nor any thought of love or hatred. (Hurvitz, 106)

Shunzei composed the poem by strictly adhering to the meaning of the passage without adding any embellishments. He adapted the idea of "moistened by the same rain" (Hurvitz, 101) by simply making "spring rain" the subject, and by using the words "grasses and trees," which appear in the sutra. In short, he simply conveys the meaning of the passage in a poetic manner. Similarly, Shunzei's other poems on the twenty-eight chapters are also very faithful to the meaning of the passages that he extracts from the sutra. His poems rarely add to or subtract from the significance of the scriptural ideas, and this is the chief characteristic of Shunzei's poetry on the *Lotus Sutra.*

The following poem by Saigyō is prefaced by the same phrase quoted in Shunzei's poem:

"Medicinal Herbs" chapter:

I, in viewing all, / Regard all without exception as equal, / Since I have neither "that" nor "this," / Nor any thought of love or hatred.

| | |
|---|---|
| Hikihiki ni | Without dividing the water |
| Naeshiro mizu o | Among the seedlings |
| Wakeyarade | I will flood them all |
| Yutaka ni nagasu | As I please, |
| Sue o tosamu. | Fully to the end. |

Just as the water is not to be allotted arbitrarily only to this seedling or to that one, but rather is allowed to flow freely through all of them to the very end, so too the Buddha allows the rain of his compassion to fall on all equally. Here there is no mention of grasses, trees, or rain. Saigyō approaches the idea of "moistened by the same rain" through a unique analogy of his own regarding the necessity of watering the entire rice paddy equally, not selectively. By comparison, Shunzei's poetic standpoint is passive, only restating the ideas. Saigyō transforms the idea into his own metaphor.

Let us compare other examples.

"Fortitude" chapter:

We do not covet bodily life, / We do but regret the Unexcelled Path (Hurvitz, 206).

| | |
|---|---|
| Kazu naraba | If my life counted |
| Oshikuya aramashi | I would have something to regret, |
| Oshikaranu | But since my wretched life |
| Uki mi zo kikeba | Is nothing to regret |
| Ureshikarikeru. | Happily do I hear the dharma. |

The "Fortitude" chapter is in the second half of the *Lotus Sutra* and the phrase comes from a passage in which the bodhisattvas pledge that after the Buddha's extinction they will endure any hardship in order to propagate the teachings of the *Lotus Sutra*. They declare that they will value only the unsurpassed path without concern for their own lives. While Shunzei frees their pledge from its context in the sutra and applies it to himself with the assertion that the dharma rather than his life is of value, he is merely personalizing the message without adding any doctrinal or poetic insight.

Saigyō and Jien also composed poems on this same theme, taking the same passage that prefaces Shunzei's poem:

We do not covet bodily life, / We do but regret the Unexcelled Path.

| Ne o hanare | Because I know |
| Tsunaganu fune o | The boat is free, |
| Omoi shireba | Untethered from its mooring, |
| Nori emu koto zo | How happy am I to climb aboard |
| Ureshikarbeki. | And take hold of the teaching. |

This poem by Saigyō recalls a Chinese-style poem from the *Wakan rōeishū:*

Mi o kanzureba kishi no hitai ni ne o hanaretaru kusa Inochi o ron zureba e no hitai ni tsunagazaru fune.

Upon reflection: I am grass uprooted from the edge of the shore;
Upon examination: my life is a boat untethered to the headland.

In other words, Saigyō plays against the image of life as an untethered boat in order to say that, precisely because his life is no more than an untethered boat, he is happy to allow it to take him where it may as long as he can grasp the dharma. Saigyō also uses a *kakekotoba* or pivot word, *nori emu,* which means both to climb aboard and to grasp the dharma. Instead of deploring the vagaries of existence, he transforms them into reasons for the joyful acceptance of the dharma and harmonizes his poetic statement with one from the past. While the theme of Saigyō's poem is similar to that of Shunzei's, the manner of incorporating the sutra passage and the attitude differ.

Jien's poem on the same passage reads:

| Morobito no | Since it is the law |
| Inochi ni kaburu | Protected by all the bodhisattvas, |
| Ho nareba | How can it be useless |
| Hiromuru kai no | To spread and expound it? |
| Nakarazarameya. | |

Jien is confident that expounding the dharma has great value because, as the passage in the sutra reveals, all the bodhisattvas have declared their willingness to discard their own lives in order to help in its promulgation. Here again Jien emphasizes the idea that the *Lotus Sutra* is preeminent among all sutras because it has the protection of

the bodhisattvas. Moreover, Jien implies that we should start immediately to expound the sutra. Shunzei, on the other hand, says that
hearing such a valuable teaching makes him happy, and he is content
to take this passive view.

Shunzei's superlative treatise on poetry, *Korai fūtei shō*, reveals
that he devoted himself to Tendai teachings. Yet an assessment of the
religious level of Shunzei's twenty-eight poems on the *Lotus Sutra*
shows that he was conservative, passive, and not very creative. These
qualities surface repeatedly in the poems, almost as if it were sufficient to be doctrinaire about doctrinal meaning.

Medieval poetry developed with many variations, but I have concentrated on only three important poets. A number of talented poets
appeared successively, producing both private and imperial anthologies. In the course of that development, the twenty-eight poems on
the *Lotus Sutra* became an accepted tradition. The Japanese concentrated on this sutra more than any other, and its ideas and stories were
widely disseminated through poetry. What I especially want to
emphasize, however, is the possibility of using the sutra as an effective gauge in registering the state of Japanese literature and poetry.
Rather than considering the three poets only in terms of literary theory, I have dealt with the twenty-eight poems on the *Lotus Sutra* by
Saigyō, Jien, and Shunzei by concentrating on the religious framework of their poems and thereby allowing the individuality of the
poets to surface. By comparing poems on the same texts and themes
to discover the poetic sensibility and religious meaning therein, I
think it is possible to gain insight into important aspects of the real
personality, character, and consciousness of medieval poets.

TRANSLATED BY WILLA JANE TANABE

## NOTES

1. Adapted from the translation in Nippon Gakujutsu Shinkōkai, trans., *The
Manyōshū* (New York: Columbia University Press, 1969), 89.

2. Leon Hurvitz, trans., *Scripture of the Lotus Blossom of the Fine Dharma*, 218.
All translations of passages from the *Lotus Sutra* are taken from this text; hereafter
the page numbers will be cited within the essay itself.

3. Nippon Gakujutsu Shinkōkai, *Manyōshū*, 274.

4. For a detailed examination of Saigyō's use of the *Dainichi kyō sho* in his poetry,
see my article "Saigyō to rokudai no uta: sono tenkyō no hakken," *Buzan kyōgaku
daikai kiyō*, no. 9 (November 1984).

# The *Lotus Sutra* and Politics in the Mid-Heian Period

NEIL MCMULLIN

To say that the *Lotus Sutra* is an extremely important Buddhist scripture is of course an understatement. Over the centuries from the seventh to the present, it has been the font of a variety of forms of inspiration for scholars and artists, monks and laity, in Japanese society. Without undervaluing the various roles that the *Lotus Sutra* played in early Japanese society, I would suggest that possibly the most important role that it played—and not just it but the other widely read sutras as well—was a political one.

The political significance of Buddhist sutras in early Japanese society is usually seen in the context of the *chingo kokka* ideology by which the ruling elite in the Nara (646–794) and Heian (794–1185) periods used the *Lotus* and other sutras as tools to guarantee the prosperity and protection of the state and the rulers thereof. The *chingo kokka* function of the *Lotus Sutra* has been the subject of many modern studies.[1] In this chapter I would like to focus on another aspect of the political role played by the *Lotus Sutra,* and specifically on the role that it played in the monastic community at Enryakuji, the head monastery of the Tendai school in Japan, during and around the time of the monk Ryōgen (Jie Daishi, or Ganzan Daishi, 912–985) in the mid-Heian period.[2] For it was with Ryōgen, who was the eighteenth head abbot *(zasu)* of the Tendai school and who is remembered in history as the "father of Mt. Hiei's revival" *(Eizan chūkō no sō),* that the Enryakuji entered its "golden age."

To put the point of this study directly: the political role that the *Lotus Sutra* played in the early to mid-Heian period is that it served as the coinage by which Tendai monks purchased power. Indeed, in terms of Buddhist institutional history, this was the most important role played by the *Lotus Sutra* and the various rituals based on it during that period. To appreciate the validity of this claim, we must first have a general understanding of the major developments in the Japanese political world—and especially the activities of the powerful families in the Kyoto area—in and just before the tenth century.[3]

## The Rise of Morosuke

Through the ninth century the imperial house, which had maintained its supremacy over the other noble families during the two preceding centuries, found its dominance increasingly challenged by the major families. The emperor gradually became a figure with the right to reign, but not necessarily to rule, as ruling power was ceded to the Fujiwara family, which had managed by and large to resolve the internal conflicts that had fractured it into a number of competing factions. The northern branch *(hokke)* of the family became dominant, and the heads of that branch came to hold, in succession, the crucially important offices of *sesshō* (regent during the reign of a child emperor) and *kampaku* (regent during the reign of an adult emperor). The first Fujiwara *sesshō* was Yoshifusa (804–872), who held that office during the reign of his infant grandson, Emperor Seiwa (r. 858–876). The first *kampaku* was Yoshifusa's eldest son, Mototsune (836–891), who assumed that title when he became regent for the Emperor Kōkō (r. 884–887). The Fujiwara family was able to solidify its control of those offices by making itself the primary supplier of imperial consorts, thus guaranteeing that the children of the emperors, the imperial princes and princesses, would be members of the Fujiwara family.

In the mid-tenth century, power struggles in the Kyoto area continued among various factions of the Fujiwara family, the most important of which were the struggles among the sub-branches of the northern branch of the family. Those struggles provided the fertile soil in which the power of the Enryakuji, and the personal power of Ryōgen, could grow.

The first Fujiwara of immediate concern for the present discussion is Tadahira (880–949), the fourth son of Mototsune and the head *(chōja)* of the Fujiwara family during the last few decades of his life. Tadahira held the title of *sesshō* from 930 to 941 during the reign of his sister's son, Emperor Suzaku (r. 930–946), and in 941 he became *kampaku*, which office he held until his death. When Tadahira died, Emperor Murakami (r. 946–967)—whose mother was a sister, and his empress (Yasuko or Anshi) a granddaughter, of Tadahira—aspired to gain some independence from his powerful Fujiwara relatives and in-laws in an effort to strengthen the power of the imperial house and his own authority. Accordingly, Murakami did not appoint a *kampaku* to replace Tadahira, beginning an eighteen-year period (949–967) in which there was no *kampaku*. Moreover, in the twenty-eight-year period from 941, when Tadahira ceased to be *sesshō*, to 969 no one held that title.

Although the offices of *sesshō* and *kampaku* were thus vacant for some time, competition continued within the Fujiwara family for the other positions of highest political authority—the offices of grand chancellor of state *(dajō daijin)*, minister of the left *(sadaijin)*, and minister of the right *(udaijin)*—and the descendants of Tadahira were deeply involved in that competition. Tadahira had two sons who are relevant here: his eldest son, Saneyori (900–970), and his second son, Morosuke (908–960). Saneyori, in turn, had several sons, the eldest of whom was Yoritada (924–989). Morosuke had twelve sons, the most important of whom were the eldest three—Koretada (924–972), Kanemichi (925–977), and Kaneie (929–990)—and the second youngest, Jinzen (943–990).

When Tadahira died in 949, his eldest son, Saneyori, succeeded him as the head of the Fujiwara family. Saneyori's younger brother Morosuke, who held great ambitions for himself and his sons, was determined to achieve a position of preeminence in both the Fujiwara family and the state, if not for himself then for his descendants. To realize that ambition he focused his attention on the issue of imperial succession. It was Morosuke's desire to have one of his seven daughters give birth to Emperor Murakami's heir, thus paving the way for Morosuke to become *sesshō* and eventually *kampaku*. There were, of course, others who shared Morosuke's ambition, notably Fujiwara no Motokata, who apppears to have been a major figure in the southern branch *(nanke)* of the Fujiwara family.[4] Thus a competition between Morosuke and Motokata developed over the issue of imperial succession, with both of them offering daughters to Murakami. Morosuke offered his daughter Yasuko while Motokata put forward his daughter Sukehime. Late in the year 949 both women became pregnant by Murakami. The result was a victory for Motokata in the first round of the contest: his daughter Sukehime gave birth to a son, Prince Hirohira, before Yasuko gave birth. Shortly thereafter, on 5/24/950, Yasuko gave birth to Prince Norihira.

With the birth of those two children, the competition entered a new stage: namely, a contest over which child would be designated crown prince *(tōgu,* or *higashi no miya).* Because Morosuke held higher court rank than Motokata,[5] and because he belonged to the more powerful northern branch of the Fujiwara family, on 7/23/950 his two-month-old grandson, Norihira, was designated to succeed Murakami. In a short time the frustrated Motokata died, and his departed spirit was said to have become a "vengeful ghost" *(onryō).*[6] Seventeen years later, upon the death of Murakami in 967, Norihira ascended the throne as Emperor Reizei (r. 967–969), fulfilling a major part of Morosuke's design.

When the office of *kampaku* was restored in 967 it was taken by Morosuke's older brother, Saneyori. With the death of the latter in 970 a new power struggle developed, this time between Saneyori's eldest son, Yoritada, and Morosuke's eldest son, Koretada, over who would succeed Saneyori as *kampaku.* This family struggle between the descendants of Saneyori, who was seen as the founder of the Ono-no-Miya sub-branch of the family, and the descendants of Morosuke, the ancestor of the Kujō sub-branch, was again resolved in favor of Morosuke's side, for it was Koretada who was appointed to succeed Saneyori, and Koretada, in turn, was succeeded by his younger brother and Morosuke's second son, Kanemichi. But because of animosity between Kanemichi and his younger brother (Morosuke's third son) Kaneie, Kanemichi designated not the overweaningly ambitious Kaneie but their first cousin Yoritada (Saneyori's eldest son) to succeed him as *kampaku,* which Yoritada did in 977.

With Yoritada's appointment as *kampaku* a new set of struggles arose centering around Kaneie. One struggle was over the issue of who would succeed Yoritada as *kampaku* when he died. To resolve that issue, both Yoritada and Kaneie offered daughters to their first cousin and the reigning emperor, En'yū (r. 969–984), who, like his immediate predecessor, Reizei, was a son of Morosuke's daughter Yasuko. Yoritada and Kaneie each hoped that his daughter would bear an imperial prince and thus give him, as that child's grandfather, access to the office of *sesshō.* As fate would have it, Yoritada's daughter was barren whereas Kaneie's daughter bore a son, Prince Kanehito, who, at the age of six, ascended the throne as Emperor Ichijō (r. 986–1011). When the boy Kanehito was enthroned, Kaneie, as his maternal grandfather, was appointed *sesshō.* With this turn of events the dominance of Morosuke's Kujō sub-branch over the Ono-no-Miya sub-branch was firmly established, and it was the descendants of Morosuke who headed the northern branch of the family thereafter, the leading members of which were to hold the highest offices in the state for the next two centuries.

The other struggle in which Kaneie was involved was over the issue of which of Morosuke's eldest sons—Koretada, Kanemichi, and Kaneie—would attain supremacy in the Kujō sub-branch of the Fujiwara family. Kaneie's daughter had born a son, Prince Kanehito, by Emperor En'yū in 980, but twelve years earlier, in 968, Koretada's daughter had given birth to a son, Prince Morosada, by Emperor Reizei, and Morosada had been designated crown prince. Therefore, when Emperor En'yū died in 984 Morosada ascended the throne as Emperor Kazan (r. 984–986). At that point Kaneie conspired to have his grandson, Prince Kanehito, designated crown prince to succeed Kazan. Once Kanehito received that designation, Kaneie schemed to have Kazan resign his office and, in 986, he was able to trick the youthful emperor into doing so.[7] Following Kazan's resignation, Kanehito, as was mentioned earlier, ascended the throne as Emperor Ichijō. Once again Kaneie was successful.

When Kaneie died in 990 his position of preeminence both in the Fujiwara family and in the state was inherited in succession by his sons, the fourth of whom was the famous Michinaga (966–1027), during whose lifetime the power of the Fujiwara family reached its zenith. With Michinaga, Morosuke's aspirations for the success of his descendants were fully realized. And as we shall see, one line of Morosuke's "descendants" was the succession of Tendai abbots at the Enryakuji.

## Ryōgen: Ritual and Power

It is against the backdrop of the foregoing set of events that we can understand the reasons for the successful career of Ryōgen, as well as the role played by the *Lotus Sutra* in his career. Much could be said about Ryōgen, but our discussion shall be confined to those points that are immediately relevant to the present topic.

First, Ryōgen appears to have come from a relatively uninfluential family. When he entered the Enryakuji monastic community at the age of ten in 923, he became a novice at the Western Pagoda *(saitō)* section rather than at the more important and prestigious Eastern Pagoda *(tōtō)* section.[8] Thus it might have been conjectured that

Ryōgen was off to a rather unpromising start: he was a minor novice with no particular prospect of advancement in the Enryakuji community.

Second, Ryōgen had the misfortune of seeing his master, a monk by the name of Risen, die in 928, just at the time when Ryōgen was due to be nominated for the reception of Buddhist orders. Given the nature of the master-disciple structure in Buddhist monasteries, and the "yearly ordinands" *(nembun dosha)* system still in effect at that time, it was necessary for an aspirant to Buddhist orders to be recommended for ordination by an influential mentor. With the untimely death of Risen, Ryōgen had difficulty obtaining an ordination license *(doen);* eventually he received the necessary license, not on the initiative of a high-ranking monk at the Enryakuji but through the intercession of one of the district governors *(gunryō)* of Ise province and his friend, a certain Fujiwara no Sadakata.[9] Once again it would appear that the young Ryōgen's stock at the Enryakuji was low. He was, in effect, an orphan in a world where connections counted for a great deal.

What Ryōgen may have lacked in connections in the Enryakuji community, however, he made up for in intelligence and ambition. Ryōgen's first public demonstration of his intellectual prowess came in 929 when he defeated his fellow monk Jōe of the Eastern Pagoda section in a debate *(rongi)* held at the Enryakuji on the occasion of Fujiwara no Tadahira's fiftieth birthday.[10] Ryōgen's success in that debate had a twofold result: he attracted the attention and admiration of high-ranking monks in the Tendai community,[11] which would prove important some years later, and, in 931, at the age of nineteen, he was assigned two disciples of his own, the brothers Senga and Shōku (or Seikyū), both of whom were to acquire high office in the Buddhist community many years later.[12] Senga and Shōku formed the nucleus of a group of disciples that Ryōgen eventually developed at the Enryakuji, a group that was to take over most of the high offices in the monastery before the end of the tenth century.

In or around the year 935 Ryōgen once again attracted attention by defeating the monk Senkan in another debate at the Enryakuji.[13] Senkan (918–983) was a Tendai monk from the Kinryūji in Settsu province who was six years Ryōgen's junior; Ryōgen's victory in this debate gained him a reputation for brilliance. In 937 Ryōgen was chosen to be one of the four monks representing the Enryakuji at the *Yuima-e,* an assembly of monks from various monasteries that was held yearly at the Kōfukuji in Nara. At that meeting the twenty-five-year-old Ryōgen debated with, and defeated, the seventeen-year-old Gishō (920–969), a Hossō monk from the Gangōji (Asukadera) and a member of the Fujiwara family.[14] Ryōgen's success on that occasion was reported to Fujiwara no Tadahira, who was then the *sesshō* and one of the most powerful men in the country.

Some time later, probably in 939 on the occasion of Tadahira's six-tieth birthday, Ryōgen was one of a large number of monks who were invited to take part in a sutra-recitation ritual *(hō-e)* at Tadahira's res-idence in Kyoto. On the completion of that ritual, Tadahira is said to have taken Ryōgen aside in order to commission a memorial service to be performed for him following his death.[15] Ryōgen was now begin-ning to find supporters among the upper ranks of the Fujiwara fam-ily. Soon Ryōgen's main patron was Tadahira's second son, Morosuke, who by 946 had begun to contribute finances for the construction of a Hokke-zammai-dō in the Yokawa section of Mt. Hiei.[16] Ryōgen had by then taken up residence in the Yokawa section, where he was developing his own base of power.[17]

On 8/14/949, ten or so years after his meeting with Ryōgen, Tada-hira died. In keeping with instructions contained in Tadahira's last will, his son Morosuke had Ryōgen perform an exceptionally long set of rituals for Tadahira's salvation. Ryōgen began the three hundred-day *goma* ritual at the Shuryōgon-in in Yokawa shortly after Tada-hira's death.[18]

Around that time Morosuke was moved to seek Ryōgen's ritual ser-vices for another reason: the contest mentioned earlier between Morosuke and Fujiwara no Motokata by way of their daughters. It will be recalled that late in 949 and early in 950 Morosuke's daughter Yasuko was in competition with Motokata's daughter Sukehime over which of the two would give birth to Emperor Murakami's successor. During Yasuko's pregnancy Ryōgen, at Morosuke's behest, conducted a series of rituals for her fetus. Although the main sources on Ryōgen state that the three hundred-day *goma* ritual that he performed through the fall of 949 and the spring of 950 was for Tadahira's salva-tion, this was not quite the case, for it appears that the rituals that Ryōgen performed during that period were also, if not primarily, for Yasuko's fetus.[19] On 5/27/950, three days after Yasuko's delivery of a son, Prince Norihira, Ryōgen sent Morosuke a *kanzu*[20] listing the var-ious rituals he had performed during Yasuko's pregnancy on behalf of the fetus. One of those rituals was called *ususama* (or *uzusama*) *no hō*, the purpose of which was to guarantee that the pregnant woman for whom it was performed would give birth to a healthy male child.

It was believed that this ritual was so potent that it could bring about a sex change in the fetus from female to male *(henjō nanshi)* in the event that the fetus was originally female.[21]

Approximately five weeks after Norihira's birth, from the second through the twenty-second days of the seventh month of 950, Ryōgen performed a twenty-one-day ritual for the health of the infant prince,[22] and on the day following the completion of that ritual Norihira was designated crown prince. From Morosuke's perspective Ryōgen's rituals had been eminently efficacious, and Morosuke accordingly rewarded him by appointing Ryōgen to the important post of protector monk *(gojisō)* to the crown prince.[23]

The disappointed Motokata, who died shortly after Norihira's investiture as crown prince, was perhaps not the only person to become a vengeful ghost as a result of these developments. While Ryōgen was performing rituals for Yasuko's success, the Enryakuji monk Kanzan (or Kansan) was performing similar rituals for Sukehime's success. Although next to nothing is known about Kanzan's life, it is said that after his death in the mid-tenth century his departed spirit haunted the court and became an evil presence afflicting the courtiers.[24]

On 10/17/954, some four years after the foregoing events, Morosuke and his eldest son, Koretada, ascended Mt. Hiei to spend a three-day period in the performance of rituals at Yokawa with Ryōgen.[25] The occasion of these rituals was the dedication of the Hokke-zammai-dō, the construction of which Morosuke had financed. On reaching the Enryakuji, Morosuke and Koretada were received by the monks of the Eastern Pagoda section, and they dispensed gifts to the 1,800 or more monks who were in residence at the Enryakuji at the time.[26] Then Morosuke and Koretada moved on to the Yokawa section, where they were received by Ryōgen.[27]

On the eighteenth day of the tenth month, Morosuke's first full day on the mountain, a "lighting" ritual *(tenka shiki)* was held at Yokawa. In that ritual the lantern of eternal light *(chōmyōtō)* which had been prepared for enshrinement in the Hokke-zammai-dō was ceremonially lit in a temporary shelter adjacent to the newly completed chapel; the new flame would then be carried in procession into the Hokke-zammai-dō in a ceremony marking the entry of the light *(hi-ire)*. In the "fire-lighting" *(hiuchi)* section of the ritual, Morosuke was the central figure: it was he who held the flint and stone with which he would produce a spark and ignite the fire. As Morosuke was about to strike a spark, he uttered the following petition:[28]

Through the power of this *sammai*[29] may the glory of my family be passed on.

May the fullness of the glory of the emperor [Morosuke's son-in-law, Emperor Murakami], the empress [Morosuke's daughter, Yasuko], the crown prince [Morosuke's grandson, Prince Norihira], the princes and princesses, the three ranks of officials [including the minister of the left, Morosuke himself], and the nine ranks of courtiers unceasingly persist for generation after generation and fill the court.

If this petition is to be granted, permit the fire to start within the first three times that I strike the stone.

So saying, Morosuke struck the stone with the flint and the fire started on the very first strike. Recognizing this as a sign that Morosuke's petition would be granted, all present rejoiced. Ryōgen then transferred the flame to the lantern of eternal light, which was thenceforth called the "inextinguishable shining light" (*fumetsu no tōmyō*) of the Hokke-zammai-dō.

Following that ceremony, Morosuke and Koretada participated in a *Hokke sembō,* a ritual that was believed to bring about the remission of sins *(sange)* through the recitation of the *Lotus Sutra.* On this occasion the ritual served to guarantee the fulfillment of Morosuke's petition and, possibly, to placate the vengeful spirits of Motokata and Kanzan.

On the nineteenth day of the month, their second full day on the mountain, Morosuke and Koretada participated in another *Hokke sembō* ritual, following which they made a pilgrimage-*cum*-sightseeing tour around the Yokawa section. On their third day on the mountain, Morosuke and Koretada participated in a recitation of a sutra, the *Amida-kyō,* and attended a *mondō,* a ritual dialogue in which, in this case, ten monks exchanged questions and answers on points of doctrine. Early the next morning, Morosuke and Koretada took part for the third time in a *Hokke sembō* ritual, following which they departed for Kyoto.

Morosuke's pilgrimage to Mt. Hiei was probably the single most important event in Ryōgen's life. During that three-day period Ryōgen and Morosuke entered into, or formally sealed, an agreement that provided a basis for the acquisition of power by Ryōgen personally and by his "line" (*ichimon*) of disciples at Yokawa. According to this agreement, Morosuke would thenceforth be Ryōgen's patron while in return Ryōgen would exercise his ritual powers for the well-being and success of Morosuke and his descendants—that is, in the words of Morosuke's petition, in order that the "glory of my family be passed on." Ryōgen thus became Morosuke's family ritualist (ichi-mon no kitōsō).

Three years later, in 957, the Morosuke-Ryōgen pact was confirmed in a dramatic fashion when Morosuke "donated" his second-youngest son to the Enryakuji. That boy, who was then fourteen years old, entered the Yokawa section of the Enryakuji as the novice Jinzen, and from that time on Ryōgen groomed Jinzen to be his successor, making him in effect the living bridge between Ryōgen and Moro-suke, and between Ryōgen's sub-branch of the Enryakuji community at Yokawa and Morosuke's sub-branch of the Fujiwara family. It might be said, therefore, that Morosuke had created a new branch of his family at the Enryakuji and that his pact with Ryōgen marked the beginning of the "aristocracization" (kizokuka)—the Fujiwara fami-ly's direct takeover—of the Enryakuji.

There was, of course, a considerable degree of self-interest in Moro-suke's decision to send one of his sons to be a monk at Yokawa. By that decision he was taking a step designed to guarantee that the finances he had donated to Yokawa, and would donate from that time forward, would be owned or at least controlled by one of his children.[30] But fundamentally Morosuke's pact with Ryōgen was a way of establishing Ryōgen and his enclave of monks at Yokawa as a sort of "ritual power unit" that would perform rituals for the well-being of Morosuke's sub-branch of the Fujiwara family. The tradi-tional family monastery (ujidera) of the Fujiwara was the Kōfukuji in Nara, but from the late ninth century some of the leaders of the Fuji-wara family had been establishing new monasteries in the Kyoto area that would function as ujidera for their particular sub-branches of the family. In 925, for example, Tadahira financed the construction of the Hosshōji, the Tendai monastery at which he was eventually bur-ied. So while the Kōfukuji served the whole Fujiwara family, the newly built institutions served the particular sub-branches of the family that had financed their construction.

For Ryōgen the major benefit was Morosuke's pledge of support for Ryōgen's line of disciples at Yokawa. The "orphaned" Ryōgen thus became the "father" (master) of a family (ichimon) of monks that eventually took control of the Enryakuji community. And just as Ryogen's family, with the support of Morosuke's family, took control of the Enryakuji, so Morosuke's family, with the ritual assistance of Ryōgen's family, took control of the state.

In 960 Morosuke died at the comparatively young age of fifty-two. A short time later, in the spring of 961, Morosuke's daughter Yasuko, the mother of the emperors Reizei and En'yū, instructed five monasteries to perform *Hokke hakkō* rituals in memory of her deceased father.[31] Those five institutions—forming the "ritual power unit" of Morosuke's sub-branch of the Fujiwara family—were the Kōfukuji; the Gokurakuji, which had been built by Tadahira's father, Mototsune; the Hosshōji, which Tadahira had built; the Enryakuji; and Yokawa. Interestingly, Yokawa was identified at that time as an independent institution, not as a part of the Enryakuji,[32] and it was there that Morosuke's older sons attended the *Hokke hakkō* ritual in memory of their father. Several months after that ritual was held, on 7/1/961, Yasuko requested that Ryōgen perform certain rituals for the health of her son, the crown prince Norihira, who was then eleven years old. In other words, with her father recently deceased, Yasuko turned to Ryōgen's ritual power to assure that Norihira would live to become emperor.

Although Ryōgen continued to enjoy the patronage of Yasuko and her powerful brothers after the death of their father—in the summer of 962, for example, Koretada contributed finances for the performance of *Hokke-zammai* rituals at Yokawa's Shuryōgon-in[33]—he evidently wanted to construct a still broader base of support. There was, it will be recalled, no *kampaku* in the eighteen-year period from 949 to 967, and no one could be sure of the direction in which the political tides would flow. In the early 960s Ryōgen could not have known that Morosuke's descendants would attain the highest offices in the state in the future, for those offices might well have gone to the descendants of Morosuke's elder (and at the time still living) brother, Saneyori, and subsequently to Saneyori's descendants. In fact, when the office of *kampaku* was reestablished in 969, it was Saneyori, not one of Morosuke's sons, who filled it. In order to broaden his base of support in those uncertain times, Ryōgen chose to rely on a talent that had served him so well in the past, namely, his debating skill.

From as early as 4/28/961, less than a year after Morosuke's death, Ryōgen began to take steps to have the court schedule a debate between the northern (Tendai) and southern (Nara) schools of Buddhism, especially between the Tendai and Hossō schools, which were traditional opponents. In response to Ryōgen's request, and the promptings of the Kegon and Sanron schools whose support in that endeavor Ryōgen had solicited,[34] the court eventually decreed that a debate be held in the Seiryōden at the imperial palace from the twenty-first through the twenty-fifth days of the eighth month of the third year of Ōwa, 963. This debate is known, therefore, as the Ōwa Debate (*Ōwa no rongi* or *Ōwa no shūron*).[35]

The form of the Ōwa Debate was a *Hokke jikkō,* a ten-session ritual in which discussion takes place on ten portions of sutra material: in the first session the *Muryōgi-kyō* (Sutra of Innumerable Meanings) is discussed; in the second through ninth sessions the eight fascicles of the *Lotus Sutra* are discussed in sequence; and in the tenth session the *Kanfugengyō* (Sutra of Meditation of the Bodhisattva Samantabhadra) is discussed. Customarily, the ten sessions are spread over a five-day period, with a morning and an evening session each day. In each session two monks carry on the discussion: one monk, the *monja*, poses questions on the assigned material, and the other, the *dōshi*, responds to those questions. All together, therefore, twenty monks take part in a *Hokke jikkō*. In the case of the Ōwa Debate, ten monks from the northern school (Tendai) and ten from the southern schools (seven representing the Hossō school, two representing the Sanron school, and one representing the Kegon school) were assigned. The northern monks were paired off against the southern monks in such a way that the seven Hossō monks would debate with seven Tendai monks in the third through the ninth sessions, the sessions in which the second through the eighth fascicles of the *Lotus Sutra* were scheduled for discussion.

In the evening session of the second day of the debate (8/22/963), in which the third fascicle of the *Lotus Sutra* was discussed, the *monja* was the Tendai monk Kakukyō (927–1014), a disciple of Ryōgen from Yokawa who later became the twenty-third Tendai head abbot. The *dōshi* was Hōzō (904–968), an eminent and considerably older Hossō monk from the Kōfukuji.[36] During their exchange, Hōzō brought up an issue that is central to the Hossō school, namely, the doctrine that not all sentient beings possess the type of buddha nature that enables one to attain buddhahood, and that there are two vehicles (*jō;* Skt. *yāna*)—the *shōmonjō* (Skt. *śrāvaka-yāna*) and the *engakujō* (Skt. *pratyekabuddha-yāna*)—that do not lead to buddhahood.[37] In response to Hōzō's argument, Kakukyō defended the Tendai position, the doctrine that all sentient beings can eventually attain buddhahood, and that ultimately there is only one vehicle *(ichijō;* Skt. *ekayāna).*[38] Evidently Kakukyō's efforts were inadequate, for Ryōgen stepped in and took over his role as *monja* in the exchange with Hōzō. The debate went on until 8:30 p.m. without a victory by either side, so it was called off for the night.

The schedule for the morning session of the third day of the debate (8/23/963) called for Ryōgen, in the role of *dōshi*, to respond to questions put by the *monja*, the monk Hyōshu of the Hossō school, on the fourth fascicle of the *Lotus Sutra*. Hōzō intervened, however, by taking the place of Hyōshu in order to continue his debate with Ryōgen. The second installment of the Ryōgen-Hōzō debate, with the antagonists' roles reversed from the previous evening, went on for several hours, at the end of which Hōzō conceded to Ryōgen, acknowledging the brilliance and clarity of his opponent's exposition.

On the fourth day of the debate the sessions went off uneventfully according to schedule, but in the morning session of the fifth, and last, day of the debate, the issue that had been discussed by Ryōgen and Hōzō resurfaced in an exchange between Chūsan (d. 969), a Hossō monk from the Kōfukuji, and the Tendai (Yokawa) monk Juchō, the former in the role of *monja* and the latter in the role of *dōshi*. Chūsan made such a good showing in his exchange with Juchō that an imperial instruction was issued for him to carry his argument over into the evening session. Chūsan would thus take over the role of *monja* from the Sanron monk who was scheduled to debate that evening with Shōku, the younger of the two brothers who had become disciples of Ryōgen in 931. In the evening session Chūsan dominated the discussion, and when he finished his oration the courtiers in attendance congratulated him on his display. Emperor Murakami then presented Chūsan with a wine cup as a symbol of his victory over his Tendai opponents. Thus ended the Ōwa Debate.[39]

Lest it be thought, however, that the Hossō school was victorious in the Ōwa Debate, the following legend must be recounted.[40] According to it, Chūsan was inspired to eloquence by the power of the Kasuga divinity *(myōjin)*, the family deity *(ujigami)* of the Fujiwara family. When Hōzō was defeated by Ryōgen on the third day of the debate, a certain Fujiwara no Fuminori hastened to the Kasuga Shrine to beseech the divinity there to deliver the Hossō school from the great danger that it was in.[41] In response to Fuminori's appeal, the Kasuga divinity empowered Chūsan to perform as eloquently as he did and thus to defeat the Tendai representatives. As things turned out, however, it was not Chūsan but of all things Ryōgen's ox that had the last word in the Ōwa Debate. As the Fujiwara lords were filing out of the Seiryōden rejoicing in Chūsan's victory, they passed near the ox-cart that had brought Ryōgen to the palace, and they noticed that a mysterious, wonderful scent was emanating from the drool dripping from the ox's mouth. While the Fujiwara lords were staring in wonderment at that marvel, a voice suddenly emanated from the ox declaring how uplifted "all beings with a heart will be when they hear that grass and trees too are buddha." The voice making that typically Tendai declaration belonged, so the legend goes, to

Sannō, the protector deity *(shugokami)* of Mt. Hiei. Sannō's victory, by way of Ryōgen's ox, over the Kasuga divinity symbolized the victory of the Enryakuji over the Kōfukuji (with which the Kasuga shrine was affiliated), of the Tendai school over the Hossō school, and, perhaps, of Morosuke's sub-branch of the Fujiwara family over the rest of the family.

Several observations might be made about the Ōwa Debate. First, as was mentioned earlier, the debate appears to have been promoted by Ryōgen as a way of attracting attention and support, and thus the primary purpose of the debate was not to demonstrate the truth of Tendai, and the falsity of Hossō, doctrine. In a sense, therefore, the debate was not a debate at all. It is in the light of this interpretation of the Ōwa Debate that we can understand the reasons for Ryōgen's curious behavior on the fifth and last day of the debate when Juchō, the Tendai representative in the morning session, and Shōku, the Tendai representative in the evening session, were being beaten by the Hossō monk Chūsan. Rather than come to their aid as he had done with Kakukyō on the second day of the debate, Ryōgen sat in silence through the last two sessions of the debate. Hirabayashi Moritoku suggests that Ryōgen maintained silence in those sessions because, having demonstrated his brilliance in his two exchanges with Hōzō, his private purpose had been accomplished; there was no need for Ryōgen to repeat such a performance with Chūsan. Besides, according to Hirabayashi, Ryōgen had more to gain by maintaining silence on that last day than by defeating Chūsan. That is to say, by maintaining silence Ryōgen could demonstrate that in addition to great intelligence he possessed moderation, tact, and the ability to compromise.[42] By demonstrating those character traits with his silence, Ryōgen could win, in addition to the admiration of the powerful Fujiwara, their esteem, trust, and patronage.

Another reason for Ryōgen's behavior during the debate is, I suggest, that whereas there was little for Ryōgen to gain by defeating Chūsan, there was good reason for him to want to better Hōzō. Although Chūsan was an important Hossō scholar, it appears that he was not a major participant in the patronage competition of the time, and thus he was not someone with whom Ryōgen had to contend.[43] Hōzō, however, was a formidable opponent in the competition for patronage by Morosuke's sub-branch of the Fujiwara family: he was himself a member of the Fujiwara family, and had been appointed by Morosuke as one of his protector monks *(gojisō)*. Indeed, Ryōgen, Hōzō, and Gishō, whom Ryōgen had defeated in debate in 937, were

known as Morosuke's "three bright stars" *(sankō tenshi),* and in that
celestial pantheon Gishō was likened to the sun, Hōzō to the moon,
and Ryōgen to Venus.[44] Just as the moon outshines Venus, so, it
might be speculated, Hōzō outshone Ryōgen in terms of intimacy
with Morosuke's family. The Ōwa Debate thus afforded Ryōgen the
opportunity to show his luster and establish his superiority over Hōzō
in the circle of high-ranking monks whom Morosuke's family patron-
ized. The fact that Hōzō took the place of Hyōshu in the morning
session on the third day in order to continue his exchange with
Ryōgen might well indicate Hōzō's recognition that there was considerably more at stake in his competition with Ryōgen than the doctrinal superiority of the Tendai or Hossō school of Buddhism. Moreover,
because Gishō and Hōzō were members of the Fujiwara family,
whereas Ryōgen was not, it might have been necessary for Ryōgen to
display exceptional ability in order to outshine those two leading
members of the Fujiwara stable of eminent monks. It appears that
Gishō, the first of Morosuke's "three stars," had smooth—that is,
noncompetitive—relations with Ryōgen. It is known, for instance,
that Gishō went to Mt. Hiei in the twelfth month of 954 to participate in a *Hokke hakkō* ritual with Ryōgen.[45] According to the *Jie
Daishi den,* both Gishō and Hōzō "submitted" *(kusshita)* to
Ryōgen.[46]

The Ōwa Debate served Ryōgen well. Less than a year after it was
held, Ryōgen was invited, in the sixth month of 964, to lead one section of a ritual that was performed at the imperial palace for Emperor
Murakami's health. In reward for that service Ryōgen was appointed
to the position of *naigubu jūzenji;* that is, he became one of the ten
protector monks of the emperor. Just over a year later, on 12/28/965,
Ryōgen was appointed to the *sōgō,* the council overseeing all matters
relating to Buddhist monks and monasteries, at the unusually young
age of 54. Then, on 8/27/966, Ryōgen attained the highest position
in the Tendai school of Buddhism, the office of head abbot. There is
little doubt that Ryōgen's promotions came about, at least in part, as
a result of his finely calculated performance in the Ōwa Debate.

During his period of tenure as the Tendai head abbot, from 966
until his death in 985,[47] Ryōgen maintained intimate relations with
Morosuke's eldest sons, Koretada, Kanemichi, and Kaneie, and they
with him, in keeping with the pact that Ryōgen had made with
Morosuke in 954. For example, Kanemichi, who was *kampaku* from
972 to 977, made several visits to Mt. Hiei to participate in memorial
services for his father,[48] and Kaneie had Ryōgen perform various ritu-

als for him. In 984 Kaneie and his grandson, Prince Kanehito, attended a *Nyoirin hō* ritual that was performed by Ryōgen at Kaneie's request. The purpose of that esoteric ritual is the eradication of one's sins and the fulfillment of one's desires.[49] The main desire that Kaneie had in 984 was most likely that Kanehito be designated crown prince and eventually succeed to the imperial throne after Emperor Kazan, whose resignation from that office, it will be recalled, Kaneie subsequently schemed to bring about. Thus Kaneie employed Ryōgen's ritual power for his own ends, just as Morosuke had done, and in reward for the exercise of that power in their service, the descendants of Morosuke financed the construction of a number of buildings at Yokawa. For example, in memory of his deceased father, Morosuke, Kaneie donated finances for the construction of the Eshin-in, the dedication of which he attended on 11/27/983.[50] Ryōgen's pact with Morosuke was honored by Morosuke's sons, and the fulfillment of that pact, an intimate union between the Enryakuji and Morosuke's family, came about shortly after Ryōgen's death on 1/3/985. On 2/27/985, Morosuke's son and Ryōgen's disciple, Jinzen, succeeded his master as Tendai head abbot.[51]

## Conclusion

It is clear from the foregoing discussion that the *Lotus Sutra* and various rituals based on it played an extremely important and practical role in mid-tenth century Japan. As we have seen in the case of Ryōgen, the *Lotus Sutra* was one of the major vehicles by which he was carried to positions of great power and prestige. The *Lotus Sutra* served two functions in that regard: first, it was the principal text whereby Ryōgen demonstrated his intellectual prowess and thus his fitness for promotions in the Tendai community; in so doing, he also attracted the attention, and later the patronage, of the powerful Fujiwara family. Second, the *Lotus Sutra* was the main text used in the various rituals that Ryōgen performed for Morosuke's family; indeed, it was by means of *Lotus* rituals that Ryōgen and Morosuke sealed their pact in 954.

Of course one reason for Ryōgen's success was his very considerable intellectual gifts, but more important was the fact that in the tenth century high-ranking monks at the Enryakuji and the other major monasteries were ever on the lookout for intelligent young monks whom they could send as representatives of their monasteries to the annual debates in which, hopefully, their representatives would do well. Should a monk perform well in those debates, both his monastery and he personally stood to gain in the form of patronage by one or other of the wealthy and powerful families.

Just as the monks sought powerful patrons, the members of the ruling aristocracy sought competent young monks whom they could sponsor and employ in their service. Accordingly, representatives of the powerful families customarily attended the debates in order to evaluate the crop of new candidates for patronage.[52] Thus it was that in 937 Ryōgen first came to the attention of Fujiwara no Tadahira on the occasion of the *Yuima-e* at the Kōfukuji. An important point to note in this regard is that in the tenth century there appears to have been a correlation made between knowledge and power. That is, a monk who demonstrated great intelligence was considered to be a prime candidate for patronage because such a monk was believed to be capable of performing especially efficacious rituals. In that climate Ryōgen was at a great advantage because there is no doubt that he was exceptionally intelligent and therefore an especially attractive candidate for patronage as a ritualist. In the tenth century, and for many centuries thereafter, it was believed that an effective ritualist could perform a variety of indispensable services: such a monk could bring about his patrons' victory over their enemies; he could effect the fulfillment of his patrons' desires; and he could even assure the remission of sins, the placation of malevolent spirits, and the attainment of happiness after death. As we have seen, Ryōgen performed rituals for the post-mortem well-being of Tadahira; for the birth of a healthy male child by Morosuke's daughter Yasuko; for the everlasting glory of Morosuke's descendants; and for the imperial ascension of Kaneie's grandson. It is impossible to ascertain what Ryōgen might have been thinking as he performed, for example, the ritual designed to assure that Yasuko would give birth to a healthy male child, but there is no reason for cynicism in this regard. It is not unreasonable for Ryōgen to have believed, with great sincerity, that the appropriate rituals properly performed would bring about their intended effects. Whatever else he may have been, there appears to be little doubt that Ryōgen was a devout monk who spent a great deal of time reciting sutras daily.[53]

It should also be noted that the period when monks were able to attain high office in the monastic communities primarily on the basis of two criteria—namely, character (i.e., virtue and intelligence) and seniority in Buddhist orders—ended around Ryōgen's time.[54] From that time on, at least in the case of the Enryakuji, blood took precedence over brains; it became much more important for a monk to have the proper family lineage than to have a profound knowledge of the sutras, a reputation for holiness, or seniority in orders. Ryōgen himself may have contributed to that change by seeing to it that the person who succeeded him as Tendai head abbot, Morosuke's son Jinzen, was noted more for his family connections than for his intellectual prowess or exemplary virtue. The main reason for the change, however, was the very success of the major monasteries in acquiring considerable economic and political power. The more powerful the monastic communities became the less likely it was that the ruling elites would allow them to go their own way. Jinzen, it will be recalled, was originally sent to the Enryakuji to watch over the materials that his father, Morosuke, had donated to the monastery.

To shift our perspective, it might be argued that the members of the ruling aristocracy needed monks for precisely the same reason that high-ranking monks needed them. After all, what ambitious people like Ryōgen and Morosuke were seeking was primarily power. In tenth-century Japan, power, when stripped of its pomp and panoply, meant the control of land and the people who lived on and worked that land. The high-ranking monks and the ruling aristocrats had basically the same goal, and the sutras and the various rituals served as tools whereby both the monks and the aristocrats could attain that goal.

In conclusion, it might be said that sutras and rituals—tools whereby monks and aristocrats gained and held power—were, in a very real sense, political tools. This is not to claim simply that the ruling aristocrats used Buddhist tools for political ends. It is to say more than that. The doing of government is the exercise of continuous controlling power in the state, and part and parcel of that exercise, at least in Heian Japan, was the doing of certain Buddhist rituals. In other words, the performance of rituals that were believed to contribute to the acquisition and maintenance of power was as much a part of the process of governing as was the detailed administration of parcels of land. In this perspective, detailed land-allotment decisions and detailed Buddhist ritual performances were, so to speak, of the same species. Rituals and the sutras on which they were based were not ancillary to the doing of government; the doing of rituals was an integral part of the governing process. To put it differently, in tenth-century Japan, Buddhism and politics, religion and politics, were not two different phenomena—to do religion was to do politics, and vice versa. Therefore it is correct to say that in early Japanese society the *Lotus Sutra* was, at least in function, a "political" text. The distinction between religion and politics is a modern one; it would not have been at home in Heian Japan.

## NOTES

1. See especially Inoue Mitsusada, *Nihon kodai no kokka to Bukkyō;* Nihon Bukkyō Gakkai, ed., *Bukkyō to seiji-keizai;* Satō Shin'ichi, *Nihon no chūsei kokka to shūkyō;* and various works by Kuroda Toshio, particularly *Nihon chūsei no kokka to shūkyō,* and *Ōbō to buppō.*

2. The primary source materials used in the preparation of this essay are *Jie Daisōjō den,* in *Gunsho ruijū,* folio 69, vol. 5 (Tokyo: Naigai Shoseki Kaisha, 1930), 553–563; *Jie Daishi den,* in *Gunsho ruijū,* folio 213, vol. 8 (Tokyo: Naigai Shoseki Kaisha, 1927), 734–742; *Shohō yōryaku-shō,* in *Zoku gunsho ruijū,* folio 724, vol. 25, pt. 2 (Tokyo: Zoku Gunsho Ruijū Kanseikai, 1924), 194–216; and Shibuya Jikai, ed., *Tendai zasu-ki* (Tokyo: Daiichi Shobō, 1939). The main secondary sources used are Hirabayashi Moritoku, *Ryōgen,* and the following articles by Hori Daiji: "Ryōgen to Yokawa fukkō" and "Yokawa Bukkyō no kenkyū."

3. Those developments are discussed in detail in all the standard histories of Japan. See especially the historical series published by Shōgakkan (1975) and Chūō Kōronsha (1966), and the first two volumes of Kyōto-shi, ed., *Kyōto no rekishi* (Tokyo: Gakugei Shorin, 1968).

4. Motokata, about whom very little is known, is identified in Hirabayashi Moritoku, *Ryōgen,* 37. It is curious that a member of the southern branch of the Fujiwara family would have been able to offer serious competition to a leading member of the northern branch in the mid-tenth century, for the northern branch had asserted its supremacy over the southern one almost a century earlier.

5. At that time Morosuke held the post of *udaijin,* the third most powerful office in the country after those of *dajō daijin* and *sadaijin,* and was a courtier of the second rank, whereas Motokata was a middle counsellor *(chūnagon)* and a courtier of the third rank.

6. See Hirabayashi, *Ryōgen,* 45.

7. For an English-language account of Kaneie's scheme, see Delmer M. Brown and Ichirō Ishida, *The Future and The Past* (Berkeley: University of California Press, 1979), 50–55.

8. *Jie Daisōjō den,* 554, and *Jie Daishi den,* 735. Information on the Eastern Pagoda and Western Pagoda sections of Mt. Hiei is contained in most of the modern Japanese works on the history of the Enryakuji. See, for instance, Kageyama Haruki, *Hieizan,* 68–79. For material in English on this topic, see my "The Sanmon-Jimon Schism in the Tendai School of Buddhism: A Preliminary Analysis."

9. See *Jie Daisōjō den,* 554, and *Jie Daishi den,* 735. Ryōgen's difficulties in obtaining an ordination license and the way he eventually acquired one are discussed in Hirabayashi, *Ryōgen,* 14–16; and in Hori, "Ryōgen to Yokawa fukkō," *Jinbun ronsō* 10 (1964): 32.

10. See Hirabayashi, *Ryōgen*, 16. The term *rongi* designates a formal question-and-answer form of exchange in which Buddhist doctrine is discussed. See Nakamura Hajime, ed., *Bukkyōgo daijiten*, one-volume ed. (Tokyo: Tokyo Shoseki, 1981), 1464.

11. It is said that Jōe's master, the monk Kikyō (889–966), who subsequently became the seventeenth Tendai *zasu*, was so impressed by Ryōgen's performance that he sent Jōe to become a disciple of Ryōgen. This probably apocryphal story, which served to point up Ryōgen's brilliance, is reported in Hirabayashi, *Ryōgen*, 16.

12. Senga (914–998) eventually became the twenty-second Tendai *zasu*, and Shōku (d. 985) received appointment to the *sōgō*, the council that oversaw all matters relating to Buddhist monks and monasteries in Japan. For information on them see Washio Junkei, ed., *Nihon Bukka jimmei jisho*, revised ed. (Tokyo: Tokyo Bijutsu, 1982), 608 and 703–704. For information on Senga's period of tenure as Tendai *zasu*, see Shibuya, *Tendai zasu-ki*, 49.

13. See Hirabayashi, *Ryōgen*, 18.

14. See *Jie Daishi den*, 736, and Hirabayashi, *Ryōgen*, 18 and 22. The *Yuima-e*, which was held traditionally from the tenth to the seventeenth day of the tenth month of the year, was a Fujiwara family event in that it was held in memory of Fujiwara no Kamatari (614–669), the founder of the Fujiwara family. The *Yuima-e* was one of three imperial assemblies *(sandai choku-e)* which were held yearly by the southern (Nara) schools of Buddhism, the other two being the *misai-e* (or *gosai-e*), which was held in the Daigyokuden (or Daigokuden) at the imperial palace, and the Yakushiji's *saishō-e*. It is curious that Ryōgen's opponents in the debates of 935 and 937 were so young. It is not clear why the monasteries assigned such young monks to represent them in the debates, or why Ryōgen and his opponents were so unevenly matched in terms of their ages.

15. See *Jie Daisōjō den*, 555. Ryōgen's relations with Tadahira are discussed in Hirabayashi, *Ryōgen*, 24–30, and in Hori, "Ryōgen to Yokawa fukkō," *Jinbun ronsō* 10 (1964): 27–28.

16. At Hokke-zammai chapels *(dō)*, rituals called *hangyō-hanza-zammai*, which are based on the *Lotus Sutra*, were performed. Those rituals, which took place over a period of either twenty-one or thirty-seven days, involved two kinds of exercises: in one of those exercises the participants circumambulated statues of the Buddha while chanting portions of the *Lotus Sutra*, and in the other exercise the participants sat and reflected or meditated on that sutra. See Taya Raishun et al., eds., *Bukkyōgaku jiten* (Kyoto: Hōzōkan, 1955), 398 and 194. The first Hokke-zammai-dō in Japan was built in 812 by Saichō (767–822), the founder of the Tendai school of Buddhism in Japan, in the Eastern Pagoda section of Mt. Hiei, and a second one was built in 835 in the Western Pagoda section by Ennin (793–864), the third Tendai *zasu*.

17. The Yokawa section of Mt. Hiei was first developed by the aforementioned Ennin in 831 when he built a cloister, the Shuryōgon-in, there. The revival of the Yokawa section, which had fallen into disuse and disrepair not long after Ennin died, began in 940 when the monk Jōzō went to the Shuryōgon-in to perform some rituals. Eventually Ryōgen developed a community of several hundred monks at Yokawa. See *Jie Daisōjō den*, 556. Ryōgen's efforts to rebuild Yokawa are discussed in detail in the articles by Hori Daiji mentioned in note 2.

18. See *Jie Daisōjō den*, 555, and *Jie Daishi den*, 737. This matter is discussed in Hori, "Ryōgen to Yokawa fukkō," *Jinbun ronsō* 10 (1964): 27–28. The term *goma*

refers to a ritual in which offerings are presented to a particular object of devotion *(honzon)* by way of being consumed in a fire. See Nakamura, *Bukkyōgo daijiten,* 386.

19. This point is made by both Hirabayashi, *Ryōgen,* 38, and Hori, "Ryōgen to Yokawa fukkō," *Jinbun ronsō* 10 (1964): 28. Hori says that Fujiwara no Tadahira instructed that those rituals be performed for Yasuko's fetus, but Yasuko did not give birth to Prince Norihira until 5/24/950 (June 12, 950), so she could not have been pregnant any earlier than late August of 949, by which time, as mentioned above, Ryōgen was performing rituals for the deceased Tadahira. Thus it is unlikely that Yasuko was pregnant before Tadahira died, and even if she was pregnant by that time she was in such an early stage of pregnancy that no one could have known of her condition.

20. See Hirabayashi, *Ryōgen,* 38. The term *kanzu* (or *kanju*) refers to a sort of "spiritual bouquet," to use a Christian term. See Nakamura, *Bukkyōgo daijiten,* 186.

21. See *Shohō yōryaku-shō,* 210–211. The *ususama no hō* ritual was directed to a divinity *(myōō)* named Ususama (Skt. Ucchuṣma) who, as the feces-eating divinity, was believed to have the power to purify unclean places and things. Thus his image was sometimes enshrined in the lavatories of the monasteries. According to early Buddhist belief, women were born with, as part of their nature, five hindrances *(goshō)* which prevented them from attaining buddhahood; certain rituals were therefore devised to assure that a pregnant woman would give birth to a male child who, at least by nature, is not so hindered. See Nakamura, *Bukkyōgo daijiten,* 90 and 368. In the case under discussion, the issue at stake was less Buddhist salvation than imperial succession.

22. See Hori, "Ryōgen to Yokawa fukkō," *Jinbun ronsō* 10 (1964): 28–29. It is not known what kind of ritual Ryōgen performed on that occasion, but given that it took place over a twenty-one-day period, it is likely that it was a *hangyō-hanza-zam-mai* ritual. See note 16 above.

23. See *Jie Daisōjō den,* 555, and *Jie Daishi den,* 737.

24. See Ōno Tatsunosuke, ed., *Nihon Bukkyōshi jiten* (Tokyo: Tōkyōdō Shuppan, 1979), 89, and Hirabayashi, *Ryōgen,* 39.

25. See *Jie Daisōjō den,* 555, and *Jie Daishi den,* 736. This event is discussed in detail in Hirabayashi, *Ryōgen,* 42–45.

26. The figure 1,800 is noteworthy. On the question of the size of the monastic community *(daishu)* at the Enryakuji in the early to mid-Heian period, see my article "The Sanmon-Jimon Schism."

27. At that time Yokawa was still under the control of the Western Pagoda section, and the names of the monks in residence there were still entered in the Western Pagoda's monks' register *(bōzuchō).* Yokawa did not become an independent, autonomous section of the Enryakuji complex, with its own monks' register, until 972, six years after Ryōgen became Tendai *zasu.*

28. See *Jie Daisōjō den,* 555, and *Jie Daishi den,* 736. Morosuke's petition is discussed at some length in Hirabayashi, *Ryōgen,* 43–44.

29. In Morosuke's petition the word *sammai,* which is a Japanese transliteration of the Sanskrit term *samādhi,* probably referred not to the profound meditative state of *samādhi* but to the ritual then being conducted or, more likely, to the Hokke-zam-mai-dō at which thenceforth rituals would be performed for Morosuke's intentions.

30. This is the view of Hirabayashi, *Ryōgen*, 55–56.

31. A *Hokke hakkō* ritual is one in which monks participated in eight *(hachi)* successive discussions *(kō)* on the eight fascicles of the *Lotus (Hokke) Sutra*. That ritual was practiced in Japan from the latter decades of the eighth century. See Ōno, *Nihon Bukkyōshi jiten*, 435–436, and Willa Tanabe, "The Lotus Lectures: *Hokke Hakkō* in the Heian Period," 393–407.

32. This fact appears to conflict with the material in note 27 above. The exact status of Yokawa in 961 is not clear.

33. See Hirabayashi, *Ryōgen*, 69.

34. Ibid., 73.

35. The record of that debate is the *Ōwa shūron-ki*, which was composed by the Kōfukuji (Hossō) monk Onkaku (d. 1162) just before he died. See *DNBZ*, folio 433, vol. 61, 1–4. See also *Jie Daisōjō den*, 556, and *Jie Daishi den*, 738. The Ōwa Debate is discussed in detail in Hirabayashi, *Ryōgen*, 69–82.

36. For information on Kakukyō's term of office as Tendai *zasu* see Shibuya, *Tendai zasu-ki*, 50. For a short biographical note on Hōzō, see Washio, *Nihon Bukka jimmei jisho*, 1053.

37. Hōzō raised this issue in reference to statements contained in the third fascicle of the *Lotus Sutra*, the one that he and Kakukyō were assigned to discuss. See, for example, references to *shōmon* in the *Myōhō Renge Kyō* in *T* 9.20. In English see verses 52 and 74 of chapter 5, the first chapter of the third fascicle of the *Lotus Sutra*, in Leon Hurvitz, trans., *Scripture of the Lotus Blossom of the Fine Dharma*.

38. In their exchange Hōzō and Kakukyō discussed an issue that had been debated by the Hossō and Tendai schools for a very long time. Saichō too debated that issue at great length a century and a half earlier with the Hossō monk Tokuitsu. Saichō's position on this issue is discussed in Paul Groner, *Saichō: The Establishment of the Japanese Tendai School*, esp. 91–101.

39. The Ōwa Debate raises a question that cannot be addressed here, namely the problem of the criteria by which the victor in a doctrinal debate was decided upon. It would appear that victory often depended less on the brilliance of a monk's argument—after all, the judges were usually courtiers who, allowing for the rare exception, would not have been experts on the finer points of Buddhist doctrine—than on the rank and power of his patrons.

40. This legend, the earliest extant source of which appears to be the fifteenth-century document called *Ainōshō*, is discussed in Hirabayashi, *Ryōgen*, 72–73.

41. Because Hōzō was a member of the Fujiwara family and a Kōfukuji monk, Fuminori's concern might have been less for the Hossō school and its doctrine than for a fellow Fujiwara and the honor of the family's *ujidera*.

42. Hirabayashi, *Ryōgen*, 77. In a doctrinal debate one type of strategy that a monk could adopt was that of "nonresponsiveness" *(fuzui)* whereby he might annoy and befuddle his opponent. It is most unlikely that Ryōgen used that strategy on the occasion in question.

43. For a biographical note on Chūsan, see Washio, *Nihon Bukka jimmei jisho*, 815–816.

44. See *Jie Daisōjō den*, 561, and *Jie Daishi den*, 739. For a short note on the "three bright stars" imagery in Buddhism, see Nakamura, *Bukkyōgo daijiten*, 461.

45. *Jie Daishi den*, 735 and 738.

46. Ibid., 742.

POLITICS IN THE MID-HEIAN PERIOD

47. For a chronicle of the main events during Ryōgen's term of office as Tendai *zasu*, see Shibuya, *Tendai zasu-ki*, 42–46.

48. See, for example, the entry for 4/25/971 in ibid., 43.

49. See Hirabayashi, *Ryōgen*, 174. For a note on the *Nyoirin hō* ritual, the full name of which is *Nyoirin kanjizai bosatsu nenju hō*, see Nakamura, *Bukkyōgo daijiten*, 1060.

50. See *Jie Daisōjō den*, 558, and Shibuya, *Tendai zasu-ki*, 46.

51. For a chronicle of the main events during Jinzen's term of office as Tendai *zasu*, see Shibuya, *Tendai zasu-ki*, 46–47.

52. It is likely that the members of the court aristocracy attended the major Buddhist debates also for entertainment purposes. Aside from the major court ceremonies, in the Heian period there would have been few other events throughout the year that would have had such style and drama as the major doctrinal debates. Those debates afforded the aristocrats the occasion to dress up and engage in a form of high theatre.

53. See *Jie Daisōjō den*, 557.

54. The abandonment of the practice of promotion to high office in the Buddhist communities on the basis of those criteria is discussed in Hioki Shōichi, *Nihon sōhei kenkyū*, 49; Hori, "Ryōgen to Yokawa fukkō," *Jinbun ronsō* 12 (1966): 20–22; and Tsuji Zennosuke, *Nihon Bukkyōshi*, 1:765.

# Historical Consciousness and *Hon-jaku* Philosophy in the Medieval Period on Mount Hiei

KURODA TOSHIO

The "Life Span of the Tathāgata" chapter of the *Lotus Sutra*[1] expounds on the existence of a fundamental buddha who achieved buddhahood eons ago in contrast to the historical Buddha, Śākya-muni,[2] who achieved buddhahood forty years before his entrance into nirvana. It explains the relationship between these two buddhas on the basis of the doctrine of expedient devices,[3] according to which the former is an essence,[4] and the latter a hypostasis.[5]

This theory or doctrine is called in Japanese *hon-jaku,* meaning a "temporary manifestation of a higher principle."[6] During the medieval period it reached the status of a philosophical principle that greatly affected in multifarious ways not only the doctrine and beliefs of Buddhism but also the secular realms of literature and the arts, as well as concepts of state and political philosophy.

In the present chapter I would like to offer a few reflections on one example of that *hon-jaku* philosophy as it appears in the scriptural activity of a scholarly lineage known as the "chroniclers" *(kike),*[7] who specialized in the study and interpretation of "documents" *(kiro-ku).*[8] I would also like to reflect on their consciousness of history as it was affected by their religiosity, in order to analyze the breadth of the impact of *Lotus* philosophy[9] on the culture of Japan.

## The *Honji-suijaku* Theory

It is unnecessary to reiterate the scholarly argument that the *hon-jaku* philosophical system was one of the doctrinally preeminent theories of the Tendai and Nichiren lineages based on the *Lotus Sutra.* The importance of that system in the history of Japanese religions—as manifested in specific doctrinal forms regarding the relationship between the *kami* of heaven and earth (the deities of Shinto) on the one hand, and various buddhas and bodhisattvas on the other hand —is well known. This body of research concerns the *honji-suijaku* theory, which appeared in texts from the latter half of the ninth century and became the basis for the combinations and associations of Shinto and Buddhist divinities.[10]

This theory holds that the buddhas and bodhisattvas (of India) are of a higher principle which manifests itself as the deities of Japan. At the time of its inception (around the ninth and tenth centuries) it was the main theory that explained in principle and in general terms the relationship between the Buddha and the *kami*. To be more precise, one should say it was a theory explaining the existence of the *kami*. However, this theory strayed from the original philosophy of the body of the Buddha expounded in the *Lotus Sutra* and became a dogma that used only one aspect of the *hon-jaku* principle to explain the divinities of Shinto in such a manner that they could be assimilated by Buddhism.[11]

In the second half of the eleventh century the *honji-suijaku* theory was taken beyond the stage of being merely a general principle. It was systematically used to establish relations between *kami* and buddhas by associating specific Shinto deities with specific buddhas and bodhisattvas; for example, it viewed the deity Hachiman as a hypostasis of Amitābha, and the deity Amaterasu of Ise as a hypostasis of Mahāvairocana. It thus became customary to emphasize the majesty and power of individual deities within a world based on Buddhist belief.[12]

From this stage on, the *honji-suijaku* theory evolved into intricate and convoluted dogmas or theories. This was due to two processes: first, a process attributed to social interest that affected the evolution of the beliefs, modes of reverence, and customs vis-à-vis Shinto and Buddhist deities; and second, what might be termed a process of Buddhist doctrinal debate over interpretations of the essential Buddha[13] and the hypostatic Buddha[14] within the framework of the doctrine of the body of the Buddha. Upon these interpretations were grafted discussions concerning the superiority or inferiority of the two parts of the *Lotus Sutra (hommon* and *jakumon).*[15] Then, from the thirteenth century on, these theories were combined with the philosophy of "innate awakening"[16] found in Shingon esotericism and Tendai doctrine. As a result, a specific formulation of the relation of essence to hypostasis appeared, in which the hypostasis was deemed superior to the essence. Normally essence was seen as superior, hypostasis as inferior; however, the combination of the *honji-suijaku* theory with the doctrine of innate awakening gave birth to a mystical and paradoxical truth according to which, in Japan, the hypostasis was deemed superior. This is the "reversed *honji-suijaku*" theory,[17] according to which Shinto deities were considered the essence and buddhas and bodhisattvas their hypostases. Moreover, it was from this reversal that such theories as the "tree" theory evolved, in which Shinto was the root, Confucianism the branches and leaves, and Buddhism the flowers and fruit. These theories prepared the first step necessary for the body of beliefs in the *kami* of heaven and earth to emancipate itself from Buddhism, under the name of Shinto.

An objective and comprehensive reflection on the *honji-suijaku* theory shows that it played the role of assimilating indigenous creeds into Buddhism and of putting them at the bottom of the Buddhist system of belief.[18] However, this was not simply a body of theories advocating what is usually derided as syncretism. There is no doubt that the indigenous *kami* of heaven and earth were worshipped in Japan from times of old. But people came to think that indigenous divinities must be an expression of the Buddhist truth, since Buddhism was a universal religion offering a truth of higher dimension. It was thought at first, up until the ninth century, that the deities indigenous to Japan were like the original divinities of India: although originally unrelated to Buddhism, they were either put in opposition to it, or in support of it, or they converted to Buddhism and positively protected it. Soon enough, however, under the impetus of the doctrines of expedient devices and *hon-jaku*, these deities came to be seen as avatars[19] of buddhas and bodhisattvas. The understanding of this relationship was not limited to anthropomorphic divinities; it included mountains, rivers, trees, oceans, and earth—that is, all phenomenal existences. As a consequence, this understanding was applied to the entirety of the national territory and history, which were then thought to be expressions and products of a religious truth.

But this interpretation of essence versus hypostasis differed semantically from those terms as they are found in the *Lotus Sutra,* in which the term *hon* refers to an original and unique Buddha, and the term *jaku* to the many historical buddhas that subsequently appeared and disappeared. Indeed, the two interpretations agree on the form of the doctrine of expedient devices, but the term *honji* in *honji-suijaku* does not refer to the ultimate, original Buddha. As for the term *sui-*

*jaku,* it indicates the practice of buddhas and bodhisattvas that benefits others besides themselves, and refers to their body of metamorphosis.[20] Furthermore, the latter interpretation did not only assume
the existence of a "clear" realm of protection by the buddhas, invisible to the eye; it also assumed the existence of a mysterious universe
beyond these two realms: a universe of secret meaning proper to esoteric Buddhism, one which this interpretation closely approximated.
The indigenous divinities, originally conceived of as mystical forces
acting in an inconceivable world, must have had something that pre-
disposed them to association with the realm of esotericism. The relation of the evolution of the *honji-suijaku* theories to that of the philosophy of esoteric Buddhism is a topic of great importance and must
be reserved for further study.

## The Evolution of Oral Transmissions and the Chroniclers

The Tendai lineage, headquartered at Enryakuji on Mt. Hiei, was
founded by Saichō in the early ninth century. It goes without saying
that the Tendai lineage is the school of thought that takes as its scriptural basis the *Lotus Sutra* and the doctrinal system founded by Chih-
i; however, already during the lifetime of Saichō, the social milieu
received the Shingon esotericism of Kūkai even more readily. As a
consequence, soon after the death of Saichō the Japanese Tendai lineage added esoteric Buddhism to its core curriculum, to the extent
that some esoteric formulations were prized even more than purely
Tendai views, and this led to the evolution of a separate Tendai esoteric doctrine. By the beginning of the tenth century the entire doctrinal body of Tendai was heavily laden with esotericism. This Tendai
esotericism was called *taimitsu*[21] and developed while relating closely
to the exoteric doctrine of Tendai proper.

There were originally two doctrinal fields in Tendai thought:
namely, the purely doctrinal and philosophical fields of research
(called *kyōsō*), and the purely practical fields of contemplation and
ritual (called *kanshin*). However, since the Japanese Tendai lineage
came early under the strong influence of esotericism, practical fields
were given more importance than doctrinal ones, a tendency that
caused a gradual decline of doctrinal and theoretical research, while
increasing consideration was given to faith earned through practice
and to religious principles gained through direct mystic intuition.
From the first half of the eleventh century onward, matters of faith

and religious principles came to be transmitted from master to disciple, not in the form of theoretical writings, but in the form of oral transmissions *(kuden)*. It can be said that this was, more than an extreme hypertrophy of the practical field of meditation, a phenomenon based on the esoteric tendency to esteem mystical affinities between people, and to set high value on the mystical power of language. In these transmissions the emphasis was on "innate awakening," a term connoting mystic achievement and flying leaps of intuition, rather than on "initial awakening,"[22] which denotes logical and gradual research or training. This accentuation was, again, akin to the practice of esoteric Buddhism. This habit or propensity received different names; when pertaining to the form of practice it was called the "doctrine of oral transmission,"[23] while in reference to its religious contents it was called the "doctrine of meditation"[24] or "doctrine of innate awakening."[25]

In the world of esotericism oral transmissions were given utmost importance, but this does not mean that all writings or tracts were completely excluded from it. As a matter of fact, one of the peculiarities of oral transmission was its systematic recording of experiences, in-depth interpretations, or essential points of doctrine and practice.[26] The contents of these oral transmissions not only included matters associated with Tendai theory, practice, and ritual at the exoteric and esoteric levels, but also embraced matters related to the different branches of the Tendai lineage—that is, to distinctions between that and other lineages; to the sacred space of Mt. Hiei, its buildings, statues, and their origin and meaning; and to matters concerning past masters, lives of great men, and legends concerning visions, miracles, chastisements, and natural disasters. Furthermore, even though one can find in these transmissions clearly expressed and logical statements, many of them consist of fragmentary knowledge gained through mystic achievement. Very soon these transmissions were copied to serve as a reminder for those who received them. Copies took the form of secret transmissions written on strips of paper,[27] and were short sentences, verses, or episodic reminiscences. These were then transmitted, and it appears that over time they received addenda, revisions, corrections, and other fragments.

During the medieval period on Mt. Hiei these "paper strips" were collectively called "documents" *(kiroku),* a term that included all ancient writings and official documents related to the traditional authority of the lineage since the creation of Enryakuji as well as all classics and scriptures pertaining to doctrine and authored by the saints and high priests of Mt. Hiei's temples. Thus these "documents," while being a product of the religious activities taking place on Mt. Hiei, were also proof of traditional authority and legitimacy. Then, at some point in history, scholarly monks began to specialize in the scrupulous study and transmission of these documents. By the beginning of the fourteenth century they came to form a specific scholarly lineage called "chroniclers" (kike). During the latter part of the medieval period it was said that the founder of this lineage was a certain Kenshin (1130–1192). As Professor Hazama Jikō has indicated,[28] the origin of the chroniclers probably belongs to that period, although it can be advanced that their period of development and systematization is limited by Gigen at the end of the thirteenth century and by Kōsō in the first part of the fourteenth century. This periodization corresponds exactly to the main stages of evolution and maturation of the doctrine of oral transmissions.

In the first part of the fourteenth century, a certain Enkan (Echin, 1281–1356), who gave all his energies to promote Tendai discipline and ordination,[29] wrote in his autobiography, composed toward the end of his life, that the doctrinal study taking place on Mt. Hiei consisted of exotericism, esotericism, discipline, and documents.[30] The text entitled *Shokoku ikken shōki,* written in 1387, notes that on Mt. Hiei since times of old one spoke of "the three ways of exotericism, esotericism, and Shugendō, and of the four degrees (of secrecy) of exotericism, esotericism, discipline, and documents."[31] Furthermore, Kōsō, who also studied under Gigen in the line of Enkan, and who was thoroughly acquainted with the documents, stated in the introduction to his monumental *Keiranshūyōshū*[32] (1318) that the documents of Mt. Hiei consisted of the four fields of exotericism, esotericism, discipline, and documents, and that each of these was completed through an "unction,"[33] a ritual symbolizing the attainment of the highest spheres. The unction in the field of exotericism was called the "secret transmission concerning the production of wisdom and marvelous understanding"; in the field of esotericism it was called the "unction of universal dharma"; in the field of discipline it was called the "transmission of the precepts of protection"; and in the field of documents it was called the "unction concerning mingling with the dust and dimming of radiance to protect and benefit the national territory."[34] The fourth field of documents was subdivided into six subjects of study: first, temples and the sacred grounds thereof; second, statues and paintings; third, miraculous manifestations in *kami* form; fourth, protection of the state; fifth, rituals; and sixth, practices of meditation. There was a compulsory study of the "Document in Twenty *kan* of the Three Saints and Two Masters"[35] concerning these six fields. (The three saints are Saichō, Ennin, and Enchin, and the two masters are Annen and Ryōgen).

Finally, the *Kuinbukkakushō*,[36] a document that seems to have been completed in 1324 and to consist of the secret transmissions of the Kajii lineage (which at the time claimed to be the correct lineage of the chroniclers), offers the following "abridged stanza" as a succinct statement of the ultimate raison d'être of Enryakuji on Mt. Hiei:

Preserve the three treasures.
Dim the radiance and appear in this world.
Purify the buddha land.
Benefit all living beings.[37]

The same text then declares that this stanza corresponds to the six subjects of study presented above in the following manner:

The first line corresponds to subjects 2, 5, and 6.
The second line corresponds to subject 3.
The third line corresponds to subject 1.
And the fourth line corresponds to subject 4.

As both the *Keiranshūyōshū* and the *Kuinbukkakushō* note, there were six degrees of transmission of the documents, going from the simple to the highest and most secret. The completion of study was marked by a secret transmission from master to disciple or by a final statement,[38] that is, either a last meeting between master and disciple in which ultimate secrets were transmitted, or a last teaching given by the master at the time of his death to only one of his disciples. Naturally, there is little doubt that these last-minute transmissions were related to the last unction within the field of documents.[39]

Thus the chroniclers defined their mission as the study and mystical interpretation of what was collectively called documents, in which secret teachings and transmissions in all forms were particularly prized. They further commented on them, organized them, offered new interpretations, and transmitted them. Although the contents of these transmissions were as outlined above, it is worth noting that Mt. Hiei was not only a huge religious institution rightly proud of constituting one of the most brilliant intellectual traditions of Japan, seated in vast temples adorned by countless statues, paintings, and scriptures studied by three thousand priests; it was also—as emphasized in the ultimate unction of the study of documents—a place where nothing was considered more important than the protection of the state and the study of history and of contemporary events surrounding a numinous site symbolized by the worship of the seven divinities of the Hie shrines, in which buddhas and bodhisattvas manifested themselves as *kami* in order to protect that state and its history. In other words, the ultimate duty of the chroniclers was the study of the *hon-jaku* combinatory Shinto-Buddhist system of the Hie shrines at the foot of Mt. Hiei. This system was known as Sannō Shinto, and the method of study of that combinatory system was the study of documents. As a result the chroniclers developed and spread the belief that the study of documents enabled one to attain the highest level of Buddhist truth.

The *Shokoku ikken shōki* mentioned earlier was written with the express purpose of describing Mt. Hiei in the latter half of the fourteenth century. Everywhere in that document one finds an emphasis marked by the terms "great matter of the chroniclers" or "secret matter of practice" (of Shugendō). Thus, even though one may speak of exoteric-esoteric Buddhism, or of exotericism-esotericism-discipline-documents to characterize Mt. Hiei, there is evidence that the chroniclers, together with the mountain ascetics *(yamabushi),* were a conspicuous presence on Mt. Hiei during the second half of the medieval period.

## The Evolution of the Documents

The exact contents, extent, genres, and purview of the documents that were maintained, edited, and transmitted by the chroniclers are unclear today. However, on the basis of the few documents transmitted to the present day, it is possible to offer hypotheses concerning the mode of editing and transmission, as well as the characteristics of the chroniclers' ways of thinking.

It appears that the fundamental basis of documentation consisted of numerous and fragmentary secret transmissions (written and oral) of old, official documents and texts, and of "secret writings." This is evidenced in a most emphatic manner by a text such as the *Sanke sairyakki* (or *Sanke yōryakki*),[40] a representative work of the chroniclers, which is almost entirely composed of countless citations claimed to be from various sources, the most authoritative of which was—or so it is said in the text—the "Document in Twenty *kan* of the Three Saints and Two Masters." This is not all. A number of addenda, corrections, and even mistakes in copying were added together with new interpretations and notes, to the point that some of these documents were organized in the form of a *summa*. On the other hand, it appears that abridged versions of some of the documents were also compiled. This practice was not confined to the chroniclers of the time, for it was widely accepted in the world of oral transmissions. For example, similar practices have already been noted concerning texts such as the *Endaragishū* and the *Sanjūshi kojishō* (the *Makura no sōshi*), which were in the mainstream of the doctrine of innate awakening.[41] In other words, the method of transmission of the documents caused an evolution of their contents.

The *Sanke sairyakki* is a classic illustration of this process of transmission. A text kept in the Library of Mt. Hiei (Eizan Bunko) with a colophon noting that it was copied on the twenty-first day of the eleventh month of 1436 is entitled *Kuinbukkakushō-narabi jūroku in;* however, next to the title is the inscription *Sanke yōryakki-shō kuju.*[42] Moreover, after the introduction, which states that the documents consist of six fields and so on, the main text is preceded by the inscription *Sanke sairyakki.* This title duplication indicates that the two texts, *Sanke sairyakki* and *Sanke yōryakki,* are in fact one and the same. Furthermore, the colophon indicates that the *Kuinbukkakushō* was transmitted as one part of the *Sanke sairyakki* and formed a "general introduction" to the study of documents. Now, a comparison with the *Sanke sairyakki* contained in *Dai Nihon Bukkyō zensho* reveals a large number of differences in the disposition and length of each chapter, while a comparison of these chapters to the version entitled *Sanke yōryakki* kept in the Library of the Imperial Household and dating from the Edo period shows that that version has, by far, much more content. Furthermore, texts such as the *Gigen kanchū* or *Sanke shibunkiroku* kept at the Hiei library overlap in many places with the contents of the texts under consideration. Finally, further comparison with the many texts bearing the same title and kept here and there indicates that there was no such thing as an authentic or standard text to begin with. This type of writing did not preserve, like other works, an original text *(teihon).*

An example of collation and editing of the theories held by the chroniclers is the *Yōtenki.*[43] This text offers comments on the history, rituals, music, palanquins, sacerdotal lineages, and miracles related to the seven shrines of Sannō at Hie. The versions current today, beginning with that contained in the *Zoku-gunsho ruijū,* consist of forty chapters to which two were later added. Although the version kept at the Library of the Imperial Household dated 1490 was thought to be the oldest, a few years ago an earlier version, entitled *Sannō engi* and dated 1292, was discovered. This earlier text, belonging to another origin and somewhat differing in content, is about one-fifth the size of the other and has only thirty-two chapters, each generally shorter than those of the *Yōtenki.* Professor Okada Seishi, who compared the two documents, suggests that the *Sannō engi* might be close to the original form of the *Yōtenki,* and that "the text might have been originally composed in a form resembling a convenient reminder for the priests and monks of the shrine-temple multiplex of Hie concerning the matters of history, rituals, and sacerdotal lineage, all taken from various documents."[44] Moreover, he suggests that "since the document lacks both date and author—which is common in this genre of documents—a number of accretions occurred over the years, as is clear in the text of the *Yōtenki,* which is much longer." The *Yōtenki* as we see it today is a sort of theoretical tract on Sannō Shinto. This example also shows that the contents of the documents did change in the process of their transmission.

The transmission of the documents, then, was not a mechanical process of preserving texts and passing them on unchanged, but was marked by an evolutionary process involving a multiplicity of sources, authors, versions, and interpretations. Although the variations are such that it is often difficult to tell whether a particular text was written by chroniclers or not, it is still possible to discern certain characteristics in terms of genre and content that make up what might be called a certain logic.

## The Logic of the Chroniclers

A second characteristic of the chroniclers is that their documents evolved into various genres. As I have mentioned, the entire contents of the documents handled by the chroniclers are obscure today, and various libraries hold quite a number of documents whose authorship remains uncertain. However, judging from the type of mission the chroniclers gave themselves, it is possible to offer a number of suggestions concerning the broad limits of their activity, and to bring to light a few of their representative works.

According to my present tentative conclusion based on the documents I have seen, there are different kinds of texts dealing with the various religious institutions of Mt. Hiei—that is, their size, the dates of their establishment, and their purpose, history, and legends—all presented in a straightforward and simple manner, as seen in documents such as the *Santōshoji engi*,[45] the *Sammon dōshaki*,[46] and the *Eigaku yōki*.[47] One might say that these texts are written in the style of basic documents and have very little mystical or philosophical content. However, there are other texts that do have a religious coloration, and their contents are even surreal. Between these two extremes there are others which, although varied and colorful, suggest a possible order.

A schematic classification attempted on the basis of the fundamental characteristics just delineated reveals two major trends. First is a group of writings concerning the sacred area of Mt. Hiei—its buildings, effigies, specific religious vocabulary, and rituals. These writings contain teachings, formulas, maxims, and mystical apothegms called *kimon, kammon,* or *mon.* A representative text of this category is the *Sanke sairyakki (Sanke yōryakki).* The same characteristics are visible in the *Kuinbukkakushō,* the *Enryakuji gokoku engi,*[48] the *Sanke yōkisenryaku,*[49] the *Hie hongi,*[50] and others. The *kimon* found in those texts are of several types: governmental decrees *(kampu)* dating back to the foundation of Mt. Hiei, theories and maxims attributed to the three saints and two masters borrowed from texts such as the *Sambō jūjishū* or the *Sambō hogyōki* (whose existence remains uncertain),[51] petitions and letters authored by these historical figures, and other authoritative fragments taken from "ancient documents," to which secret transmissions have been added in many cases. The text entitled *Wakō dōjin riyaku kokudo kanjō,* which belongs to the highest rank of secret transmission among the chroniclers, belongs to this group.

The second trend is represented by texts describing the origins and the history of Mt. Hiei's institutions and rituals, as well as all kinds of legends, miraculous occurrences and chastisements caused by Buddhas and *kami,* and various tales relating popular beliefs. These texts often take the form of painted scrolls and edifying tales; as such they received the generic name of *kenki* (chronicle of miracles). Examples are the *Sannō engi (Yōtenki),* the *Gonjinshō,*[52] the *Hie Sannō rishōki,*[53] and the *Sannō reigenki.*[54] It can be said that the *Shintō-shū,* which belongs to an unrelated proselytizing lineage known as Ago-in, displays a close resemblance to these texts.[55]

Antithetic characteristics of these two trends can be noted; one could say that the texts belonging to the first trend are doctrinal and tend toward secrecy or mysticism, whereas those of the second tend toward fiction or historicism. Moreover, the first originate in *kimon* and end up in secret oral transmissions, and are made up of poetry and formulas expressing the sacred and secret character of a mystical world, while the second originate in historical events *(koji)* and end up in prosodic and episodic fabulations expressing the profane world and its legends or miraculous events. Furthermore, symbolic expression stands out in the documents belonging to the first trend and displays thought patterns characteristic of painted shrine-mandalas, whereas narrative and descriptive traits stand out in the texts representative of the second trend. These prosodic works display a certain similarity to the texts offering the history of shrine-temple multiplexes and the hagiographies based on the fundamental Buddhist notion of *engi* (interdependent origination; Skt. *pratitya-samut-pāda*), although it is unclear how removed or close those texts are, philosophically and logically, to that notion. Finally, from the point of view of their contents, it is remarkable that many texts belonging to the first trend deal with matters related to the "essence" *(honji,* i.e., Buddhism,) while those representing the second trend relate matters pertaining to the "hypostasis" *(suijaku,* i.e., Shinto).

I would like therefore to characterize the two trends in the following fashion. Generally speaking, the first trend indicates a logic that develops spatially, symbolically, and as a mandala. It is doctrinal, mystical, and secretive while tending to indicate the "essence." The second trend evidences a logic that develops temporally, is descriptive, and partakes of the *engi* while tending to indicate the "hypostasis." One might say that these two trends represent the surface *(omote)* and the underside *(ura)* of the documents and the thought of the chroniclers.

## Conclusion: Historical Consciousness in the Medieval Period

It has become clear from the foregoing discussion that among the documents were some that were descriptive and tended to have a character of historicity, since they recounted past events. Although texts such as the *Santōshoji engi* show quiescent signs of a sense of history, it is the other texts like the *Sannō engi* (the *Yōtenki*) and the

*Sannō reigenki,* in spite of their religious coloration, that display in a partial but unmistakable manner those configurations that are characteristic of historical writings. One might say that they show a certain consciousness of history.

Does this mean that the texts that exhibit symbolic, spatial, and mandala-like characteristics show no consciousness of history? Not necessarily so. These texts were not only based on or woven into descriptive documents but, given the argument that they formed the other side of the coin, their symbolic, mandala-like expression has given them the character of prophecies. They are therefore based on what might be called a historical sense or consciousness. This historical consciousness corresponds to the notion expressed in Jien's *Gukanshō* and other medieval texts according to which both chronicles (past history) and prophecies (history to come) were apprehended at the same time. This phenomenon is to be associated with the concept of the "sacred nation," based on religious notions concerning the past and the future of the nation and the state.[56]

This means that within the aforementioned framework of the historical consciousness of the chroniclers, history was a matter to be extolled according to the fundamental principles of "essence" and "hypostasis," that is, of what is prior and what necessarily follows. This historical consciousness of the chroniclers was representative of a medieval consciousness which, it must be said, did have a tremendous impact in Japan, all the way from the intellectuals to the common people.

TRANSLATED BY ALLAN G. GRAPARD

## NOTES

1. *Nyoraijuryō-bon.*

2. Translator's note (hereafter abbreviated as *trans.*): *kobutsu,* lit. "old buddha"; and *kombutsu,* lit. "present buddha."

3. *Trans.:* This central doctrine within the Mahāyāna system is known under different names in English: expedient devices, salvific means, or clever means. It is the doctrine of *upāya,* or *hōben* in Japanese.

4. *Trans.:* The term *hon* is difficult to translate; here it means "principal," "original," or "fundamental."

5. *Trans.:* The term *jaku,* which literally means "trace," denotes the temporary manifestation on earth of a transcendent principle. I have therefore used the term "hypostasis," which seems adequate in this context.

6. *Trans.:* There is no fixed or universally accepted translation of terms which, in Chinese and Japanese, have extremely concrete connotations, such as footsteps left on the ground.

7. *Trans.:* This term has never been translated before, and the rendering of it by "chroniclers" is tentative. In light of the discussion proposed by Professor Kuroda in the fourth paragraph, the emphasis on the historicist aspect of the term "chronicle" may render that choice of word inadequate for this context. The term *ki* in *kike* means "record" or "chronicle" whereas the term *ke* means "specialist" or "house" in the sense of lineage. One could propose the term "scribe," but the connotations of writing and copying seem to warrant its exclusion. The term "recorder," because of its contemporary connotations, seemed inadequate.

8. *Trans.:* Here again discussions with colleagues might lead to a fixed translation; literally, the term *kiroku* means chronicles and records. Finding that sense too long and heavy, I opted for the easier term "documents," though its connotations are loose.

9. *Trans.:* The term *hokke shisō* includes both the philosophy of the *Lotus Sutra* proper and the doctrinal systems surrounding it in China, Korea, and Japan.

10. *Trans.:* The term *honji-suijaku shisō* has been rendered in varied ways. I reject the phrase "philosophy of assimilation" because of the inherent bias it may imply: there is much more to *honji-suijaku* than assimilation. Why not say "doctrine of hypostasis"? The term hypostasis has the advantage of having at least two closely related connotations: the first meaning of the term is "sediment" (as in *jaku* 'trace'), and the second meaning, in the Nicene use, is "substance of godhead" (as in *honji* 'original ground or substance').

11. *Trans.:* The dogma of the body of the Buddha is an extremely important one, and not only for the question at hand. For a good survey of the origins and evolution of the term, see the *busshin* entry in the *Hōbōgirin* encyclopedia of Buddhist terms.

12. On the evolution of the doctrine of hypostasis in Japan, see Murayama Shūichi, *Honji-suijaku.*

13. *Hombutsu.*

14. *Jakubutsu.*

15. These two main divisions of the *Lotus Sutra, hommon* and *jakumon*, were established by Chih-i.

16. *Hongaku shisō.*

17. *Han-honji-suijaku setsu.*

18. On the relations between Buddhism and the belief system associated with the *kami* of heaven and earth in Japan, see Kuroda Toshio, *Chūsei shūkyō-shi ni okeru Shintō no ichi*, in *Ienaga Saburō Kyōju taikan kinen ronshū: kodai, chūsei no shakai to shisō* (Tokyo: Sanseidō, 1979). See also Toshio Kuroda, "Shinto in the History of Japanese Religions," *Journal of Japanese Studies* 7, no. 1 (Winter 1981).

*Trans.:* The rest of Professor Kuroda's chapter does not deal with the reversed theory, which is an entirely separate problem even though it seems to have evolved among the chroniclers on Mt. Hiei.

19. *Gongen*, lit. "temporary manifestation."

20. *Ōge-shin.* See note 11 above concerning the dogma of the body of the Buddha.

21. *Taimitsu*, as opposed to *tōmitsu*, which is the Shingon form of esotericism.

22. *Shikaku.*

23. *Kuden hōmon.*

24. *Kanshin hōmon.*

25. *Hongaku hōmon.* On this topic, see Shimaji Daitō, *Tendai kyōgaku-shi*, in Nakamura Hajime et al., eds., *Gendai Bukkyō meicho zenshū*, vol. 9 (Tokyo: Ryūbun kan, 1964).

26. See Hazama Jikō, "Edan ryōryū kuden hōmon no shujusō to sono taikei," *Nihon Bukkyō no tenkai to sono kichō* (Tokyo: Sanseidō, 1948).

27. *Kirigami.*

28. See Hazama Jikō, "Chūsei Hiei-zan ni okeru kike to Ichijitsu Shintō no hatten," *Nihon Bukkyō no tenkai to sono kichō.*

29. *Endon-kai.*

30. *Ken-mitsu-kai-ki.* See *Godai kokushi jiki* in Tokyo Daigaku Shiryō Hensanjo, comp., *Dai Nihon shiryō* (Tokyo: Tokyo Daigaku shiryō hensan-jo, 1901–), vol. 6, pt. 20, p. 380.

31. Kyōto daigaku bungaku-bu kokugo-kokubungaku kenkyūshitsu, ed., *Shokoku ikkenshō-monogatari*, in *Manjū-in-zō, Komakawadera-zō* (Kyoto: Rinsen shoten, 1981).

32. *Keiranshūyōshū.* *T* 76.7.

33. *Kanjō*; Skt. *abhiṣeka.*

34. (1) *Shōchi myōgō hiketsu*, (2) *Zuhō kanjō*, (3) *Chingo jūkai*, (4) *Wakō dōjin riyaku kokudo kanjō.*

35. *Sanshō nishi nijukkan kiroku.*

36. *Kuinbukkakushō*, in Hanawa Hokiichi, comp., *Gunsho-ruijū*, vol. 24 (Tokyo: Naigai Shoseki Kaisha, 1928–32).

37. Sambō jūji.
    Wakō suijaku.
    Jō bukkoku-do.
    Riyaku shūjō.

38. *Menjū kuketsu; matsugo no ikku.*

39. For a text that seems to indicate the contents of that function, see *Wakō dōjin riyaku kanjō*, in *Tendai-shū zensho*, vol. 12.

40. *Sanke sairyakki, Sanke yōryakki*, in *DNBZ, jishi sōsho*, 4.

41. *Endaragishū; Sanjūshikojisho.* See Tamura Yoshirō, *Kamakura shin-Bukkyō no kenkyū* (Kyoto: Heirakuji shoten, 1965); and "Tendai hongaku shishō gaisetsu," *Tendai hongakuron* in *Nihon shisō taikei*, vol. 9 (Tokyo: Iwanami shoten, 1973).

42. *Sanke yōryakki-shō kujū*, in *Gunsho-ruijū*, vol. 24, under the title *Sanke yōryaku kujū.*

43. *Yōtenki*, in Zoko gunsho ruijū Kansei Kai, comp., *Zoku gunsho ruijū*, vol. 2, 2 (Tokyo: Zoku gunsho ruijū Kansei Kai, 1932).

44. Okada Seishi, "Yōtenki no ikkōsatsu—'Sannō engi' Shō-ō shahon no shutsugen o megutte," *Kokushigaku*, no. 108 (1979).

45. *Santōshoji engi*, in *DNBZ, jishi sōsho*, 4.

46. *Sammon dōsha-ki*, ibid.

47. *Eigaku yōki*, in *Gunsho ruijū*, vol. 24.

48. *Enryakuji gokoku engi*, in *DNBZ, Tendai kahyō*, 2.

49. *Sanke yōkisenryaku*, in *Zoku gunsho ruijū*, vol. 27, 2.

50. *Hie hongi*, in *Zoku gunsho ruijū*, vol. 2, 2.

51. *Sambō jūjishū; Sambō hogyōki.* Some edited versions of fragments, under the

name of *Sambō jūjishū zanketsu* or *Sambō hogyōki zanketsu,* are published in *Nihon daizōkyō, Tendai-shū kengyō shōso,* 2.

52. *Gonjinshō,* in *Zoku gunsho ruijū,* vol. 2, 2.

53. *Hie Sannō rishōki,* ibid.

54. *Sannō reigenki.* See "Sannō reigenki emaki shisho," *Bijutsu kenkyū,* no. 99 (1940).

55. See *Akagi bunko-bon Shintō-shū,* in *Kijū koten sekisō,* vol. 1 (Tokyo: Kado-kawa shoten, 1968).

56. See Kuroda Toshio, "Gukanshō to Jinnō shōtōki," in *Nihon chūsei no kokka to shūkyō* (Tokyo: Iwanami shoten, 1975). See also Kuroda Toshio, "Gukanshō ni okeru seiji to rekishi ninshiki," in *Ōbō to buppō.*

# The Textualized Mountain—
# Enmountained Text:
# The *Lotus Sutra* in Kunisaki

### ALLAN G. GRAPARD

The earth contains a number of remarkable regions and it is not
—in its nature or in its space—what authors who have ordinarily
dealt with the earth have to say about it.

Socrates, in the *Phaedo*

The following pages present some reflections on aspects of the adoption of the *Lotus Sutra* in the Kunisaki Peninsula in Kyūshū, as exemplified in the *Rokugō kaizan Nimmon Daibosatsu hongi,* a nineteenth-century text.[1] The approach taken in this discussion issues from the following questions: What significance is to be attributed to the ways in which a culture adopted a scripture that had been conceived in yet another culture? Did the epistemological framework of Japan influence the ways in which the scripture was accepted, interpreted, and put into practice? How did the *episteme* represented by the *Lotus Sutra* impact Japanese culture? Was the inception of the *Lotus Sutra* the same throughout Japan, or was it influenced by local factors? Finally, was the Japanese interpretation of the *Lotus Sutra* significantly shaped by institutional or ritual frameworks?

In view of these questions, the discussion will address two sets of problems, examining local factors at the concrete level, and the cognitive framework at the abstract level. Both types of considerations reflect a concern with the *milieu,* which is both a specific ground of human experience within a geographical setting and what could be termed a cultural mood. That mood was shaped by an epistemological framework which consisted of the dominant notions according to which the Japanese people defined "knowledge," developed certain practices, and interpreted their existence and the texts to which they attributed importance.

## Local Considerations

It is useful to study Japanese religious phenomena *in situ,* starting from the basic territorial unit and community in which they developed rather than from the more traditional focus on sects or major thinkers. It becomes evident from a study of specific cults that the basic unit of coherence in the overall pattern displayed in their world of meaning and practice was a territory symbolized by a specific *kami* which was enshrined there and was said to protect the area and to be the ancestral *kami* of the actual rulers of the area. That territory was reinforced by the sacerdotal lineages whose duty it was to legitimize the power of the rulers who employed them, and by zones of influence of the expanding cult that were delimited either by land possessions that had been "offered" to the cultic center or, later, by links in roads of pilgrimage, or by symbolic relations and concrete exchanges established between various cultic centers through the formulation of a comprehensive sacred geography.[2] These cultic centers, which are today euphemistically referred to as "numinous sites" *(reijō)*, became during the medieval period the object of pilgrimages, in the course of which the pilgrims used guides that were written by ecclesiasts or mountain ascetics, or in which they were accompanied by religious guides. Such sites were conceived and ritually treated on the basis of fundamental conceptions and formulations of space, of ritual and social organization, and of time. In other words, a certain type of cultural geography based on native categories promises a more comprehensive approach to Japanese religious systems not only because it pays attention to spatial and temporal schemes of representation of power, but also because it takes as its basic unit of research a geographical area where Buddhist and non-Buddhist institutions, creeds, rites, and practices interlocked and formed combinatory systems. These systems shared a number of features while keeping their own characteristics.[3] Each of these units produced a cultural system that was open to outside influences, but that was closed onto its own patterns. Each unit evolved into a specific cult with its own institutions, its own rituals, its own arts, and its own literature. And for the present purpose, it is important to emphasize the fact that each unit interpreted the *Lotus Sutra* in significantly different ways.

## Cultural Considerations

For the purpose of the present discussion, let us stipulate that a geographical area with the self-contained characteristics I have described is inseparable from the culture that evolved in it, as well as from the culture of the "center" with which it had some necessary links. The French term *milieu* suggests a link between a specific area and a specific culture; this term has both abstract and concrete meanings. However, in order to propose a comprehensive analysis of any given milieu, we must come to terms with the fact that we are confronting spatially expressed representations of social, religious, and political notions and practices which together form what could be called a mindscape—that is, a place which is also a representation.[4] Considerations such as these lead to the following thesis.

First, the adoption of the *Lotus Sutra* in Kunisaki occurred along epistemological lines which conditioned the elaboration and the resolution of an opposition between nature and culture; that opposition was itself inferred from mythology, as that mythology survived in the Hachiman cult and as it was thought to be mirrored by the *Lotus Sutra* itself.

Second, the disappearance of the influence of the *Lotus Sutra* as a cultural operative in the Kunisaki Peninsula was due to changes in economic and political structures, and to a change (that is possibly related) in the dominant interpretive modes and techniques—what Michel Foucault has termed an "epistemological shift."[5]

To clarify matters immediately, let us state that the *episteme* that underlies Japanese mythology and that was upheld by the Hachiman cult over the centuries saw the world (nature) and words (culture) in the specific light of similitude, reflection, identity, and communication. Under those conditions, the world of meaning that was thought by the Japanese to be that of the *Lotus Sutra* was in fact a world of meaning issuing from specific frameworks of interpretation of the existential situation, frameworks that might have had little to do with the *Lotus Sutra* per se. Furthermore, when epistemological shifts occurred, the perception of the position of the *Lotus Sutra* in relation to nature changed drastically. However, that observation requires more discussion than can be offered by way of introduction; for the time being, let us simply underline the possibility that the oppositions between the natural and cultural worlds were a dynamic phenomenon subject to change, and that this phenomenon was a significant aspect of the development of Japanese religious and political thought in Kunisaki.

## The Kunisaki Peninsula

The specific geographical unit of the Kunisaki Peninsula was chosen for study for several reasons. First, the area has an easily observable physical integrity: consisting of a volcanic dome of great antiquity, the peninsula is fairly circular and deeply eroded. Its summit, called Futago-yama (Twin Peaks) because of its double peak, was seen as the abode of twin divinities, a phenomenon that led to a combination with symbolism found in the *Lotus Sutra*.[6] Second, the peninsula developed during the Heian period as a major center of religious practice in which the *Lotus Sutra* enjoyed a prominent position. Third, the peninsula came to be conceived of as a self-contained cultic center in which influences of various kinds were felt over the centuries; it was related to a single community as well as to the state at large; it was an economic and institutional entity of some complexity; it developed rites and ceremonies in which one can see structured interactions of Buddhism, Shinto, and Taoism. And finally, the rich interactions between this area and the minds of its viewers—the mindscape—reveal a great deal about the culture which evolved in that part of Japan.[7]

The Kunisaki Peninsula developed as a major religious center during the Heian period (794–1185) and reached its apex during the late Heian and Kamakura periods (1185–1333). It evolved mainly as a multiplex for mountain asceticism (Shugendō) under the associated influences of the Tendai lineage of Shugendō and the combinatory cult dedicated to Hachiman in Usa. The multiplex of Kunisaki was a highly combinatory religious and political (i.e., ideological) system related to the protection of the national territory by the Hachiman cult, and therefore needs to be studied in terms of the relations that obtain between political and religious discourses. The name Rokugō (Six Districts), which was often used to refer to it, comes from the fact that the peninsula originally consisted of six administrative districts, though it properly consisted of eight. The general term used to refer to the multiplex was Rokugō-zan, or Rokugō-manzan, in which case the appellation referred to the (Buddhist) temples and (Shinto) shrines of the area and to their population as well.

## The Hachiman Cult

The Hachiman cult evolved from several complex origins in northeastern Kyūshū and reached religious and organizational coherence in the first half of the Nara period, especially after Emperor Shōmu established the Tōdaiji as the overall Buddhist emblem of the state in Nara. When the monk Dōkyō attempted to establish a theocracy in 764, he claimed that he had been instructed to do so by an oracle received from Hachiman. The oracle was then checked by Wake no Kiyomaro, who received other oracles to the opposite effect. Dōkyō was exiled, and Hachiman became the protector *(chinju)* of the Tōdaiji and, by extension, of the state.[8] It is probable that these historically unclear events express specific relations between the center and the periphery, in which the periphery (Kyūshū) tended to play an important role. Scholars usually say that Dōkyō attempted to establish a Buddhist quasi-theocracy; however, if that was the case, why did he bother to back his claim with the authority of Hachiman, an originally non-Buddhist entity? The quasi-theocracy in question was, in all probability, a combinatory phenomenon issuing from the fundamental Japanese tendency to merge religious and political power (or to hide a political discourse behind a religious one), which took the form, among others, of merging indigenous and imported deities, and of drawing distinctions between status and power in such a manner that the religious discourse was relegated to the mere function of legitimating the power of rulers.

The Hachiman shrine-temple multiplex of Usa in Kyūshū became thereafter a powerful system that variously symbolized relations between the center and the periphery, between "Shinto" and "Buddhism," and between religious and political power. The main priestly group charged with the cult was the Miwa sacerdotal lineage, which lost its hegemony in the middle of the eighth century and was replaced by the Usa lineage, which thenceforth ruled the Hachiman cultic center of Usa. Just as the former sacerdotal lineage had erected Buddhist temples in the compounds of shrines *(jingūji,* in this case the Kokuzōji), the Usa lineage erected its own Buddhist temple (the Mirokuji) near the shrines, and the Nakatsuoji near Mt. Omoto, the mountain dedicated to Hachiman in Usa. The Hachiman cult further evolved in the Kinai area when, around the middle of the ninth century, a major shrine-temple multiplex, the Iwashimizu cultic center, was created to protect both the imperial lineage and the national territory. Finally, the Minamoto warriors took Hachiman as their tutelary divine entity and erected a major cultic center in the thirteenth century, the Tsurugaoka Hachimangū in Kamakura. Under various religious and political influences, the Hachiman cult thus evolved over the centuries in several parts of Japan and became a central aspect of the politico-religious establishment.

Mountain religion developed in Kyūshū rather early in the area of Hiko (Hikozan), probably under the combined influences of Buddhism and Taoism, which themselves interacted with native concep-

tions of space and with ritual practices.[9] After the creation of the Tendai and Shingon lineages at the beginning of the Heian period, and
as these lineages branched out into separate systems for mountain
asceticism, the influence of the Tendai lineage and of its main center
in Kyoto, the Enryakuji of Mt. Hiei, came to be felt in Kyūshū. It was
under the combined influences of the esoteric form of Tendai
(taimitsu) and the Hachiman cult that the mountain religion of
Kunisaki developed.

It may be surprising to hear of the Hachiman cult in connection
with mountain religion, but in this particular case the connection is
rich. The Hachiman cult retained, as one of its primary ritual features, litholatry, which was an original characteristic of the world of
meaning and ritual related to the early interpretations of the putative
conquest of Korea by Jingū Kōgō. It is probable that prehistorical
forms of litholatry fused with the stone cult that would have been
imported by the putative invaders of Japan in the fourth century.[10]
These stones are worshipped on Mt. Omoto, to the west of the Usa
shrines, and throughout the Kunisaki Peninsula and Kyūshū, as well
as in most shrines that are dedicated to Hachiman in the entire country. A second connection between the Hachiman cult and Shugendō
resides in the fact that the ascetics who were seen in later periods as
the founders of the mountain multiplex came to be conceived of as a
single entity named Nimmon Daibosatsu, who was viewed as a reincarnation of Hachiman. Hachiman himself was regarded as an avatar
of Śākyamuni, the historical Buddha to whom the exposition of the
Lotus Sutra on the Mount of the Numinous Eagle is attributed. Furthermore, it is necessary to point out that both the Hachiman cult
and Shugendō were fundamentally related to the processes of formation of the Japanese state, and, more particularly, to the formulation
of the national territory as a space of a sacred character: the conquest
of Korea by Ōjin's mother, Jingū Kōgō, was rationalized in Buddhist
terms by claiming that Ōjin/Hachiman was a manifestation of
Śākyamuni, and Buddhism became an element of the myths of conquest as well as of the protection of Japan. It was in those conditions
that the Hachiman cult came to be represented in the mountains as
well.

The structure of the cultural system that evolved in the Kunisaki
Peninsula cannot be understood or appreciated if it is seen only in the
light of Buddhism, or if Hachiman is treated as a "Shinto god"—as
has generally been the case in the past. From its inception, the cult was

a ritual and cultural system marked by highly elaborate and systematic associations between Buddhist, Shinto, and Taoist entities and ritual practices. The terms Buddhism, Taoism, and Shinto might lead one to think of them as separate, but this would be incorrect, for the ritual and cultural reality of Kunisaki was essentially a combination of specific entities rather than of sects and doctrines, and was inscribed within certain discursive practices and ideological formulations whose relation to "Buddhism" or "Shinto" is not altogether clear.

## The *Rokugō kaizan Nimmon Daibosatsu hongi*

Kunisaki was under the influence of the Hachiman cult, but it also came under the influence of Mt. Hiko and the specific mountain asceticism which developed there, first through the impact of Taoism, and second, the impact of the Tendai form of Shugendō that had developed in Kumano. These influences have been studied by Nakano Hatayoshi; the following remarks are limited to the evolution of the sacred geography of the peninsula as it relates to the *Lotus Sutra*, a phenomenon mentioned but not studied by Nakano.[11] Though it was written at the end of the Edo period, the *Rokugō kaizan Nimmon Daibosatsu hongi* is based on several other versions written earlier. The text of a painted scroll kept at the San Francisco Museum of Asian Art and dating from the Muromachi period, for example, is similar, in parts, to the *Rokugō kaizan Nimmon Daibosatsu hongi*.[12] The Edo version of the *Hongi* not only gives clues concerning the character of the cult, but also suggests that the text is a kind of *Lotus Sutra* itself; most of the events described in the text are rewritings of events described in the *Lotus Sutra*, or are based on various chapters of the scripture. This loose "intertextuality" will serve as the main interpretive device in the discussion that follows. The contents of the *Rokugō kaizan Nimmon Daibosatsu hongi* are separated below into different parts for the sake of convenience:

1. Record of the Former Life of Hachiman
This part deals exclusively with mythology; starting with the origins of the Japanese islands, it soon passes over to the putative conquest of the Korean Peninsula by Jingū Kōgō and to the birth of her son (the future "emperor" Ōjin/Hachiman) on the northern shore of Kyūshū.

## 2. Immaculate Conception and Rebirth in China

The spirits of the mother and child are reborn in China: the daughter of an emperor, the mother conceives through penetration by the radiance of Nittenshi (Sūryaprabha), and gives birth to Hachiman. Mother and child are put into a dugout and set afloat. They reach the country they are to rule by divine right, and land in Chōshi in Kyūshū.

## 3. The Sacred Stone

A stone surges forth from the earth and is inscribed with a text stating that the Buddha expounded the *Lotus Sutra* on the Peak of the Numinous Eagle, and that he manifested himself in Japan as Hachiman. Hachiman practices his devotion in front of the stone and possessed of supernatural powers he flies off to visit various parts of the country. A blacksmith sees three stones that emit a great radiance. Perched atop those stones, a golden falcon (or eagle) suddenly undergoes metamorphosis into a dove, Hachiman's theriomorphic symbol. A miraculous well appears near the stones.

## 4. Mortification of the Flesh

A space is set apart in Kunisaki to practice mortification of the flesh through fire, in emulation of the fire-sacrifice by the bodhisattva Medicine King in the *Lotus Sutra*.

## 5. Protection of the State

The Kunisaki temples are ordered during the medieval period to perform rites dedicated to the protection of the state and to ward off the Mongol invasions.

## 6. The Lotus in the Mountain

Description of the transformation of the peninsula into a spatial natural embodiment of the *Lotus Sutra*.

## 7. Visit to China

Hachiman visits China in order to receive the teachings of the Tendai lineage of Buddhism. He returns to Japan and practices under the guidance of Hōren on Mt. Hiko.

## 8. Hayato Rebellion

Hachiman protects the island of Kyūshū against insurgencies, thanks to "the power of the mother."

9. Release of Living Beings
This passage describes the rationale for the creation of the *hōjō-e* ceremonies, which, through the symbolic release of animals, release spirits of those who died in war or through forced conversion.

10. Hachiman's Entrance into the Cave
Toward the end of his life Hachiman enters a cavern, takes the vows and tonsure, and receives the ordination name of Nimmon Daibosatsu.

11. Pilgrimage Rediscovered
The course of pilgrimage around the peninsula being lost, a monk decides to recreate it. This monk undergoes austerities in a quest for a vision of Nimmon Daibosatsu in his flesh-body, achieves this vision, and is taught the correct peregrination routes. The mountain's sacred geography is then described in the last segments of the text.

## Kunisaki and the *Lotus*

All major aspects of the Hachiman cult appear in this text written in the nineteenth century after the cultic center had been "rediscovered" and a major effort was under way to reconstruct some of its parts, obviously for ideological reasons. The text is composed in the manner of the texts of the medieval period that relate the origins, history, and structures of major cultic centers *(jisha engi)*. However, the main interest of the document resides in a hidden depth which consists of an intertextuality with the *Lotus Sutra* operating on two levels: the structure of the sacred geography of the peninsula on the one hand, and on the other, the structure of the legends associated with the Kunisaki mountains. As was stated earlier, the Kunisaki multiplex developed as a center of mountain asceticism under the combined influences of the Hachiman cult and the Tendai lineage of Shugendō, therefore in connection with the Kumano cult. The central scripture of the *yamabushi* of that lineage was the *Lotus Sutra,* and a central devotion of the *yamabushi* was a creed to Kannon (Avalokiteśvara, the bodhisattva of compassion); the two are represented prominently in Kunisaki. The Tendai tradition of the mountain ascetics emphasized the fact that the *Lotus Sutra* is associated with mountains, since that scripture was expounded by the Buddha on the Mount of the Numinous Eagle (Ryōjusen). That is also why many paintings that depict the exposition of the *Lotus Sutra* represent the bird-head shape of the mountain. It was natural, therefore, that the teachings of the *Lotus* would be sought for in mountainous areas seen as "lesser Mounts of the Numinous Eagle" in Japan. The mountains of Kunisaki were viewed in this manner, as was Mt. Hiei itself.[13]

## Mystical Visions

For the purpose of this presentation, however, the word "viewed" should be qualified, and the key to its interpretation, which unlocks the mysteries of the sacred character of the mountains of the Kunisaki Peninsula, is offered by the *Lotus Sutra*'s treatment of perception.[14]

The sense organs, when used without adequate preparation, deliver biased views of the universe. The term "biased views" ought to be taken literally: the *Lotus Sutra* is dealing with inadequate "mental views" or ideas people make about the world, but it is also talking about ways in which the universe at large is perceived through the sense organs. According to the *Lotus Sutra,* perceptions of the world that lead one astray must be "corrected" in order to deliver an adequate representation from the point of view of nonduality. This correction is achieved mainly through a purification process associated with penance *(sange).* The purification of the sense organs then leads to an undefiled perception of the cosmos, which is said to be that of the Buddha. It is a quest for vision. And it was that vision that the followers of the *Lotus Sutra* projected onto the geographical area of Kunisaki, realizing it concretely in the establishment of temples, of a "sacred" geography, and of practices that were derived from the *Lotus Sutra* and from indigenous rituals of purification. Like most scriptures of Mahāyāna Buddhism, the *Lotus Sutra* is based on visionary experiences. Almost every chapter of that scripture begins or ends with a vision of cosmic proportions, the most famous of which—and most widely depicted in art—are the description of the Buddha expounding that scripture on Mt. Gṛdhrakūṭa (Mount of the Numinous Eagle, also known as Vulture Peak), and the apparition of the bodhisattva Samantabhadra. Located near the ancient city of Rājagṛha, where the Buddha dwelled for some time, the Mount of the Numinous Eagle was granted a cosmic status early in history. Often represented in Buddhist art in Japan, it was thought to be a sacred peak existing in a transcendental space. Various Japanese paintings related to the *Lotus Sutra* represent the Buddha, seated on the mountain's slopes, surrounded by a huge assembly of saints and disciples, and emitting from his forehead a ray of light that illuminates eighteen thousand worlds to the east. This supernatural light pervading the universe is a sign that "the Buddha is about to preach an excellent, unsurpassed teaching." Light is such an important and repetitive motif in the *Lotus Sutra* that the first exposition of the scripture is attributed to the Sun-And-Moon-Glow Buddha, and it pervades the world of its adoption in Japan.

It is under that supernatural light that the teaching of the Buddha, profound, abstruse and difficult to penetrate, is finally visible, even though that too may be—ultimately—no more than an expedient device related to the parable of the conjured city in the seventh chapter. Indeed, throughout the text we are told that one needs to "see," that the teaching of the *Lotus* is a matter of adequate perception, and that those who succeed in seeing that teaching will immediately realize a transcendental space described as an unadulterated, tranquil, splendid "buddha realm." This "buddha realm" can be reached through strenuous practices and through the exercise of wisdom, which is precisely what enables the Buddha to see through the cosmos and focus on those who practice his teaching:

Then I see bodhisattvas
Striving with courage and determination,
Entering deep into the mountains,
And aspiring to the Path of the Buddha.
Again, I see them separating themselves from desire,
Constantly dwelling in desolation and serenity,
Profoundly cultivating *dhyāna*-concentration
And attaining the five supernatural penetrations.
. . . . . . . . . . . .
Further I see . . .
Every individual stūpa-shrine
Having on it a thousand banners . . .
To which gods, dragons, and spirits,
Humans and nonhumans
Of sweet flowers and skillfully played music
Constantly present offerings.[15]

These lines set patterns for the Japanese inception and practice of the *Lotus Sutra*. Nevertheless, the question still remains as to whether such visions could be seen by simple, untrained eyes. Just as the untrained mind could not discern the depth of the Buddha's teachings, the untrained eye remained blind to the transcendental nature of space, and thus could not see the Buddha that was thought to be hidden in mountains. Chapter 19 of the *Lotus Sutra*, on the "Merits of the Dharma Preacher," provides some indications to this effect:

> If any good man or good woman shall accept or keep this Scripture of the Dharma Blossom, whether reading it, reciting it, interpreting it, or copying it, that person shall attain eight hundred virtues of the eye, one thousand two hundred virtues of the ear, eight hundred virtues of the nose, one thousand two hundred virtues of the tongue, eight hundred virtues of the body, and one thousand two hundred virtues of the mind, by means of which virtues he shall adorn his six faculties, causing them all to be pure.
>
> . . . . . . . . . . . . . . . .
> This man shall attain eight hundred
> Virtues distinguishing his eye,
> With which adorned
> His eye shall be very pure.
> With the eye engendered by father and mother
> He shall thoroughly see the thousand-millionfold world,
> Its inner and outer mounts Meru,
> Sumeru, and Iron-Rim,
> As well as all other mountains, forests,
> Great Seas, rivers, streams, and rivulets,
> Down as far as the Avīci prison
> And up to the gods of the Pinnacle of Existence.
> The living beings in their midst,
> Everyone of them, shall he see.
> Though he may not yet have acquired a divine eye,
> Such shall be the power of his fleshly eye.[16]

The chapter goes on to describe the various virtues that come to adorn the senses as the practice along the Buddha path unfolds according to the teachings of the *Lotus*. The eye-vision promised by the scripture is a vision that results from the purification of the sense organs as set forth in ritual treatises and texts of meditation, a purification that takes the form of practices of penance *(sange)*: as one expresses the multitude of sins one and others are guilty of, a cleansing occurs in the mind and the body. This purification is the prerequisite to the faculty of seeing things as they are, of seeing the various dharmas with the eye, with the other senses, and with the mind. The *Kanfugen bosatsu gyōhōgyō* teaches that when an ethical state of being is achieved through rituals of penance, a "pleasurable vision" *(rakken)* takes place. It was this pleasurable vision, this aesthetic sense born out of ethics, that the mountain ascetics achieved. And it was these pleasurable visions that the architecture of sacred spaces in Japan tried to offer through the agency of viewing platforms set in groves below mountain temples, or architectural devices set in such a manner as to offer apertures to direct the sight onto gardens that replicated the Pure Land. That architecture was intimately tied to this specific vision of transcendental space which was itself achieved through the junction of ethics and esthetics. The *Lotus Sutra* played a major role in these developments, but it alone could not have been responsible for those visions that received concrete architectural formulation in Kunisaki. It is as though the scripture merely gave an impetus to the underlying structures of the Japanese perception of space which were intimately related to indigenous notions and practices of purification, and to the dialectic between nature and culture which had found its earliest expression in mythology. These phenomena of light, of the achievement of a perception that leads to truth, and of the realization of a transcendental space through practices of such character that space is traversed as if it were an acquisition of truth, characterize in no mean fashion the establishment of the sacred geography of Kunisaki that will be described below.

## Intertextuality and Sacred Geography

Certain Japanese cultic sites are said to be sacred because specific events occurred in them that changed their character, or because they came to be seen as the residence of combined *kami* and buddhas or bodhisattvas. The sacred space of residence of a combinatory divinity then came to be viewed as a buddha land or a Pure Land, the transcendental abode of buddhas and bodhisattvas, *in this world*. This vision was made possible by several factors. First, the site of residence of a non-Buddhist divinity was, before the inception of Buddhism, sacred because it was ritually defined, and because Japan was born from the sexual union of demiurges and thus shared in their character. Second, from the Buddhist perspective, this vision was possible because basic tenets of esoteric Buddhism (both *taimitsu* and *tōmitsu* lineages) provided a rationale grounded in the philosophy of nontwoness, according to which there was a relation of nonduality between transmigration and nirvana *(shōji soku nehan),* between awakening and passions *(bonnō soku bodai)*, and between this lower world and the Pure Land *(gekai soku jōdo)*. Thus a "natural" landscape could be the residence of a buddha or bodhisattva associated with a *kami*. These landscapes were in geographical areas of great beauty and were viewed by monks who, from the summit of the mountains, thought that they were confronted in their ecstatic discovery by a manifestation of the combined *kami* and buddhas to which they had dedicated their arduous ascent. Since such and such *kami* had manifested itself there, and since that *kami* was considered to be the Japanese manifestation of a buddha or a bodhisattva, the mountain came to be seen as their residence and to symbolize the supernatural protection of the territory. A mountain thus sanctified came to be described in literature as a visionary land of a buddha in the scriptures: this is the first level of intertextuality.

Temples were then erected on the slopes or on the tops of the mountains, and the numinous figures that were enshrined there were represented according to ritual and iconographic directions provided in the scriptures. Those who held a particular faith in those figures, or who held those scriptures in special reverence, went on pilgrimage to those mountains, anxious to climb them while reciting the scripture, to make their devotions in front of the statues and paintings, and to "see" the sacred landscape. All these activities were the central ingredients of a quest for vision. This relation of intertextuality between the *Lotus Sutra* and the Kunisaki Peninsula led to the establishment of a sacred geography that was essentially the embodiment of a mystical and political vision which received several formulations, of which the first one was concrete and direct: the *Rokugō kaizan Nimmon Daibosatsu hongi* states that, in the eight major valleys that correspond to the eight fascicles of the scripture, there are as many temples as there are chapters in the *Lotus Sutra*, twenty-eight. These temples were administratively and ritually organized according to traditional distinctions made in commentaries on the *Lotus Sutra*, which viewed that scripture as being made of three distinct parts. Therefore the temples were ranked in three groups: eight corresponded to the "introduction" of the sutra, ten corresponded to the "exposition," and ten corresponded to the "means of dissemination." Another type of distinction consisted in the fact that the first group of eight temples specialized in the study of the scriptures, the second group of ten specialized in mountain austerities, and the last group of ten specialized in proselytism.[17]

The text says, moreover, that there are as many Buddhist statues in

the Kunisaki Peninsula as there are ideographs in the Chinese version
of the sutra: some 69,380 representations. Thus the paths on the
mountains had become the text of the scripture, and on that level
too, intertextuality was the integrative factor, but that intertextuality
was more subtle and abstract. Reading the scripture, one discovered
the mountain; walking on the mountain became the equivalent of
reading the scripture: the mountain was textualized, and the text
was, if this term can be coined, *enmountained.* The worlds of nature
(the mountains) and culture (the *Lotus Sutra*) were unified in a harmony that was thought to characterize the teaching of the *Lotus Sutra*
and to express, at the same time, indigenous and foreign conceptions
of sacred space. This was achieved, in part, by a strict adherence to
the practices recommended in the *Lotus Sutra,* as for example in the
second chapter, "Expedient Devices," which states that a number of
practices should be understood not as mere vehicles leading to the
Buddha, but as the Buddha path itself:

Or there are those who in open fields,
Heaping up earth, make Buddha-shrines.
There are even children who in play
Gather sand and make it into Buddha-stūpas.
Persons like these
Have all achieved the Buddha Path.
If any persons for the Buddha's sake
Erect images,
With carvings perfecting the multitudinous marks,
They have all achieved the Buddha Path.
Some fashion them completely with the seven jewels,
Or with nickel, or copper, or bronze,
Or with white tin, or with alloys of lead and tin,
Or with iron, or wood, or, again, with clay.
Some coat them with resin and lacquer,
With art creating Buddha images.
Persons like these
Have all achieved the Buddha Path.
Those who with many-colored designs create Buddha images,
Adorning them with the marks of hundredfold merit,
Making them themselves or having them done by others,
Have all achieved the Buddha Path.
Even children in play,
With grass, sticks, and brushes
Or with their fingernails,
Draw Buddha images,

Persons like these,
Gradually accumulating merit
And perfecting thoughts of great compassion,
Have all achieved the Buddha path.[18]

The *Rokugō kaizan Nimmon Daibosatsu hongi* states, as if in echo:

The subtemples of these head temples number more than one hundred, and the total number of representations of the Buddha is based
on the number of words in the *Lotus Sutra*. Having conceived the wish
to enshrine these 69,380 august representations in the sacred space of
the twenty-eight temples, ninety-nine sacred caverns, and more than
one hundred subtemples, Hachiman and his three companions made
their spirits as one and founded these temples one by one. On days and
directions determined by divination, carpenters, stonemasons, statue-
carvers, and painters joined them and created images of the buddhas.
Upon the cliffs Hachiman and his three companions portrayed the
seed-letters and the mantras. That is, they themselves carved the sacred
images of the buddhas of the two mandalas and drew *siddham* representations of the buddhas. The light of the Buddha radiated fully at
that time and like grass in the wind their will conformed to it.[19]

There is little doubt that the creation of the Kunisaki temples was
interpreted according to the rationale exposed in the second chapter
of the *Lotus Sutra*. Moreover, the *Lotus Sutra* proposes other ration-
ales for the type of behavior that is portrayed in the text on Kunisaki
under consideration. The presence of the Buddha in Kunisaki was
perceived, by those who participated in that universe of meaning, in
a manner in which the Buddha appeared as a huge cloud of rain
(chapter 5) pervading the mountains and cracks in the valleys, adorning many a shape with its mists, infusing life to all plants and herbs,
forgetting nothing. The Kunisaki Peninsula was lived as a world that
was pervaded and suffused with transcendental characteristics. This
existential stance vis-à-vis the peninsula was in a direct relation of
similitude with the attitude found in mythology. Furthermore, as
mentioned above, the sacred geography of Kunisaki could be "seen"
only by those who had purified their sense organs and thus reached
what is technically known as the supernatural penetrations. The fifth
chapter, "Medicinal Herbs," proposes that just as a blind person who
is cured can finally see the world, a common person who reaches an
understanding of the teachings can achieve a superknowledge and
*see*. He who wishes to attain this superknowledge should "live in the

forest; or think of the Dharma, seated in mountain caves! And [his] defilements are to be forsaken."[20] This is what countless numbers of ascetics did in the caves and temples of the Kunisaki mountains. Most prominent was Nōgyō, who, in 855,

> secluded himself in the cavern of Mt. Tsunado and began ascetic practices with the vow of beholding Nimmon Daibosatsu in his flesh-body. . . . As Nōgyō was performing the sixth-hour penitence with tears in his eyes, his prostrated body drenched with perspiration, an extraordinary fragrance pervaded the cavern and a thousand lights illuminated the entire mountain. A serene, solemn-faced priest appeared, hovering above the cavern, and spoke thus: "I am an ascetic who performed austerities on this mountain in the past. You have been doing excellently! Your sins are now extinguished and all obstacles to your awakening are removed."[21]

In chapter 14 of the *Lotus Sutra*, "Comfortable Conduct," the Buddha says:

> He shall see the Thus Come Ones
> Seated on their lion thrones,
> A multitude of bhikṣus
> Surrounding them as they preach the Dharma.
> He shall also see dragons and demons, Asuras and the like,
> In number like to Ganges' sands,
> Their palms joined in humble reverence,
> To whom, showing his body,
> He preaches the Dharma.
> He shall also see Buddhas,
> One of their marks being their gold color,
> Emitting incalculable rays,
> Wherewith they illuminate all,
> And with a voice of Brahmā sound
> Expounding the dharmas.
> [To such a man the Buddha says:]
> "Your land shall be adorned and pure,
> Broad and great and without equal.
> You shall also have a fourfold assembly
> Who shall listen to Dharma with palms joined."
> He also sees himself
> In the midst of mountains and forests
> Cultivating and practicing good dharmas,
> Bearing direct witness to the marks of Reality,

Deeply entering into dhyāna-concentration,
And seeing Buddhas in all ten quarters."[22]

Little doubt remains that this is the type of vision the devotees of the
*Lotus Sutra* searched for in their peregrinations in the Kunisaki Peninsula, in their ascetic exercises on the high cliffs, and in the medita-
tions they conducted in the recesses of dark caverns. Those visions
served to sacralize the peninsula and formed a rationale for the establishment of the temples, the placement of stones, and the performance of rituals. The quest for vision grounded in the *Lotus Sutra* and
in the mountain which was its natural embodiment was a quest for
golden radiance, for a sight of the Buddha, and for a vision of Kunisaki as the buddha land in this world.

Yet another, but less obvious, type of intertextuality becomes evident when the *Rokugō kaizan Nimmon Daibosatsu hongi* is read in
close reference to the *Lotus Sutra.* A near-simultaneous reading of the
two texts reveals that the mountains of Kunisaki were to be viewed as
if they were the Mount of the Numinous Eagle on which the *Lotus
Sutra* was expounded. This reading is inferred from the composition
of the text itself, though it might be argued that this similitude of
composition may have been unconscious on the part of religious individuals who repeatedly read the *Lotus Sutra.* However, definite traces
of intentionality on the part of the author(s) can be seen in the use of
motifs such as those of radiant light, the search for awakening and
understanding of the arcane meanings of the *Lotus Sutra,* the parable
of the conjured city, the description of the buddha realm, and the rituals that are to be performed on the mountains. Moreover, there are
clear borrowings from various chapters of the scripture.

On that level, the *honji-suijaku* doctrine, which proposes that the
*kami* are local manifestations of buddhas and bodhisattvas, functions
as the basis for the relationship of intertextuality between the *Lotus
Sutra* and the *Rokugō kaizan Nimmon Daibosatsu hongi.* It is
expressed in the vision of the Kunisaki mountains as a cosmic zone of
residence of Hachiman (Nimmon), which is itself seen as the manifestation of the Buddha Śākyamuni in this world. The indigenous
hypostasis is the bridge between the Buddha's realm of essence and
the world of duality that is the common residence of nonawakened
beings. Thus one can expect that what happens in the realm of the
Buddha, namely, the exposition of the *Lotus Sutra,* also happens—in
its hypostatic "translation"—in the realm of Hachiman, the hypostatic character of the Buddha in Kunisaki. The mystical vision of

Kunisaki as the Mount of the Numinous Eagle is reserved for those who put the teachings of the *Lotus* into practice, and who can therefore reach the supernatural penetrations allowing them to *see*. A definite clue is provided early in the text when it is stated that a large stone spontaneously sprang forth from the earth, and that this stone was inscribed with the following verse:

> In time of old on the Mount of the Numinous Eagle
> [The Buddha] expounded the *Lotus Sutra;*
> Now residing in the main shrine [at Usa]
> He manifests himself as a *daibosatsu.*[23]

Mt. Omoto (formerly called Mt. Maki), on which this stone stands, is treated as if it were the equivalent of the Mount of the Numinous Eagle, a Japanese "translation" of the original Indian context. This is further indicated by the name Ryōzenji, "Temple of the Mount of the Numinous Eagle," which was given to the temple that is set next to the shrine on that mountain. Using the expedient devices that are expounded in the *Lotus Sutra,* the Buddha manifested himself in Japan on a mountain of his choice as a *daibosatsu* named Hachiman, and he used the favorite support *(mishōtai)* of Hachiman, a stone, to "inscribe" his presence. Readers are thus entitled to predict that what Hachiman did in this mountainous area should not be different from what the Buddha expounded in the *Lotus,* and that the peninsula protected by Hachiman is, even more than a mere replica of the Indian mountain, the earthly equivalent of the Pure Land of the Buddha. The message of intertextuality comes into sharper relief with each major paragraph of the text. The motif of radiance appears early, as when a great radiance seen from afar causes people to wonder about its origins; someone is dispatched and finds a "golden falcon" that emits a great radiance and suddenly undergoes metamorphosis into a golden dove—the theriomorphic symbol of Hachiman. Thus the relation between the Buddha and Hachiman is equivalent to, and mediated by, the relation between the Mount of the Numinous Eagle and Kunisaki, itself evidenced by an equivalence between the eagle (or falcon) and the dove. These morphological equivalences serve to suggest the structural equivalences between the two texts. Later in the text a radiance is seen near three stones, atop which a golden eagle sits emitting that radiance. Next to these stones is a miraculous well whose waters never increase or decrease, thus displaying characteristics of the teaching of the Buddha in the *Lotus Sutra.* In the para-

graph on the mortification of the flesh, we are told that an area of
Kunisaki is known as Mt. Aburatori (Mt. Oil-Take), since it is there
that mountain ascetics burn the wood on which they then walk: this
is the "fire crossing" *(hi-watari)* that the *yamabushi* perform as an act
of penance and purification. This practice is directly related to chapter 23 of the *Lotus Sutra,* in which the former affairs of the bodhisattva Medicine King, who offered his body in fiery sacrifice to the
Buddha, are recalled. The practice of self-immolation in fire occurred
in Japan and in China, as it did in Vietnam. There is a document that
describes it in Kumano; no document relating this practice in Kunisaki has yet been found, but it would not be surprising if it were.

Another chapter of the *Lotus Sutra* is reflected in the text when
Hachiman is told by the divinity of the Pole Star *(hokuto)* to practice
under a monk on Mt. Hiko in order to gain the jewel that symbolizes
the quest for awakening:

> The old man [Hachiman] rejoiced and served Hōren for three years,
> just as Rintō Dannō did when he served the immortal in total self-
> abnegation in his quest for the dharma. . . . Before thirty years
> elapsed a divine dragon emerged from the rock, clutching the pearl in
> its claws, and presented it to Hōren. Spreading the left sleeve of his
> garment in front of him, Hōren gently bore the pearl aloft, finally in
> possession of it. However, conceiving thoughts of attachment to it, he
> did not comply with Hachiman's earlier request. The old man pleaded,
> saying, "Without actually giving the pearl to me, simply acknowledge
> in words that you grant it to me."
>
> Unable to remain silent, Hōren then said, "I grant this pearl to you.
> It is now yours."
>
> As this utterance was made the pearl flew of itself into the old man's
> hand. Shouting, "My wish has been fulfilled!" the old man leaped in
> ecstasy and hurled the pearl into the air. From the very place where it
> landed a crystal-clear spring gushed forth, its water emitting rays of
> light.[24]

This passage seems to be based on the twelfth chapter of the *Lotus
Sutra,* in which we read:

> At that time, the dragon girl had a precious gem, whose value was the
> [whole] thousand-millionfold world, which she held up and gave to
> the Buddha. The Buddha straightway accepted it. The dragon girl said
> to the bodhisattva Wisdom Accumulation and to the venerable Śāripu-
> tra, "I offered a precious gem, and the World-Honored One accepted
> it. Was this quick or not?"

He answered, saying: "Very quick!"

The girl said, "With your supernatural power you shall see me achieve Buddhahood even more quickly than that!"

At that time the assembled multitude all saw the dragon girl in the space of an instant turn into a man. . . . The Spotless world-sphere trembled in six different ways.[25]

Thus the *Rokugō kaizan Nimmon Daibosatsu hongi* echoes the *Lotus Sutra* in subtle ways, on the various levels of setting, spirituality, parables, teachings, practices, and ritual. On the level of setting, we find the *Lotus Sutra*'s structure of twenty-eight chapters and three parts reflected in the number of temples and their arrangement in three classes in the sacred geography of the Kunisaki Peninsula; there are further equivalences in the number of words in the scripture and statues in the mountains, and in the numinous correspondences between Kunisaki and the Mount of the Numinous Eagle. On the spiritual level, the *Lotus Sutra* advocates visions of cosmic proportions and of a golden radiance that are echoed in Kunisaki by a quest for vision accompanied by the remission of sins *(metsuzai),* and manifested by various events that are symbolized by a golden radiance. On the level of parables, a number of direct "translations" occur in the text that were used to qualify the practices which developed in the multiplex. On the level of teachings, the fundamental aspect is that of the *honji-suijaku* theory, according to which the Buddha is an infinite and transcendental being that manifests itself in various parts of the world and in various guises. These equivalences allowed systematic combinations to take place between the *Lotus Sutra* and the Hachiman cult, so that they mutually reinforced each other. On the level of practices, the quests for vision depended on a purification of the sense organs and were accompanied by confession and penance: they are therefore technologies of the self that functioned in relation to the formation of the state, which required control over the body and mind.[26] It has been noted that the merits promised to the devotees if they copied, chanted, recited, or interpreted the scripture, or if they established temples, performed rituals, and created images, were primarily responsible for the immense amount of energy and wealth that formed the basis of the creation of the Kunisaki system of temples and shrines. On the ritual level, both the magical formulas *(dhāraṇī)* and the various rites described in commentaries on the *Lotus Sutra* were performed in Kunisaki. In sum, these fundamental equivalences functioned in such a manner that Kunisaki could be seen as the earthly embodiment—politically, socially, spiritually, and culturally—of the transcendental Pure Land of the Buddha.

That being said, the view of the Kunisaki Peninsula as the natural embodiment of the *Lotus Sutra*—what I have called the enmountain-ment of the text/textualization of the mountain—deserves more attention because it is closely related to the question of the relation between the space of experience and the experience of space. That question is itself related to definitions of religious experiences and to issues of an epistemological character.

## Mountain-Being-Text: A Unified Triad

The definition of being that was proposed in Kunisaki was the result of a system of equivalences postulated between mountain and text, or between the world and words, nature and culture. These equiva-lences were codified, or made possible, by a certain epistemological realm and were expressed in the linguistic combinatory devices that characterize the associations between *kami* and buddhas or bodhisatt-vas in Japan. Furthermore, space was used as a fulcrum for these interactions. Merleau-Ponty wrote in *Phenomenology of Perception:*

> Thus, either I do not think, and I live then among things and vaguely consider space as the milieu of these things or as their common attribute, —or else I think, and then I grasp again space at its source, I actually think the relations covered by this word, and I realize then that things live only because of a subject that perceives and bears them, and I move thus from a spatialized space into a spatializing space.[27]

These lines refer to a central ambiguity manifested by the phenome-non of sacred geography: How is it possible for Kunisaki to be within the world at the same time that it posits itself as a principle thereof? What camouflage or subterfuge in the nature of their experience pushed ascetics to see in Kunisaki more than what was, while claim-ing that what they saw was all there was to "see" in the world? What was responsible for the choice of certain natural sites as privileged *milieu* for a quest for meaning? What was responsible for that pecu-liar management of space, the sacred territory? Were visions such as those described above related to, and/or limited by, concepts of the sacredness of Japan *(shinkoku)* within a given sociocosmic and politi-cal perspective? These questions are in some way related to a cogent definition of sacred geography. However, much more research is needed before theoretical propositions can be offered, and the following remarks should be seen as mere musings.

It may well be that the wall onto which the shadows of objects were cast in the cave described by Plato was not like a flat screen, and that the shadows of the objects were therefore distorted, phantasmagoric, or conducive to an aesthetic reverie. Metaphorically speaking, is it possible that the mountains that appeared to the minds of the ascetics of Kunisaki, "corrected" as they were by a perception trained by austerities, took on a phantasmagoric aspect? Or that the dominance of visionary practices tended to throw a specific light onto certain objects of the world and thus gave them an aesthetic dimension? Is it possible that the natural configurations of the world were then to be thought of as forms that informed and determined the interpretation of that world as a set of signs that called for an intellection of their latent meaning? As a tentative answer to those questions, it might be pointed out that all Buddhist philosophical lineages have paid a significant amount of attention to perception; treatises dealing with the subject were written and sutras devoted to the question were expounded. The nature of dharmas, the existence of things independently from our being, and the world as it was lived were questioned, investigated, sometimes affirmed, and sometimes denied. Some lineages, like that of Yogācāra Buddhism, went so far as to postulate that the world exists only as thought, that it is "mere representation."

The ascetics of Kunisaki lived within a world from which they would not detach themselves by denying its being, or the possibility that it was, in and of itself, the bearer of a fundamental message. The preferred tendency on the part of those mountain ascetics was a kind of visual thinking, an aesthetic contemplation in which neither the objects of perception nor the perceiving mind would ever totally disappear. If the subject dominated, the emphasis on the mind as the producer of reality would ensure that the perceived world would have no more status than a dream; if the object dominated, it would have been subjected to rules of representation that have little to do with the theories we are considering. The Kunisaki anchorites conceived of space first and foremost as something that is lived, if not living. As a consequence, mountains never appeared as "things" devoid of a character that urgently required decoding; the objects on the mountain appeared as signs filled with a meaning to be discovered, or pointing to a meaning not entirely extraneous to them. That meaning was itself, it was claimed, no less than the meaning of existence. In other words, a mountain, a stone, a cliff, a waterfall, a source, or a cavern were all treated as pregnant presences, signatures to be deciphered, and as potential texts to be read, understood, translated, and communicated. Were it not the case, all those natural objects would have been perceived as "alien," as if exiled from the world of experience. Therefore, one is not surprised to find in the texts that nature helps: the *Hachiman takusenshū* states that, as Nimmon Daibosatsu had no water to write with, he planted his bamboo brush into the earth and a source of clear water sprang forth.[28] Of the many techniques that were recommended for copying the *Lotus Sutra*, that which was called *nyohōkyō*, or "natural text," enjoined one to refrain from using an animal-hair brush and to use instead grass and plants as brush, stones as ink, and to bow after each graph was copied, so that the natural character of the tools that were used would fit the natural character of the scripture that was copied. In the epistemological orientation of the mountain ascetics, natural objects *signified* of themselves, and the world was endowed with speech. This epistemological direction led them to postulate that natural sounds were the sermon of the Buddha, and that the natural world was the body of the Buddha. This *"episteme* of identity" led them to manage a natural area in accordance with a vision which held that the *Lotus Sutra* was embodied in the mountain, and that the mountain was a "natural discourse" expounding the *Lotus Sutra*. In other words, their perception of the world was already a sophisticated interpretation that was doctrinally related to the Tendai motto to the effect that "all animate and inanimate beings possess the buddha nature," and to the proposition that "inanimate beings can expound the doctrine of the Buddha."

A comparison with Europe may not be totally unwarranted. Michel Foucault proposed in *The Order of Things* that the *episteme* which dominated Europe up to the end of the sixteenth century was that of resemblance, which he broke down into the four components of *convenientia, aemulatio, analogy,* and *sympathies.*[29] These categories seem applicable to Japan as well. *Convenientia* was the adjacency of places: "those things are convenient which come sufficiently close to one another to be in juxtaposition,"[30] and this convenience was the sign of a relationship, however obscure it may be. This was true for Japan, where Kūkai, for instance, used the device constantly, as when he stated that the surface of Lake Chūzenji was the manifestation of the mirror-wisdom *(kyōchi)* because of the convenience induced by the shared phenomenon of reflection. For Kūkai, if the environment was influenced by the mind, conversely the mind was influenced by the environment: they shared a structural intimacy, which might well be that of *convenientia*.[31]

*Aemulatio* was a convenience freed from space, such as an association of the two eyes with the sun and the moon.[32] That is the case, in mythology, of Izanagi, whose two eyes became Amaterasu and Tsukuyomi through the act of purification. *Aemulatio* tends to let one see the world as a series of concentric circles, or of envelopes. The "five elements" *(gogyō)* were not only constitutive of the universe, they were also constitutive of the body. A case in point is that of the *gorintō,* a symbol in the Shingon lineage which represents, at the same time, the elements of the universe according to esoteric Buddhism and those that constitute the body: the top droplike part of the symbol represents the head, the oval part represents the neck, the triangular part represents the arms, the global part represents the stomach and trunk, and the cubic part represents the legs of a person seated in meditation, while all five material elements are suffused with the sixth element of consciousness.[33]

*Analogy* was an aspect in which *convenientia* and *aemulatio* were superimposed, so that, for instance, "man's body is always the possible half of a universal atlas."[34] Japanese mythology indicates that the sociocosm was conceived of as the body of Izanagi: the main functions of society, symbolized by Amaterasu, Tsukuyomi, and Susano-o, were issued from his head, while the functions of defense (the Sumiyoshi *kami*) were issued from his legs, out of a process of purification in the ocean.[35] Thus Izanagi's body was a "text" from which information concerning the structure of the sociopolitical world could be inferred.

*Sympathies* "play through the depths of the universe in a free state" and "alter objects in the direction of identity,"[36] so that any object could be charged with a specific meaning that was claimed to be encoded in its form or appearance. Thus, in the *Rokugō kaizan Nimmon Daibosatsu hongi,* stones were thought to carry meaning and the behavior of a monkey was thought to correspond to specific human tendencies.

Foucault stipulates that the world, by means of this interplay of resemblances and likenesses, was as if forced to remain "identical," an identity in which "the same remains the same, riveted onto itself."[37] The world was filled with "signatures" in which similitudes could be recognized, and through which the relation of the visible to

the invisible was reversed. This reversion was responsible for divination, an act in which, essentially, similitudes were used in such a
manner as to charge natural phenomena with "messages" that
encoded and prescribed behavior. The Hachiman cult was first and
foremost an oracular religion in which divination played a central
role. Oracles are not possible without claiming an identity and inter-
communication between the realms of forms in nature and language
in culture. In this *episteme* of resemblance, Foucault tells us, the
notion of microcosm/macrocosm played a fundamental role in the
field of knowledge.[38] That notion pervaded the world of thought in
Japan, at least until Neo-Confucianism (through which the first epistemological shift occurred) and until the introduction of western science caused an epistemological break. This was most evident, of all
places, in Kunisaki. Miura Baien (1723–1789), who lived on the
slopes of Mount Futago in the center of the peninsula, wrote poems
about his love for the mountains.[39] However, Baien was a "modern"
man, who answered in his own way Parmenides' call for the distinction between perceiving and reasoning that was picked up, later still,
by Ernst Cassirer in his *Philosophy of Symbolic Forms.*[40] Miura Baien
attempted to harmonize the western knowledge *(yōgaku)* he had
gained in Nagasaki with Neo-Confucianism and, in that process,
revolted against the epistemological conditions that had been instru-
mental in the evolution of Kunisaki as a cultural system.

## The Ideology of the Sacred Nation

The epistemological considerations outlined above were structurally
related to particular technologies of power through which dominion
over land and people was achieved and legitimated. An element that
appears only indirectly in the *Lotus Sutra,* but is directly related to
the Tendai lineage in Kunisaki, is the theory of the protection of the
state *(chingo kokka)* by the scripture. The theories and ritual practices
that concern the protection of the territory overseen by the emperor
had a central function in the evolution of Kunisaki as a cultural system. The term *shinkoku,* which could be used to refer to it, is essentially ambiguous because it can be interpreted to mean both "sacred
nation" and "land of *kami.*"[41] There is little doubt that during the
medieval period both meanings were assumed by those who used the
term, but it should be emphasized that this term had—at the same
time it expressed a religious vision—important characteristics of a

political nature. The concept of the "Pure Land in this world" *(gense jōdo),* proposed indirectly by Kūkai in the ninth century and directly by Kakuban in the eleventh century, and fully operative in Kunisaki, is closely associated with the inception of the concept of the sacred nation during the medieval period and is related to the epistemological realm alluded to in the preceding section, since the buddha land can be construed at the macrocosmic level, and the territory of the nation can be construed as its microcosmic dimension. Moreover, even though the term came in use during the medieval period, it is clear that the notion existed long before in both religious and political realms. A systematic study of combinatory cults supports this claim, and Kunisaki is a case in point because of its relation to the Hachiman cult. It is important to note that the apparent lack of distinction between religious and political realms in Japan means simply that Japanese society had a mythical vision of itself: first expressed in the *Kojiki* and in the *Nihongi* in the eighth century, it served as a structuring device of the sacred geographies that developed thereafter. In that vision, society and the world were conceived of as a single sociocosm in which the pantheon of *kami* and its hierarchy were a mirror-image of the social construct and a mirror-image of the Buddhist pantheon. Furthermore, the world in which people lived was thought to be impacted by symbolic forces (such as those of stars or of diseases believed to originate in symbolic realms). In such a scheme, the position of ritual was central, because people used it as an effective means to act over symbols. One could qualify this as the socio-ritual aspect of the sociocosm. What one could qualify as the cosmonatural aspect of the sociocosm was the definition of nature according to mythology. That definition is clearly, though indirectly, given in the *Kojiki* in the myth relating the birth of fire, in which all the *kami* born before the birth of fire belong to the realm of nature whereas all the *kami* born after belong to the realm of culture. The nature *kami* are born from a sexual union and out of the lower orifices of Izanami's body, while the culture *kami* are "born" from a process of purification and out of the head of the male Izanagi.[42] This structural interpretation of mythology brings to light specific conceptualizations concerning the position of nature; it is obvious that even though nature was subject to decay and to impurity, it came into a dialectical relationship with culture, since the purification of Izanagi took place within nature. Thus nature was both pure and impure; the dominance of one aspect over the other depended on the type of activity taking place in nature. Therefore, if Izanagi could create cul-

ture by purifying himself within nature, it is only "natural" that the
ascetics of Kunisaki created a cultural realm by undergoing purification in fire, water, caverns, and the like. Furthermore, it is only "natural" that they searched for sites in the natural world in which to
purify themselves, and later, under the impact of Buddhism, to
purify their organs of perception—in which case again native and
imported ritual forms were combined. In the realm of external, natural purification, they purified their bodies, while in the realm of
inner, cultural purification, they purified their minds. The notion of
the sacredness of certain natural sites comes from this reasoning, and
the sacredness of the land *(shinkoku)* is tightly related to it: Amaterasu (imperial rule) was born from a process of purification within a
natural world. This point could be demonstrated by looking at the
rituals surrounding the ascension of the emperor to the throne as well
as the rituals for protection of the country performed by Buddhist lineages. Japanese society was fundamentally organized on the basis of
the opposition between purity and pollution: the imperial house
represented purity and was opposed—particularly during the medieval and premodern periods—to the polluted status of the "non-per-
sons" *(hinin)*.[43] Thus the opposition between purity and pollution
was not just one of the devices whereby the opposition between
nature and culture was expressed; it was also intricately related to
power and social hierarchy.

In Kunisaki, the Hachiman cult insists on its relation, through the
legend of the "conquest" of Korea, to the Sumiyoshi divinities that
were born from the purification of Izanagi's body right after he
created Amaterasu, Tsukuyomi, and Susano-o. It was not by chance,
then, that the Hachiman cult was related to the protection of a country thought to be divine, and it is not surprising to note that it is as
though the doctrines of all the major lineages of Buddhism had been
called upon in the *Rokugō kaizan Nimmon Daibosatsu hongi* to
express the sacred character of the Kunisaki Peninsula. The last seg-
ment of the text, for example, states that the peninsula should be
seen, by those who perform austerities properly, as the triple sections
of the *Lotus Sutra*; as the nine realms of the Pure Land *(kubon jōdo)*;
as the nine sections of the diamond mandala; as a double three-
pronged thunderbolt *(vajra)*; as the diamond and womb mandalas; as
the site of Maitreya's coming; as the eight petals of the lotus in both
mandalas; as the twenty-eight chapters of the *Lotus Sutra* according
to its double distinction in *hon* and *jaku*; and as Mahāvairocana's
Pure Land.

These elements indicate the various ritual influences that impacted the peninsula over several centuries. The vision of Japan or of some of its parts as a ritual object appeared in the thirteenth century in the *Keiranshūyōshū,* a rich document that issued from the *kike* specialists of Mt. Hiei; in that text Japan is depicted, for instance, as a *vajra,* one extremity of which is marked by the Suwa Shrine in eastern Japan, and the other by the Sumiyoshi Shrine in western Japan. The center is marked by Lake Biwa and the Sannō shrines, surrounded to the north by the Kehi Shrine in Tsuruga Bay and to the south by the Ise Shrine in Ise Bay.[44]

Bearing such images and similitudes in mind, the Kunisaki ascetics would identify the space of their experience with a transcendental space. This being achieved, they engaged in the practices of penance to ensure that their ordinary experience would be engulfed in the remission of sins and thereby in the realm of undifferentiated suchness. This was what we would call the "religious" dimension of their experience. However, that experience was also closely related to the political dimensions of the formation of the state and of the national territory, which was regarded as being under the control of ruling agents who were seen as the native manifestations on earth *(suijaku)* of Buddhist figures *(honji).* In this sense, then, the ascetics' experience was neither purely religious nor purely political: it was what might be called "poligious."

The Kunisaki Peninsula thus represented a complex cultural system, the multitudinous aspects of which were related to mythology, to ancient views of the sociocosm, to specific forms of adoption of Buddhism, and to fascinating techniques combining Japanese and non-Japanese ritual systems. All were inscribed within the premodern epistemological realm out of which Japan's sacred geography evolved to coalesce into a specific form of nationalistic ideology.

## NOTES

1. Contained in Sakurai Tokutaro et al., eds., *Jisha engi* (Tokyo: Iwanami, 1975), 306–325. See the translation of the text in Allan G. Grapard, "Lotus in the Mountain, Mountain in the Lotus."

2. For a general survey of the establishment of sacred geography in Japan, see Allan G. Grapard, "Flying Mountains and Walkers of Emptiness: Toward a Definition of Sacred Space in Japanese Religions."

3. That is the reason why Japanese scholars speak of the Kumano Cult, the Hachiman Cult, the Ise Cult, the Kitano Cult, the Sannō Cult, the Kasuga Cult, etc.

4. I began using this term at about the same time Maruyama Magoroh used it in several articles he brought recently to my attention. See, for instance, his "Mindscapes: Meta-principles in Environmental Design," *Garten + Landschaft,* October 1981. However, my use of the term in the present context is different from Maruyama's.

5. The era of disappearance of the *Lotus Sutra* from Kunisaki is not discussed in this paper. It was related to the surge to power of the warrior class and to the ensuing collapse of the *shōen* system in the medieval period, as well as to the spread of Christianity in Kyūshū. The text under consideration was written shortly before the final blow to the system was given by the Japanese government in 1868, when it ordered that all native *kami* be disassociated from their Buddhist counterparts. A fledgling group of *yamabushi* survives today in Kunisaki.

6. I have used the translation of the *Lotus Sutra* by Leon Hurvitz, *Scripture of the Lotus Blossom of the Fine Dharma,* hereafter referred to as Hurvitz. The present reference is to fasc. 4, chap. 11.

7. On Kunisaki, see Umehara Kazuo, *Kunisaki hantō no rekishi to minzoku;* Kagawa Mitsuo and Fujita Seiichi, *Usa;* Ōtake Junkō and Watanabe Shinkō, *Kunisaki bunka to sekibutsu.*

8. See Ross Bender, "The Hachiman Cult and the Dōkyō Incident," *Monumenta Nipponica* 34 (1979): 125–153.

9. On the mountain religion of Kyūshū, see Nakano Hatayoshi, *Hikozan to Kyūshū no Shugendō* (Tokyo: Meicho Shuppan, 1977); on the topic of Kubotezan, which is one of the mountains related to the Hiko complex, see Shigematsu Toshimi, *Yamabushi mandara* (Tokyo: NHK Bukkusu, 1987).

10. See Gary Ledyard, "Galloping Along with the Horseriders: Looking for the Founders of Japan," *Journal of Japanese Studies* 1, no. 2 (1975): 217–254.

11. Nakano Hatayoshi, *Hachiman shinkō-shi no kenkyū* (Tokyo: Yoshikawa kōbunkan, 1976), 2 vols., offers the most wide-ranging discussion of the topic.

12. The painted scroll at the San Francisco Museum of Asian Art is called *Hachiman engi emaki* and has been edited and studied by Miya Tsugio in *Shinshū Nihon emakimono zenshū* (Tokyo: Kadokawa, 1981), supplement 2: 17–26.

13. For a study of the painted representations of the *Lotus Sutra* in Japan, see Willa Jane Tanabe, *Paintings of the Lotus Sutra.*

14. The notion of adequate perception as the result of correct practice appears in several chapters of the *Lotus Sutra,* but especially in chaps. 5, 14, 19, and 28. The exercises of purification of the sense organs are prescribed in the *Kanfugen bosatsu gyōhōgyō,* in *T* 9, no. 277.

15. Hurvitz, 8–11.

16. Hurvitz, 264–265.

17. Nakano, *Hikozan to Kyūshū no Shugendō,* 781.

18. Hurvitz, 38–39.

19. Sakurai, *Jisha engi,* 316.

20. Hurvitz, 113.

21. Sakurai, *Jisha engi,* 324. The date 855 is offered by the *Usa no miya takusenshū,* quoted in Nakano, *Hikozan to Kyūshū no Shugendō,* 7.

22. Hurvitz, 222–223.

23. Sakurai, *Jisha engi,* 312.

24. Ibid., 317.

25. Hurvitz, 201.

26. See Luther Martin et al., eds., *Technologies of the Self: a Seminar with Michel Foucault* (Amherst: University of Massachusetts Press, 1988), 16–49.

27. Maurice Merleau-Ponty, *Phénoménologie de la Perception* (Paris: Gallimard, 1945), 281–282. My translation.

28. Nakano, *Hachiman shinkō-shi no kenkyū*, 712.

29. Michel Foucault, *Les mots et les choses;* translated into English as *The Order of Things* (New York: Vintage, 1970), 17–45.

30. Ibid., 18.

31. This is clearly indicated in a text composed by Kūkai which is the oldest extant text documenting the ascent of a mountain for religious purposes. See Allan G. Grapard, trans., "Stone Inscription for the Monk Shōdō, Who Crossed Mountains and Streams in His Search for Awakening," in Michael Tobias and Harold Drasdo, eds., *The Mountain Spirit* (New York: Overlook Press, 1978), 54–59.

32. Foucault, *The Order of Things*, 19.

33. This is best described in Kakuban's *Gorinkuji-myōhimitsu-kaishaku*, in *T* 79.11–22, no. 2514.

34. Foucault, *The Order of Things*, 22.

35. See Donald Philippi, trans., *Kojiki* (Tokyo: University of Tokyo Press, 1968).

36. Foucault, *The Order of Things*, 23.

37. Ibid., 25.

38. Ibid., 32.

39. Very little work has been done on Miura Baien. A short treatment can be found in Theodore de Bary, ed., *Sources of Japanese Tradition*, vol. 2 (New York: Columbia University Press, 1958), 480–488. A short study by Rosemary Mercer of Victoria University, New Zealand, is published in *Baien gakuhō*, no. 10 (Tokyo: University of Tokyo Press, 1986).

40. See Ernst Cassirer, *The Philosophy of Symbolic Forms*, tr. Ralph Manheim, vol. 2 (New Haven and London: Yale University Press, 1975), 29–59.

41. Kuroda Toshio, "Nihon chūsei no kokka to shūkyō." See also Kuroda Toshio, *Jisha seiryoku* (Tokyo, Iwanami shoten, 1980).

42. Philippi, *Kojiki*, 49–70.

43. On these oppositions, see the stimulating discussions between Noma Hiroshi and Okiura Kazuteru, *Chūseihen*, vol. 2 of *Nihon no sei to sen* (Kyoto: Jimbun shoin, 1985).

44. *Keiranshūyōshū*, in *T* 76.626, no. 2410. On the *kike*, see the essay by Kuroda Toshio in this volume.

# Tanaka Chigaku: The *Lotus Sutra* and the Body Politic

GEORGE J. TANABE, JR.

One of the most salient features of Japanese Buddhism of the late nineteenth and early twentieth centuries is its need to justify itself as a religion suitable for modern Japan. This vindication was necessary as a response to Confucian and Shinto critics who held in various ways that Buddhism, an alien system, was incompatible with Japan. With the Meiji Restoration of 1868, ideological criticism of Buddhism, once a matter of debate alone, was incorporated into government policies which officially supported Shinto at the expense of Buddhism.[1] It did not matter that Buddhism and Japanese culture had become integrated over the course of many centuries; by force of argument and policy, they were now disassociated and it was the task of Buddhists at that time to reintegrate them.

Making the best of their defensive posture, many of the Buddhist reformers actually welcomed the criticism as a challenge. Takaoka Zōryū of the *Shoshū Dotoku Kaimei* (Pan Sectarian Ethics Council) criticized Buddhist monks for cohabiting with women, eating meat in the temples, visiting brothels, gambling, selling religious implements, and so forth, all in an attempt to convince fellow Buddhists to reform their ways. Fukuda Gyōkai (1806–1888), another of the Buddhist reformers, even went so far as to say that the anti-Buddhist movement *(haibutsu kishaku)* had really been brought on by Buddhists themselves, who were more interested in splendid robes and officious titles than they were in the promotion of the dharma. Shaku Unshō (1827–1909), follower of the Shingon precepts master Jiun (1718–1804), saw in the *haibutsu kishaku* movement an opportunity for moral reform, and threw himself into a round of activities that left him little time for the upkeep of his own temple buildings, much to the dismay of his superiors whose reprimands he ignored. The anti-

Buddhist movement, then, offered Buddhists an opportunity for
self-reform, which was also a chance to show Buddhism to be a modern religion worthy of a Japan that took pride in itself as a modern
nation.[2]

Nationalism was always a part of the reform agenda. Buddhism
had to recover its moral worth in order to earn, once again, its place
in the nation's ideology. It also had to demonstrate its claim to truth,
for nothing less than the truth would be worthy of the allegiance of
the nation. Inoue Enryō (1858–1919) accordingly coined the phrase
*gokoku airi* (protect the country, love the truth) as his motto. For
Inoue, the truth of Buddhism could be demonstrated by its compatibility with western philosophy and science, a compatibility that could
not be claimed by other religions, not even by Christianity. Others
tried to show Buddhism to be not just a corroborating partner of science, but superior to it and all other systems, and therefore worthy to
be the foundation of modern Japan. In reviewing the Buddhist
accomplishments of the late nineteenth and early twentieth centuries, Yabuki Yoshiteru, writing in 1934, pointed out what he perceived to be the qualitative and quantitative superiority of Buddhism:

> The doctrine of Japanese Buddhism, on the side of its philosophical
> foundations, holds a position of superiority over all other religions.
>     The vast numbers of temples, scriptures, books, scholars, and educa-
> tional institutions connected with Buddhism surely give Japan the
> crown among all the nations of the world. These are matters that can-
> not be passed over in relation to the progress of the national destiny.[3]

As a general description, Yabuki's comments apply to the beliefs of
Tanaka Chigaku (1861–1939), one of the most ardent of the Buddhist nationalists, who called for a return to truth and the principles
of Japan, perceiving them to be one and the same.

Tanaka's sense of truth was defined specifically by the *Lotus Sutra,*
not by any sense of Buddhism as a comprehensive whole. And since
truth for Tanaka was the justification of the national essence *(kokutai),* or the body politic, his political ideology can accordingly be
called a species of "Lotus nationalism." Actually a second source for
Tanaka's nationalism is to be found in Shinto, for unlike the other
Meiji reformers, Tanaka took the very foundation of the Shinto critics
and turned it into a defense of Buddhism. This accomplishment, the
reintegration of Buddhism and Shinto as the basis for nationalism, is

perhaps, as Edwin B. Lee suggests, "Tanaka's most important contribution to Japanese thought,"[4] but is best left for a separate inquiry. We shall be concerned in this chapter with how Tanaka used the *Lotus Sutra* to justify the superiority of Japan's national essence. Despite its anti-Buddhist policies, the new Meiji order was not, in Tanaka's eyes, an obstacle; on the contrary, it would become the very manifestation of the *Lotus Sutra* if the unity between the *Lotus Sutra* and the body politic could be asserted.

## The New Age of *Shakubuku*

In an attempt to nationalize the training of all clergy, Shinto and Buddhist alike, the Meiji government established a seminary called the Daikyō-in in 1872. The selection and training of priests was accomplished through three levels of "seminaries": the lower seminaries *(shōkyō-in)*, which actually consisted of every shrine and temple in the country; the middle seminaries *(chūkyō-in)*, which were established in each province; and the "great" seminary (Daikyō-in), located at the Zōjōji in Tokyo. Based on the three dogmas of obeisance to the Shinto deities, clarification of the principle of heaven and the way of humanity, and reverence for the throne and government authority, this "great teaching" *(daikyō)* was meant to replace the old forms of religion known as Shinto and Buddhism. As an attempt to create a new civil religion by government fiat, the policy proved cumbersome and utterly failed to root out centuries of traditional religious forms. The Daikyō-in, an interesting experiment, was abolished in the spring of 1875, much to the relief of the Buddhist leaders who actively opposed it.

Each sect was thereafter left to establish its own educational system, and the Nichiren leadership took advantage of this new beginning to set up a comprehensive training center called the Daikyō-in of the Nichiren Sect. In the fall of 1875, Tanaka Chigaku, then fifteen years of age, was sent to the Daikyō-in to be trained for the Nichiren priesthood. There he soon found himself at odds with the prevailing teaching on the issue of *shakubuku,* or the forceful propagation of the *Lotus Sutra.*

By Tanaka's time, Nichiren orthodoxy had been defined largely by the efforts of those who opposed the tendency to interpret the *Lotus Sutra* along Tendai lines.[5] The movement to return to Nichiren's emphasis on the latter half, or *hommon* section, of the *Lotus Sutra* was begun by Nichidō (1724–1789) of Ichimyō-in, who made a deep impression on many. One of those was Nichiki (1800–1859) of Udana-in, who himself became extremely influential, many of his disciples becoming leaders in the sect's hierarchy. Foremost among them was Arai Nissatsu, the man who was primarily responsible for the establishment of the Daikyō-in of the Nichiren Sect, serving as its first headmaster. These men defined the new orthodoxy which called for less dependency on Tendai interpretations.

Tanaka certainly concurred with this return to Nichiren's understanding of the *Lotus Sutra,* but he felt that it did not go far enough. While the new orthodox masters rejected Tendai dogmatics, they also avoided the aggressive, argumentative style characterized by *shakubuku.* Nichiki, for example, took a moderate approach in deemphasizing *shakubuku* and gave greater validity to its opposite value, *shōju,* the gentle, diplomatic way of presenting one's claims. Tactfulness, he said, was necessary in response to the times. Nichirin, one of the scholars of his school, even espoused the principle of *shakutai shōshin,* retreating from *shakubuku* and promoting *shōju.* It is necessary, he argued, to keep on good terms with Buddhists from other schools. Nichiki's *Gukyō yōgi* fully explained this preference for the moderation of *shōju,* and it was used as a textbook in the Daikyō-in.

Moreover, the religious practices which Tanaka was obliged to engage in at the Daikyō-in proved to be reflections of the moderate approach. On the first and fifteenth days of the month, everyone had to recite the "Peaceful Practices" chapter *(Anrakugyō-hon)* of the *Lotus Sutra,* which was the scriptural basis for the *shōju* doctrine. That was acceptable enough, but the chanting took place to the beating of the *mokugyo,* a hollowed-out piece of wood in the shape of a stylized fish, used to set the rhythm of the chanting. Recalling this experience, Tanaka writes:

> Until then, I had never beaten the *mokugyo* for the *Lotus Sutra.* I now use something called a wooden bell, but this came later. In the past, there were only drums and wooden clappers. Beating the *mokugyo* while reciting the sutra or chanting the *daimoku* was performed in the Gensei style of Fukakusa, and this situation was almost entirely a matter of another style from outside the sect. Therefore no one doubted that it would not gain wide usage. But in the school of the Udana-in masters, we used the *mokugyo.*[6]

Although some priests objected to the inclusion of this non-Nichiren practice in the Daikyō-in, the moderate opinion prevailed.

The Daikyō-in teachers did allow for the legitimate use of *shaku-buku* in discussions about the superiority of the *Lotus Sutra,* but pro-hibited it in any argument about the worth of other sects. In other words, it was all right to declare that the truth was revealed by Śākyamuni in the *Lotus Sutra,* but arguments about sectarian dif-ferences, being offensive to human feelings, incurred only the oppo-sition of others, were detrimental to the possibility of having any influence over others, and damaged social harmony. In the distant past, it used to be that if a person won a debate with someone, the loser had to convert to the victor's sect, or if a head priest lost the debate, his entire temple had to convert. But under Tokugawa law, changes of sect by individuals or institutions were forbidden, so it was useless, argued the Udana-in teachers, to engage in aggressive propa-gation. Furthermore, since Buddhists had a common enemy in the Confucian, Shinto, and National Learning camps, it was wise to avoid animosity within the *saṃgha.* This, Tanaka explained, is what was taught in lectures, sermons, and Nichiki's *Gukyō yōgi.*

Tanaka could accept this approach within certain limits, but at the point of adopting a wrong teaching such as the *nembutsu,* which could destroy the nation, he felt he had to draw a line.

> Evil and wrong teachings must be entirely discarded or else they will destroy the world. For that reason Nichiren fought against wrong teachings even at the risk of his own life, and this teaching, which he preached throughout his whole life, must not be eradicated. As for myself, my own father told me this ceaselessly day and night.[7]

The establishment of new teachings in response to contemporary con-ditions was to be expected, but how could it be justified if it went against Nichiren's teachings? Was it not the case that the teachings of the Udana-in masters stood in opposition to Nichiren's? These ques-tions were raised by Tanaka early on, and throughout his life he would hold to the answer implicit in them. The Udana-in masters, Tanaka noticed, were contradicting themselves in a certain way, for the new Meiji era was no longer bound by the old Tokugawa laws. If vigorous debate was once useless because religious conversion was for-bidden by law, how could that rationale apply in an age of religious freedom, when a new law allowed for voluntary changes between sects? This would seem to be precisely the time which calls for the use of *shakubuku.* For Tanaka the Meiji policy of religious freedom, often seen by Christians as an implicit sanction for their missionary work, was an open invitation for his own kind of *shakubuku* missionary activity. Like the other reformers who saw opportunities in the adverse policies of the government, Tanaka thrived in the new age of Meiji.

## *Honge shōshaku ron*

In *Honge shōshaku ron* (Nichiren's Theory of *Shakubuku* and *Shōju*), published in 1902, Tanaka resolved his doubts about the moderate orthodox position on *shakubuku*. He begins by pointing out that propagation is not just a part of Buddhism, but is its entirety, for Buddhism exists to be propagated. Forceful and gentle ways must both be used, and Tanaka makes it clear that he is not against *shōju*; he is simply opposed to those who would deemphasize or reject *shakubuku*. In the *Śrīmālā Sutra*, *shakubuku* is recommended for use against those who have committed serious sins, while *shōju* is applicable to those with lesser offenses. Since the most aggressive interpretation of *shakubuku* is actually in the *Nirvāṇa Sutra*, which speaks of the use of military weapons, and the fullest explanation of *shōju* is in the *Lotus Sutra*, should the *Lotus* be thought of as the teaching of moderation? Tanaka's reply is decidedly negative, and he proceeds to argue that the *Lotus Sutra* actually places a higher priority on forceful propagation than on moderation.[8]

In Tanaka's exegesis of the *Lotus* the reciprocal relationship between a text and its interpreter can be seen, for the text can exert its influence only after the reader works his or her influence on it. The hermeneutic Tanaka used was a kind of structural analysis reminiscent of the traditional Buddhist exegetical technique whereby meaning is derived from an analysis of the order and structure of the text. The division of the *Lotus Sutra* into two parts, the fundamental teaching contained in the latter fourteen chapters of the sutra *(hommon)* and the secondary teaching in the first fourteen chapters *(shakumon),* is the most prominent example of the application of this technique to the *Lotus*. Tanaka accepted this division of the *Lotus Sutra* and Nichiren's understanding of it, and further devised his own unique structural interpretation of several chapters relating to *shakubuku*.

Tanaka identified three chapters in the *Lotus* as the *loci* of the teaching on propagation: chapter 13, "The Encouragement of Keeping This Sutra" *(Kanji-hon);* chapter 14, "Peaceful Practices" *(Anrakugyō-hon);* and chapter 20, "The Bodhisattva Never Despising"

*(Jōfukyō-hon)*. *Kanji-hon* ends with the "Hymn in Twenty Lines" in which the bodhisattvas sing with one voice about how they will endure persecution by others:

Ignorant people will speak ill of us,
Abuse us, and threaten us
With swords or sticks.
We will endure all this.[9]

The difficulties encountered by propagators of the *Lotus Sutra* are so frightful, says Tanaka, that they make one's "hair stand on end."[10] Anyone contemplating these difficulties will naturally be apprehensive about promoting the *Lotus,* and it is out of sympathy for those with apprehensions that the Buddha preached the next chapter, *Anrakugyō-hon,* which recommends the more passive approach of moderation, even-handedness, and noninflammatory speech. In short, *Kanji-hon* advocates *shakubuku* while *Anrakugyō-hon* teaches *shōju*. Does the latter invalidate the former? Of course not. They are simply meant for different kinds of bodhisattvas: *Kanji-hon* for those of profound depth, *Anrakugyō-hon* for those who are shallow.[11]

Tanaka's use of a structuralist argument comes with his observation that *Kanji-hon* precedes *Anrakugyō-hon* and thus takes precedence:

*Kanji-hon* is the thirteenth chapter and *Anrakugyō-hon* is the fourteenth. In terms of the relationship between things, it is clear that *Kanji-hon* gives birth to *Anrakugyō-hon*. Therefore, *Anrakugyō-hon* develops in an opposite direction from it, and is the ancestral text for *shōju*. It is as if a literary person were born as the child of a military man.[12]

Borrowing biological metaphors, Tanaka explains that while the child is not a duplicate of the father, the blood line is the same, and therefore at some later point in the lineage, a hereditary trait from the parent will reemerge. This would be a case of atavism *(kankatsu iden)*, a latter recurrence of an ancestral trait, and this is indeed seen in chapter 20, *Jōfukyō-hon*. This chapter embodies the "bones of *Kanji-hon* and the blood of *Anrakugyō-hon*," and thus "is an heir to the house of *shakubuku*."[13] In Tanaka's argument, the order of the chapters is crucial: *Kanji-hon*, as the teaching of *shakubuku*, takes precedence over the rest quite simply because it precedes the rest.

This argument is developed further in Tanaka's analysis of the relationship between *Kanji-hon* and *Jōfukyō-hon*. On the surface, the Bodhisattva Never Despising would seem to be a model of the gentle approach, for even when slandered and attacked for predicting that his hostile audience would become buddhas, he continued to praise and respect them. However, this act of reverence, according to Tanaka, is not to be mistaken for moderation, but is actually a form of aggression.

> This unyielding reverence is a *very significant manifestation of righteousness* and, furthermore, will invite a *great attack which he is morally obliged to bear.* It is an act which can be called the essence of *shakubuku* action.[14]

Tanaka's interpretation suggests that there is merit in being persecuted by people angered by a stubborn, aggressive righteousness based not so much in concern for the other as in the conviction of one's truth. This is *shakubuku* kindness, not that of *shōju*, which would be free of any provocation.

The relationship, then, between *Kanji-hon* and *Jōfukyō-hon* is that the latter is the experienced fulfillment of what was prophesied in the former. The latter is also the outer aspect of the inner condition of the former. Both *Anrakugyō-hon* and *Jōfukyō-hon* are descendants of *Kanji-hon,* but they have different emphases. Insofar as *Jōfukyō-hon* teaches the *shakubuku* of reverence, it stands in a direct line with *Kanji-hon*. Citing the Chinese T'ien-t'ai master Miao-lo's ten distinctions between *Anrakugyō-hon* and *Jōfukyō-hon*, Tanaka reinforces his conclusion that the latter chapter is essentially concerned with *shakubuku*. Each of Miao-lo's distinctions consists of two four-character phrases, one from each chapter, set in juxtaposition. Tanaka adds his own short commentary to each pair of phrases, and expands on his comments on the tenth pair. From the *Anrakugyō-hon,* the phrase "to be in accord with others and have rituals" is paired with "to oppose others and forget what is usual" from *Jōfukyō-hon*. The former phrase, says Tanaka, means that the situation of the other person must be preserved, and the teachings must be explained gently with the use of many rituals. The phrase from *Jōfukyō-hon,* however, means that one must ignore the hatred of others and make them hear in order to establish a forceful karmic connection *(shakubuku)*. The usual rules of politeness can be dispensed with, and extraordinary methods are justifiable.[15] The priority given to *shakubuku* is seen in the ordered relationship between the three chapters: *Kanji-hon* establishes the fundamentals of *shakubuku* and predicts the consequent persecutions, making the moderate teaching of *Anrakugyō-hon* necessary for those beginners who cannot bear such difficulties. *Jōfukyō-hon,* coming after the other two, confirms both of them by recognizing the aggressive quality of kindness.

The *Lotus Sutra,* then, essentially teaches *shakubuku* though it does find a place for *shōju.* Propagators of the *Lotus Sutra* must ultimately carry out their tasks with force. In *Shūmon no ishin* (The Reformation of the Sect), written in 1901, Tanaka called *shakubuku* the "martial art of the *Lotus Sutra.*" Since the *Lotus Sutra* is the source of all good, if something is found to be in opposition to it, then such opposition cannot be good and must therefore be attacked. If this aggressive approach is separated from the *Lotus Sutra,* it would be like taking the flavor out of wine. Even the way of moderation is a battle insofar as it must persist until victory is won. "If even for a single instant, any thought against *shakubuku* should arise, then the *Lotus Sutra* will be dead, and that will be the spiritual death of the nation."[16] Tanaka, of course, never regarded his unshakable conviction as sectarian self-righteousness; it was Absolute Righteousness. His grandson, Tanaka Kōho, writes that his *shakubuku* transcends time, and does not involve a relative dualism which rejects others, as it is misunderstood by many, but embraces the universal principle of Truth.[17] In this can be seen a familiar religious attitude which presumes the sacred responsibility of carrying out the ultimate act of altruism, spreading the truth everywhere, by aggressive means if necessary. All that is necessary is some concrete structure through which that task can be accomplished in fact.

## The *Lotus* and *Kokutai,* the Body Politic

If Hirata Atsutane (1776–1843) saw in Buddhism a foreign system that was not suitable for Japan, Tanaka saw in Hirata's interest in Western knowledge something even more incompatible. Both men were patriots; both saw that the foreign elements in each other's system could never promote Japan's interests.[18] Tanaka was not in principle opposed to western influences, but he felt that the fad for foreign things had contributed to a loss of interest in *kokutai,* the essence of Japan. If, however, the Japanese could hold fast to *kokutai,* then it would not matter if Freemasons, Communists, or Marxists came to Japan, for the nation's identity would be secure. Hirata and Tanaka were convinced that Japan could not survive without an understanding of its essence, but contrary to Hirata, Tanaka found the source of its essence in Buddhism, and specifically in the *Lotus Sutra*. By failing to realize this, Hirata's brand of patriotism amounted to what Tanaka called a "national essentialism" *(kokutai shugi)*, [19] which was simply a theory about *kokutai* but not the essence of the nation itself.

Furthermore, the difference between Hirata's "national essentialism" and Tanaka's "national essence" was nothing less than Truth itself. Unless *kokutai* is a manifestation of the *Lotus Sutra*, it will not embody the Eternal Truth:

> Where does the spirit of the national essence come from? If our understanding of the national essence is not a manifestation of the *Lotus*, and is not illuminated in terms of the great insight of the *Lotus Sutra*, then it will not amount to the great principle which exists forever and does not pass away, and which penetrates throughout the true heaven and earth. If it is not this great principle which exists forever and does not pass away, then it cannot be said to have the nucleus of the national essence. That which exists forever and does not pass away possesses an eternal nature. This must be the Truth. [20]

The "great principle which exists forever and does not pass away" is not as abstract an idea as it might seem, for the "principle" is specifically the Buddha of chapter 16 of the *Lotus Sutra*, in which he reveals himself to be eternal: "I am always here. I shall never pass away." [21]

Chapter 16 is the foundation on which the truth of the *Lotus* is built. All religious movements make some claim to truth, and the great emphasis given to truth in the *Lotus*-inspired groups is what gives them their aggressive, dynamic quality. Tanaka Kōho makes this point clearly when he says that the Buddha and Nichiren did not establish a religion so much as they discovered the Truth. Absolute Truth is not simply a concept which stands in contrast to relative existence, for if it were so, it would not be absolute and would be relative instead. Nichiren, continues Tanaka Kōho, advocated the *Lotus Sutra* as the teaching of Truth because for the first time it did not stand in contrast to other schools but embraced them all, including the Hīnayāna believers. The fundamental Buddha, being eternal, also unifies all the other buddhas and deities as well, even the Christian God, who is therefore a partial reflection of the eternal Buddha.

Whereas other religions claim but cannot prove the absolute quality of their deities, the *Lotus Sutra* is the proof of the eternal Buddha.[22]

The importance of locating truth in the *Lotus Sutra* lies in the fact that it is now made a fact. The truth which transcends time and space is now embodied in a text such that every word is the Buddha himself. This is what is portrayed in the *Lotus Sutras* done in the *ichiji ichibutsu* style in which a buddha is painted next to each character. This "incarnational" thinking whereby the Buddha as the truth is transformed into a text is extremely important for understanding so many other aspects of *Lotus* culture. For if the truth can be embodied in a text, then, by extension, the text can be embodied in a poem, or a mandala, or a mountain, or in its own title, or a person, or even a nation. Masaharu Anesaki, a Nichiren scholar who was a good friend of Tanaka Chigaku, uses the word "embodiment" over and over in his work *Nichiren, the Buddhist Prophet*. The title of the sutra *(daimoku)* is not just a symbol but is "the embodiment of the whole truth." Anesaki cites Nichiren's explanation that "all the letters of this Scripture are indeed the living embodiments of the august Buddhas. . . . " The *Lotus* must not be read simply with the eyes or understood just by the mind but "must be read by the body." It is not surprising, then, that "Nichiren deemed himself to be an embodiment of the scripture, a personal version of its teachings and prophecies, and a living testimony to them."[23] As the embodiment of the Truth, the *Lotus* as a book can be compared to the Koran, but unlike the Muslim scripture, it can be reembodied in a wide variety of ways to produce the articles of *Lotus* culture.

The unique ability of the *Lotus Sutra* to embody itself in concrete form means that its truth will never become vague or abstract. It thus lends itself to practical use and is not just a matter for theoretical discussion. Tanaka's youngest son, Satomi Kishio, published in English a book called *Japanese Civilization* in which he explained how religion must be practical not just on an individual basis but on a national scale as well:

> Religion has the State and the world at large as well as the individual as objects of its salvation. But the unit of salvation is the State. In this respect religions in nine cases out of ten have vague ideas. The religion we need should assuredly be the authoritative principle of our actual life, and of course that of the countries and the world as well.[24]

The "authoritative principle," of course, is to be found in the *Lotus Sutra* as had been declared by Nichiren so many times before. The

*Lotus* and Japan have a unique relationship of mutual fulfillment: "The *Hoke kyō* [*Lotus Sutra*] must have a state like Japan in order to validate its pregnant value, and Japan should have the *Hoke kyō* for the sake of the realization of her national ideal."[25] Tanaka himself put it in no uncertain terms: "the form that it [the truth of the *Lotus*] takes is the national essence of Japan."[26]

Over and over in the writings of Tanaka and his descendants, the equation is drawn between the *Lotus Sutra* and Japan. When Emperor Meiji died, Tanaka conducted a grand *Hokke hakkō* (Eight Lectures on the *Lotus Sutra*) in which he used the interpretive technique of correlating or associating a word or passage from the sutra with an idea that is not found explicitly in the text. For example, the word "Thus" in the opening lines of the sutra ("Thus have I heard . . . ") was interpreted to refer to the thusness or essence of Japan *(kokutai)*. The Meiji Constitution was seen as the completion of the ten worlds in the "Expedient Devices" chapter *(Hōben-bon)*, Japan was likened to the jeweled stupa appearing in chapter 11, and the national essence and the *Lotus* were said to form "a single essence, not two."[27] Emperor Meiji himself, far from being seen as the symbolic head of a government that opposed Buddhism, was described by Tanaka in terms drawn from traditional Buddhist/ Shinto syncretic diction as one whose "trace" *(jaku)* is the manifestation of the "original ground" *(honji)* of the Buddha.[28] Even though Emperor Meiji was not a believer in the *Lotus Sutra,* he was in effect carrying out the work of the *Lotus,* and therefore was a bodhisattva.[29] The structure of the national essence is completely unified with the structure of the *hommon* section of the *Lotus Sutra,* which takes as its objective the reality of the nation and the original Buddha.[30] In a statement of the purpose of *Dokku,* one of several journals Tanaka founded, he wrote:

> *Dokku* clarifies the true aspect of the essence of the country by proclaiming the great significance of the unification of the dharma with the nation in which the *Lotus Sutra* is the heart of Japan and Japan is the body of the *Lotus Sutra*.[31]

When the Meiji Constitution was first proclaimed publicly, Tanaka gave a series of lectures lasting ten days, and interpreted that political document in terms of its spiritual significance. In his concluding remarks, he said:

The country is to be ruled by means of the spirit of the *Lotus Sutra*. The spirit of the *Lotus Sutra* is manifested precisely in the essence of the country of Japan. The *Lotus Sutra* in form is Japan, and the heart of Japan is the *Lotus Sutra*.[32]

Insofar as politics and religion are intimately bound together in government, Tanaka might be said to have been advocating a theocracy. The deity, however, who stands at the center of this government is incarnated in a book whose essence becomes polity, and as such, Tanaka's idea of government might also be called, to coin a new term, a "bibliocracy." At times, the specific contents of the book become important in the understanding of how it is that the text and the nation are identified; thus the constitution is equated with the ten worlds spoken of in *Hōben-bon,* or the jeweled stupa is likened to Japan itself. But by and large, the details are not as important as the overall essence of the sutra, whatever its specifics might be, which is then equated with the essence of the nation, whatever its specific organization might be. The nation is the sutra, which is the Buddha, who is incarnated in the emperor, who embodies the nation. The circle of identities is made complete through these series of mutual embodiments or incarnations, and, like all incarnations in which the Truth is made concrete, there is a mystique if not a mystery, which makes the inclusion of specifics unnecessary. The argument is not by rational development but by correlation through successive embodiments. Nor is the circle fixed, for it can be extended by that same process of correlation to include the entire world.

## Lotus Nationalism and the World

In the *Hokke hakkō* conducted for Emperor Meiji, Tanaka and his followers clearly expressed their understanding of the *Lotus Sutra* in geopolitical terms. In the verse summary of all the extraordinary events surrounding the illumination of the worlds by the Buddha in chapter 1, there is one line which says, "Heavenly drums sounded by themselves."[33] According to Tanaka's *Hokke hakkō* text, which was read in turns by his followers, this line is to be understood as follows:

The explanation of this from the standpoint of the essence of the nation is that the Heavenly Task of unifying the world is the actual

realization of [the phrase], "Heavenly drums sounded by themselves."
Already we have had the great victories in the wars against China and
Russia; there is also the annexation of Korea. Great auspicious signs for
the nation have numerously appeared. The great work of spreading the
Heavenly Task has begun, and the single great country of Japan has
appeared on this earth as the single sacred master of the one heaven
and the one earth. . . . Ah! How exalted is this mysterious text![34]

The promulgation of the Meiji Constitution is the realization of the
passage "the ten worlds were all completed" in the *Hōben-bon*,[35] the
Imperial Rescript on Education is the manifestation of the "mysterious preaching" in chapter 16 ("The Life Span of the Tathāgata"),
and the attacks against China and Russia are expressions of the ten
supernatural powers referred to in chapter 3.[36] The geopolitical reasoning by correlation is strikingly clear in the section dealing with the
chapter on "The Life Span of the Tathāgata," which Tanaka himself
read during the ceremony:

> Śākyamuni appeared in this world in order to preach the *Lotus Sutra;*
> the *Lotus Sutra* [appeared] in order to preach the "Life Span" chapter;
> the "Life Span" chapter [appeared] in order to bear witness to the fun-
> damental disciple [Nichiren]; the fundamental disciple [appeared] in
> order to manifest Japan; and Japan [appeared] in order to save the
> world.[37]

Indeed, the *Lotus Sutra* establishes a blueprint for Japan's role in the
world.

As a religious man, Tanaka was motivated by a thoroughgoing
sense of altruism and idealism. The objective of his journal, *Dokku,*
was to declare to the world its aim of rebuilding the world in terms of
Japan's national essence, and to reach out to humanity to make them
take refuge in the *Lotus Sutra* and Japan so that the world may be
unified.[38] The theme of the reconstruction of the world also runs
throughout Satomi's *Japanese Civilization.* In order to fulfill the
hopes of all people for world peace, all nations must undergo "moral
reconstruction" along the lines of Nichirenism and the Japanese
national principles, which are the "general basis of life and of the
world." It is Japan's mission to propagate the *Lotus Sutra* and thereby
"redeem the world."[39] Not just the world but even God himself will
be reconstructed in terms of Japan:

> . . . The world, the morality, the humanity, the Buddha, the God or
> the truth, all things of life and being would start anew from the Reality

of Japan. Thus, Japan as the Truth of the world, Japan as the Foundation of Human salvation and Japan as the Finality of the world concerning her moral essence and aspects is Japan in her reality.[40]

All of this, of course, was an accurate reflection of his father's views. In Tanaka's *What Is Nippon Kokutai?*, which Satomi translated into English, Japan's mission to the cosmos is reiterated many times:

> The world begins with Nippon and ends with Nippon. The right interpretation of "Nippon Kokutai" should be "if Nippon were well understood, the world or mankind would get on perfectly."
>
> The Kokutai of Nippon has the duty of controlling and arranging everything in the universe, so it may be called "the science of sciences" if we take it as an object of study, and is not to be interfered with by men's trifling arguments or by logic among foreign countries.
>
> Now our neighbour state, Manchoukuo, has taken the lead in establishing the state on "the Way of the Prince" as its basis, and for Nippon it is one of the realizations of our ideal in one corner of the globe, so that we should naturally be glad of it and help it and pray for its sound growth, and it is the very mission of the founding of Nippon to hope for and help the effects of Manchoukuo's birth to spread first to China proper . . . and then be expanded to the various countries both in the East and in the West, and change the whole world into a great paradise. . . .
>
> The paramount mission of Nippon lies in realizing perfect universal peace by drawing the whole world to one goodness and one way. . . .
>
> Nippon is, needless to say, the model state for all mankind. Nippon [is] the fundamental organ for unifying the whole world. . . . [41]

The altruistic note is unmistakable: Tanaka sincerely believed in the welfare of all the people in the world, so much so that the spread of peace by force if necessary was justifiable.

Tanaka found in the *Lotus Sutra* not only justification but even a prediction of Japan's use of force. In accordance with his interpretation of chapter 14, "Peaceful Practices," which he saw as supporting *shakubuku* as well as *shōju*, Tanaka interpreted the "powerful, wheel-turning-holy-king,"[42] who went to war against the kings of smaller countries, as referring to Emperor Meiji. The word "powerful" was a "prediction of the Emperor's military might."[43] Military aggression, however, had to be undertaken for the right reasons. In and of itself, world conquest was an "empty idea of floating clouds in the dreams of conquerors" such as Napoleon, Hideyoshi, and the

Kaiser, all of whom failed miserably.[44] World unification must be understood correctly according to the *Lotus Sutra* and the essence of Japan, but this does not mean that the objective of unification can only be pursued in a fragile and frail manner. Obviously, Tanaka noted, the power for unification must be supported by military power, but it is "military power for the protection of righteousness, which is necessary in order to crush wrong views and to disperse ignorance . . . not military power in the sense of attacking others and suppressing them."[45] Military power for the sake of righteousness was justifiable, and Emperor Meiji was righteous because he in fact was the *cakravarti-rāja*, the sage king who turns the wheel of the dharma throughout the world. It is in his capacity as *cakravarti-rāja* that Emperor Meiji acts, not as a world conqueror, and therefore when it is time to wield the power of sanctions against those who are not in accord with righteousness, "military power is to be used."[46] The Buddhists in Burma were not wise in eschewing military power, and mistakenly believed that they could prevail simply by waving their faith in the face of the enemy. But they were all killed as they sat in superstitious prayer to Avalokiteśvara, who they believed could stop the bullets of the heretics.[47]

War, then, cannot be won by prayers alone, but righteous war waged by force of arms can be aided by prayers. When the Sino-Japanese War broke out in August 1894, Tanaka and several hundred of his followers went to a small deserted island called Sakurajima located in a river near Osaka. There they built a two-storied prayer platform and enshrined a sword in front of a statue of Nichiren on an altar set up to face Peking. The cutting edge of the sword was also made to face the Chinese capital. Three times a day for over a month they prayed for the defeat of the enemy, and on the day when they concluded their services, word was received that Pyongyang had fallen to the victorious Japanese army. This was powerful vindication of the invocation prayer which called for the wisdom of the Buddha to be brought to bear upon the evil sphere of China, and praised the *Lotus Sutra*, Nichiren, and the "exquisite practice of *shakubuku*."[48]

## Conclusion

The constellation of ideas comprising Tanaka's religious and political thinking is formed by the lines connecting several points: the *Lotus Sutra*, *shakubuku*, *kokutai*, Japan, and the world. Shinto forms one of those points, and in *What Is Nippon Kokutai?* Tanaka drew solely on Shinto for his geopolitical interpretations, seldom mentioning the *Lotus Sutra* at all. The *Lotus Sutra* was another point from which Tanaka drew a clear line to his nationalism, and that connection took the form of ideological arguments based on conceptual and structuralist correlations linking the scripture with politics. The relationship between the text and his interpretations is intimate, and it is not possible to say which is prior. Another way of putting it would be to say that the text is nothing but his interpretations, or that the text, which exists prior to his interpretations, is an "empty" text which is "filled" by his interpretations.

Every text is caught in an intricate web with its interpreters. But the *Lotus Sutra* possesses one characteristic which lends itself more easily to this process. In a real way, the text is empty insofar as the real *Lotus Sutra* is never preached. Since the text is empty, it means that what Tanaka saw was not his own personal interpretations drawn in the context of the Nichiren tradition, but a clear mandate issued by a scripture whose meaning, as far as he was concerned, was as absolutely self-evident as it was absolute.

## NOTES

1. See Notto Thelle, *Buddhism and Christianity in Japan: From Conflict to Dialogue, 1854-1899* (Honolulu: University of Hawaii Press, 1987), 1-17; Kathleen Staggs, "In Defense of Buddhism," Ph.D. diss., Princeton University, 1979; and Allan G. Grapard, "Japan's Cultural Revolution: The Separation of Shinto and Buddhist Divinities in Meiji *(shimbutsu bunri)* and a Case Study: Tōnomine," *History of Religions* 23, no. 3 (February 1984): 240-265.

2. Staggs, "In Defense of Buddhism," 55-121.

3. Yabuki Yoshiteru, *Nippon seishin to Nippon Bukkyō,* 3 and 6. This work was written at the request of the Bukkyō Rengōkai (Buddhist Federation of Japan) and went through fifteen editions in two years. The passages cited are translated in D. C. Holtom, *Modern Japan and Shinto Nationalism* (Chicago: University of Chicago Press, 1947), 137.

4. Edwin B. Lee, "Nichiren and Nationalism: The Religious Patriotism of Tanaka Chigaku," 22.

5. The following account of Tanaka's experiences at the Daikyō-in is based primarily on his autobiography, *Tanaka Chigaku jiden,* 1:197-316.

6. Ibid., 199.

7. Ibid., 201.

8. Tanaka Chigaku, *Honge shōshaku ron,* 1-20.

9. Senchū Murano, trans., *The Lotus Sutra,* 187.

10. Tanaka, *Honge shōshaku ron,* 21.

11. Ibid., 21–22.

12. Ibid., 23.

13. Ibid.

14. Ibid., 27. Tanaka's emphasis.

15. Ibid., 30–32.

16. Tanaka Chigaku, *Shūmon no ishin,* 176.

17. Tanaka Kōho, "Tanaka Chigaku no Nichirenshugi to kokkakan," 59.

18. Hirata Atsutane, of course, died nearly twenty years before Tanaka was born and therefore could not have criticized him directly. Hirata's criticism, however, would still have applied to Tanaka as a Buddhist.

19. Tanaka, *Jiden,* 1:335.

20. Ibid., 335.

21. Murano, *Lotus Sutra,* 220.

22. Tanaka, *Nichirenshūgi no kenkyū,* 111–112.

23. Masaharu Anesaki, *Nichiren, the Buddhist Prophet* (Cambridge: Harvard University Press, 1916), 16–32.

24. Kishio Satomi, *Japanese Civilization* (Plymouth: The Mayflower Press, 1923), 8.

25. Ibid., 27.

26. Tanaka, *Jiden,* 1:335.

27. Tanaka, *Jiden,* 7:102, 107, 142, 163.

28. Tanaka, *Jiden,* 3:155.

29. Tanaka Kōho, *Tanaka Chigaku,* 149–152.

30. Tanaka Kōho, *Nichirenshūgi no kenkyū,* 114.

31. *Dokku* 1, no. 6 (June 1920): 1.

32. Tanaka, *Jiden,* 2:100.

33. Murano, *The Lotus Sutra,* 16.

34. Tanaka, *Jiden,* 7:103.

35. The exact passage Tanaka is referring to is not clear. It may be the section in which those who hear the sutra are said to become buddhas (hence, their "completion") in any of the ten worlds. See Murano, *The Lotus Sutra,* 33.

36. Tanaka, *Jiden,* 7:107.

37. Tanaka, *Jiden,* 7:163.

38. *Dokku* 1, no. 6 (June 1920): 1.

39. Satomi, *Japanese Civilization,* 10, 11, 111.

40. Ibid., 210.

41. Tanaka Chigaku, *What Is Nippon Kokutai?,* 56, 75, 121, 145.

42. Murano, *The Lotus Sutra,* 199–200.

43. Tanaka, *Jiden,* 7:155.

44. Tanaka, *Jiden,* 3:146.

45. Ibid., 147.

46. Ibid.

47. Ibid., 148.

48. Ibid., 158–159.

# The *Lotus Sutra* in Modern Japan

HELEN HARDACRE

## Introduction: Lay Centrality

In all areas of Japanese religions, the trend to lay centrality is among
the most conspicuous historical developments of the nineteenth and
twentieth centuries. By lay centrality I mean an increasingly important role for laity in all aspects of religious life and a weakening of the
distinction between clerical and lay status. Lay centrality characterizes
the nineteenth- and twentieth-century history of both Buddhism and
Shinto and is closely related to the appearance of new religious
groups outside the ecclesiastical hierarchy of either tradition. Lay centrality in Buddhism was stimulated after the Meiji Restoration by
*haibutsu kishaku* (movement to destroy Buddhism), which became
the occasion for serious reform within temple Buddhism. Early Meiji
Buddhism witnessed the appearance of popularizers, ecumenical
thought, and moves to initiate laity in the precepts, all aspects of the
trend to lay centrality.

Lay centrality provides the context for the use of the *Lotus Sutra* in
modern Japan. Not surprisingly, use of the *Lotus Sutra* in the modern
period is most closely associated with the Nichiren school. Lay centrality has been at work there since the mid-nineteenth century, when
the trend was manifest in doctrinal arguments over interpretation of
the sutra. Since the questions at stake then are still central to the use
of the sutra in the twentieth century, this essay will examine them in
some detail. In brief, the issues are the importance of the sutra in
merit transfer *(ekō)*, the relation to the sutra of ancestral and mortuary ritual, and the use of the sutra in repentance and the destruction
of karmic hindrances *(sange metsuzai)*.

This essay will examine the use of the *Lotus Sutra* in modern Japan
by three stages. First, I will discuss the mid-nineteenth century Bud-

dhist group Butsuryūkō, in which lay centrality was intimately connected to the founder's understanding of the *Lotus Sutra*. Second, I will discuss the use of the *Lotus Sutra* in two twentieth-century new religions, Reiyūkai Kyōdan and Risshōkōseikai. Third, I will offer tentative conclusions on the use of the *Lotus Sutra* in the modern period, stressing the importance of ritual and the efforts of modern Japanese to implement the sutra in daily life.

## Butsuryūkō

Founded in 1848 by Nagamatsu Nissen, also known as Seifū (1817–1890), Butsuryūkō is a distant ancestor of most twentieth-century lay Buddhist groups of the Nichiren line.[1] In 1983 it had 512,379 members, 269 temples, 8 churches, and 796 priests and preceptors *(kyōshi)*. Presently its official name is Honmon Butsuryūshū.[2]

Nagamatsu Nissen was born to a Kyoto merchant's family and was educated in *waka* poetry, painting, calligraphy, National Learning thought *(kokugaku)*, and Confucian philosophy. In 1848 he entered the Eight Chapter sect (Happon ha) of the Honmon Hokkeshū.[3] The Honmon Hokkeshū, founded by Nichiryū (1389–1464), took a strong stand on the principal doctrinal debate in the Nichiren school during the Edo period (1600–1868): the unified *(itchi)* versus the superior-inferior *(shōretsu)* conflict. The debate pitted the idea that the *Lotus Sutra* is uniformly valid throughout (the claim of the unified proponents) against the idea that the second half was proclaimed by the eternal Buddha and hence is more valid (the position of the superior-inferior side). The superior-inferior side, which included the Honmon Hokkeshū, accepted a distinction arising from the Tendai school between the eternal Buddha *(kuon honbutsu* or *kuonjitsujō)* and Śākyamuni, held to be but a temporary manifestation *(suijaku)* of the eternal Buddha.[4] Since the eternal Buddha was identified as the source of chapters fifteen to twenty-eight of the *Lotus Sutra*, those chapters were regarded as "superior," that is, more true than the "inferior" first half of the sutra.[5]

Within the second, "superior" half of the scripture, the Eight Chapter sect identified the following eight chapters as the true law adapted to the latter days of the dharma *(mappō)*:

1. Apparition of the Jeweled Stupa, chapter 15
2. The Life Span of the Tathāgata, chapter 16

3. Discrimination of Merits, chapter 17
4. The Merits of Appropriate Joy, chapter 18
5. The Merits of the Dharma-Preacher, chapter 19
6. The Bodhisattva Never Disparaging, chapter 20
7. The Supernatural Powers of the Tathāgata, chapter 21
8. Entrustment, chapter 22.[6]

In the same year that he took the tonsure, Nissen founded the True Gate Eight Chapter Confraternity (Honmon Happon kō), later and hereinafter called Butsuryūkō, in collaboration with an Awaji Island priest, Nichiyō (1811–1863), and other compatriots.[7] Their arrangement was that Nissen would manage the Kyoto branch of the confraternity while Nichiyō tended the followers on Awaji. Nissen entered his sect's seminary partly in hopes of preparing himself to lead lay members of the confraternity, but he was disappointed by seminary life. He found that his birth as a commoner made him the object of his fellow students' scorn, and far from offering him guidance on the care of lay followers, the seminary did not encourage contact with the unordained commoner classes. Becoming a priest at thirty-two, Nissen was older than most of his colleagues and better educated, characteristics they viewed with little enthusiasm. Nissen became disgusted with the seminary and left.[8] However, just at that time the Eight Chapter sect became embroiled in divisive dispute.

The argument of the efficacy of priestly transfer of merit to beings in the three lowest realms of existence laid the groundwork for the birth of new lay religious groups. On the traditionalist side were those who held that beings born in hell, among the hungry ghosts, or as animals (the three lowest realms, *sanzu*) could be saved by priestly transfer of merit. The traditionalist side was known as the proponents of the attainment of buddhahood in these three realms *(sanzu jōbutsu)*. The reformist side, including Nissen, held that in the age of *mappō* priestly merit transfer cannot effect the salvation of these beings. This side was hence named the proponents of nonattainment of buddhahood in the three realms *(sanzu fujōbutsu)*. The reformist side followed Nichiren's position that merit transfer by priests is null and void in the latter days.[9]

To question the clergy's capacity to transfer merit constituted a threat to the position of the priesthood in Tokugawa Japan. Clerical revenue depended heavily on the performance of mortuary and ancestral rituals, and merit transfer played an important role in both. Only clergy could transfer merit to the deceased, in part because of their training in liturgy. Also, the purity they possessed on account of their renunciation of marriage and meat-eating made them an appropriate "field of merit" for lay donations. Thus parishioners depended on clergy to transfer the merit of lay donations to ancestors at funerals and periodic ancestral rituals. The relations of parishioners (*danka*) to the clergy was based on hereditary agreements that a certain temple perform a lineage's funerals and ancestral rites, and in some cases provide for burial. The Tokugawa shogunate required everyone to become a parishioner of some Buddhist sect, and temple records came to be used as census data.[10] To deny the clergy's qualifications to transfer merit thus had radical implications and threatened thoroughly to undermine Buddhism's prestige and economic base of support.

While the performance of funerals and ancestral liturgy became commonplace in all the Japanese Buddhist schools during the Tokugawa period, these practices had a special relevance to the *Lotus Sutra*. The new sects of the Kamakura age offered funerals to their believers, and this is thought to have been a significant source of their appeal in the early days. In the Nichiren school priests performed last rites even for fishers and leather workers, who were despised in other sects.[11] After Nichiren's death, funeral rites provided proselytizers access to potential converts. Nichiren's successors allied themselves with provincial landholders, who entrusted Nichiren priests with maintaining and developing the power of control at the local level. Funeral rites became one expression of Buddhism's place in the network of social control.[12] Nichiren himself advocated recitation of the title of the *Lotus Sutra* (*daimoku*) and of the *Lotus Sutra* itself for a deceased person.[13] The *Lotus Sutra* thus became the core of funerary and ancestral rites throughout the Nichiren school and remains so today.

Meanwhile, the formation of local chapters of Butsuryūkō proceeded apace. Besides Nissen, other priests such as Nissō founded chapters in Edo, Sakai, through the Kansai, in Aomori, and in Kyūshū.[14] Matsudaira Yorikane (1807–1868) founded a chapter in Takamatsu, and Nissen joined forces with him. A high-ranking samurai, Yorikane cut a very unusual figure among religious leaders of the period by preaching with a gold and silver fan in one hand and a sword in the other. Preaching in Awaji temples and in believers' homes, Yorikane was a zealous proselytizer. Nissen corresponded with Yorikane between 1853 and 1855, and in 1856 they decided to cooperate in Kyoto and Takamatsu.[15]

Nissen and Yorikane were united in placing their priority upon lay participation in the confraternity, and doctrinally they justified their stance by reference to one of the Eight Chapters, "The Merits of the Dharma-Preacher" (chapter 19). There five types of preachers of dharma are elaborated without reference to a distinction between cleric and lay person.[16] Both Nissen and Yorikane shared the view of Nichiryū, who held that distinctions between clerics and laity were not essential to true followers of the *Lotus Sutra*.[17] In Nissen's eyes, the work of a layman like Yorikane was far more valuable than the pretensions of the priests he had known in seminary.

Nissen began living a half-lay life, attached to no temple on a permanent basis.[18] Butsuryūkō was officially linked to the Honmon Hokkeshū, and Nissen's disciples among its priests continued to lead the confraternity, but no soteriological significance was attributed to the distinction between priest and laity.

While Nissen and Yorikane were in sympathy in their incipient anticlericalism, they grew apart on other issues. As a samurai, Yorikane could not but take a stand on the foreign threat, and he and his many samurai followers in the confraternity became involved in the call to "revere the emperor and expel the barbarians" *(sonnō jōi),* supporting their sentiments with preaching on Nichiren's patriotic essay, *Risshōankokuron,* and large monetary contributions. This political activity was of little interest to Nissen and his followers, most of whom were merchants and other townsmen. Yorikane and his followers were critical of Nissen's outspoken forceful proselytization *(shakubuku)* and of practices such as healing, which were very prominent among Nissen's followers.[19] Furthermore, Nissen came under attack from secular authorities, who several times investigated and arrested him for preaching and proselytizing without sectarian authorization.[20] When Yorikane died in 1868, his followers went over to Nissen.[21] At that time the Takamatsu group had 4,459 members.[22] Nationwide there were 33 chapters of the confraternity and a rough total of 10,000 members.

Nissen's Butsuryūkō developed a distinctive organization and ritual. Word of the group spread mainly through merchant followers who traveled for business.[23] A cure of a wealthy man from Ōtsu led to the building of a worship hall there in 1861. Followers contributed their labor, and a statue of Nichiren was installed as the main object of worship.[24] Meetings were also held in believers' homes ten times a month on a rotating basis.[25] Nissen's copies of Nichiren's calligraphic mandala were used in communal worship, and Nissen made a formulaic, vernacular rendition of the *Lotus Sutra* for liturgical use.[26] Recitation of it and the title of the sutra constituted the core of group ritual. Funerals were also conducted, even for nonmembers.[27]

In 1871 at the age of fifty-five, Nissen married a believer's daughter. Their marriage was not publicly announced until 1872, however, when the government officially permitted clerical marriage for the first time.[28]

Nissen continued writing in *kana* for followers, and developed a unique form of doctrinal study. A preceptor read a scriptural passage slowly to a group, followed by two interpretations. Followers had to opt for one of the interpretations as the correct one, and they were questioned by preceptors about the reasons for their choice. Preceptors were ordained priests, but they were not significantly elevated above the laity. These meetings were arranged like *sumō* tournaments, so that correct doctrinal interpretations resulted in rising ranks, up to *ōzeki,* which were posted around the walls of the hall.[29]

Sermons were delivered by Nissen or his disciples on themes expressed in his poetry *(kyōka)*. Nissen rendered Tendai writings on repentence *(sange)* into vernacular, and these were also recited in group meetings.[30] Proselytism was an important practice, taken as proof that a believer possessed absolute faith, a *sine qua non* for salvation. Many joined to be healed, and some believed they had been revived from the dead by a custom called *jōgyō,* in which members gathered at the bedside of the dying and recited the *Lotus Sutra* and its title.[31] Use of holy water in healing also developed.[32]

Near the end of Nissen's life, an issue regarding the role of women in the group threatened to divide it. Confraternity leaders resented the growing prominence of female members, who routinely did the cooking and cleaning of the temples, helped Nissen's disciples with various tasks, and were beginning to speak out on matters of substance. Some male leaders wanted to eject them, but since Nissen was living in a group temple with his wife, they could not get rid of the women without evicting Nissen. Nissen threatened to abandon Butsuryūkō entirely if the women were thrown out, and with that the opposition backed down.[33]

Butsuryūkō mirrors the doctrinal and organizational issues that lie in the background of modern Japan's use of the *Lotus Sutra.* In his own life and in the organization of the confraternity, Nissen increasingly downgraded the significance of distinctions between clergy and laity. He married twice, and while pre-Meiji clerical marriage was by no means a rarity, Nissen's choice to live a married life openly removed a major difference between himself and his followers. In confraternity management, priests and laity held equal votes, and ordination was not held to privilege a cleric beyond a lay person. We can see in Butsuryūkō a "Protestant" impulse to put scripture into the hands of the laity, both in the literal sense of translating the *Lotus Sutra* into Japanese and rendering it in phonetic script, and in the sense of engaging the laity in doctrinal study, and granting rank on the basis of intellectual mastery of scripture.

The doctrinal heritage of the Honmon Hokkeshū bequeathed the most pressing issues in Butsuryūkō's use of the *Lotus Sutra.* These concerned the transfer of merit. The practice of lay funerals and the relatively prominent role accorded to women, as well as the sect's stand on merit transfer to beings in the lowest three realms, tended to undermine any notion of special status for the clergy in this regard. I suspect also that healing was justified by reference to the *Lotus Sutra*'s parable of the physician and other passages regarding healing. The issues at stake in Butsuryūkō were echoed by later developments in Meiji Buddhism.

## The Heritage of Meiji Buddhism

While it is impossible to treat Meiji Buddhism here in the detail it deserves, it is appropriate to mention developments bearing upon the use of the *Lotus Sutra* in the twentieth century. The early part of the period, roughly 1868 to 1890, was dominated by the question of how to achieve a viable relation with the state. The Meiji state chose Shinto as its official ideology, and Buddhism was abruptly divested of the state patronage it had enjoyed through the Tokugawa period. An official order for the separation of Buddhism from Shinto in 1868 was followed by a wave of attacks upon Buddhism called *haibutsu kishaku,* in which hundreds of temples were closed, priests defrocked, and priceless images destroyed. The violence varied regionally in its ferocity, but everywhere it caused reflective Buddhist leaders to call for reform. *Haja kenshō* (trounce evil and uphold righteousness) was a general slogan covering many types of proposed reforms.[34]

Recognizing that pre-Meiji Buddhism had been too preoccupied with sectarian concerns and too little involved in the religious lives of the laity, leaders such as Shaku Unshō (1827–1909) and Fukuda Gyōkai (1809–1888) tried to revive lay interest in the precepts. In these two figures ecumenism and popularization merged. Unshō held that keeping even one precept is a meritorious act and that sincere repentance can absolve sins. Gyōkai advocated a pan-Buddhism transcending sectarian boundaries.[35] Ouchi Seiran (1845–1918) of the Sōtō school was another advocate of Buddhist ecumenism, and he believed the laity should be the clergy's main concern. Not only that, he spoke of lay bodhisattvas, an idea popularized in the twentieth century.[36] These writers and others published simple doctrinal explications in great quantity, priced low, and written in a style that could be understood by ordinary people. Stress upon observance of the precepts and on repentence were pervasive themes in both clerical and lay writings.

The problem of coexistence with the state dramatized by *haibutsu kishaku* took a different form in the twentieth century as Buddhist leaders strove to revive the ancient theme of "Buddhism for the protection of the state" *(gohō Bukkyō)* and became apologists for imperialism and war. Nationalistic theories claiming inspiration from the *Lotus Sutra* appeared, mainly among clerics and lay leaders of the Nichiren line, such as Tanaka Chigaku (1861–1939), founder of the nationalistic Buddhist association Kokuchūkai.[37]

## Use of the *Lotus Sutra* in Reiyūkai and Risshōkōseikai

The second section of this essay is devoted to an examination of the use of the *Lotus Sutra* in Risshōkōseikai and Reiyūkai. Reiyūkai was founded by Kubo Kakutarō (1892–1944) and his sister-in-law Kotani Kimi (1901–1971) between 1919 and 1925 in Tokyo. At present it has about three million members in Japan and seventeen foreign countries.[38] Its chief practice is lay ancestor worship based on recitation of the title of the *Lotus Sutra* and an abridged version of the *Lotus Sutra* called the *Blue Sutra*. Kubo Kakutarō poured scorn upon the clergy, accusing them of vice and mediocrity, and calling for temples to be turned into kindergartens and schools. Priests, he said, are good for nothing but guarding the bones of the dead. They do nothing to help humanity, to guide them in pursuing an ethical life.

Kubo was studying the *Lotus Sutra*'s chapter on "Expedient Devices" *(Hōben bon)* and its prophecy of the advent of the evil world of the five impurities *(gojoku akuse)* on 1 September 1923, the day of the great Taishō earthquake. That he was actually studying the prophecy of terrible disaster at the time of the earthquake greatly strengthened Kubo's conviction. Kubo came to believe that the earthquake, war, and social turmoil were caused by corrupt priests taking charge of ancestral rituals which rightfully should be performed by descendants. Everyone must recite the *Lotus Sutra* for their ancestors, or else the ancestors would fall into hell, become hungry ghosts or wandering spirits. If ancestors were not set at rest (a condition he equated with the attainment of buddhahood [*jōbutsu*]), the human world would continually be in chaos. The first step to rectifying the situation is repentance and resolution to undertake "spiritual training" *(shugyō)*.

In Reiyūkai we can see a continuation of the debate over merit transfer that we saw in Butsuryūkō. Reiyūkai holds the belief, found commonly through the Buddhist world, that karma is partially inherited. Thus ancestors and their descendants have a shared bond of karma, and it is possible for descendants to improve the ancestors' karma by sutra recitation and by living an ethical life (which in Reiyū-kai implies adhering to the traditional role hierarchy of the family, *ie*). Besides improving karma with sutra recitation, repentance can destroy karmic hindrances (the *sange metsuzai* theme introduced above), and thus repentance as a way of life, rather than a one-time act, is recommended.

Repentance and merit transfer are principally relevant to the karmic bonds between ancestors and descendants, and priests have no rightful place here. What is the clergy's qualification for transferring merit? Reiyūkai asks. Whereas former ages could point to the purity of the priesthood based on their renunciation of marriage and meat, in the twentieth century they are no longer distinguished from the rest of society in that way. Merit can genuinely be transferred, holds Reiyūkai, only by living descendants.

Reiyūkai has constructed its *Blue Sutra* in accord with this position on merit transfer to the ancestors. That is to say, Reiyūkai makes a selection from the *Lotus Sutra* for the purpose of transferring merit to the ancestors. In so doing, it has added its own prayer for merit transfer and emphasizes passages dealing with repentance. As I have treated this matter in some detail elsewhere, I will not recapitulate my analysis of the *Blue Sutra* here, but will simply introduce an outline which illustrates the sutra's construction.

The ritual purpose of the *Blue Sutra* is to encapsulate the *Lotus Sutra* and to unlock the power its doctrines proclaim by surrounding the core with merit transfer and repentance pieces (the two excerpts dealing with Samantabhadra). These merit transfer and repentance pieces direct the power of the *Lotus Sutra* to the destruction of evil

## The Construction of the *Blue Sutra*

Invocation
Merit Transfer *(ekōshō)*
Sutra of Innumerable Meanings (excerpt) *(Muryōgi-kyō jūkudoku)*
Sutra of Meditation on the Bodhisattva Samantabhadra *(Kanfugen bosatsu
    gyōhōgyō)*
Expedient Devices *(Hōben)*
Devadatta *(Daibadatta)*
The Life Span of the Tathāgata *(Nyorai juryō)*
The Bodhisattva Never Disparaging *(Jōfukyō bosatsu)*
The Supernatural Powers of the Tathāgata *(Nyorai jinriki)*
The Bodhisattva Medicine King *(Yakuō bosatsu)*
The Universal Gate of the Bodhisattva Avalokiteśvara *(Kanzeon bosatsu fumon)*
The Encouragements of the Bodhisattva Samantabhadra *(Fugen bosatsu kambotsu)*
Sutra of Meditation on the Bodhisattva Samantabhadra *(Fugen bosatsu gyōhōgyō)*
Invocation *(Kiganshō)*

karma through repentance. The merit of repentance and the karma-destroying force of the ritual of sutra recitation, begun and ended with recitation of the title of the *Lotus Sutra,* are trained upon the ancestors by the merit transfer section, strategically placed at the beginning, instead of the end, as is often the case in the clerical use of the *Lotus Sutra.*

The *Lotus Sutra* has been used to benefit ancestors through repentance and merit transfer since 847, when Ennin (794–864) brought the rites from China. He caused a pagoda to be constructed at the Cryptomeria Cave on Mt. Hiei in 848 for ceaseless meditation on the *Lotus Sutra,* and its object of worship was a statue of Samantabhadra. These lotus pavilions *(hokkedō)* were later erected in many places to provide masses for the dead. The imperial court sponsored rites using the *Lotus Sutra* for repentance and merit transfer to ancestors *(Hokke sembō)* down to the Meiji period.[39]

Seen in light of this long history of utilizing the *Lotus Sutra* in ancestral rites, Reiyūkai's use of the sutra in that way is less innovative than continuative, perpetuating a long tradition. It is also worthy of note that most of the fourteen groups that have arisen by schism from Reiyūkai also use the sutra in this way, as well as carry over many other Reiyūkai beliefs and practices virtually intact. However, besides the act of interpretation of the sutra per se, there remains a question of a different order concerning the general type of religious approach to the sutra.

In the 1930s an event occurred which sounded the death knell for doctrinal study in Reiyūkai. At that time two branch leaders of the organization, Naganuma Myōkō (1899–1957) and Niwano Nikkyō

(b. 1906) were holding study groups for doctrinal analysis, and they attracted many followers in this way. Kotani Kimi, however, saw in their efforts a specious logic-chopping that subverted believers' simple devotion to the sutra. For her, an analytic approach to the sutra was not only misguided but dangerous. She recited the sutra as a means to train and discipline the spirit, and to gain the powers prophesied for faithful believers. She publicly castigated Naganuma and Niwano, who left Reiyūkai with all the members in their charge and founded Risshōkōseikai in 1938. Since this incident there has been no serious attempt at doctrinal instruction in Reiyūkai.

This incident illustrates a basic difference between the two organizations. While both make similar use of the *Lotus Sutra*, Reiyūkai assumes an essentially devotional attitude to scripture and discourages discussion and analysis. Scripture is to be cherished as sacred writing, recitation of which can give the devotee power and aid in the solution of personal or familial problems.

In Risshōkōseikai one finds a devotional attitude, but the group also rewards doctrinal study.[40] It has a seminary for the development of doctrine, and in ordinary meetings of followers, called the "dharma seat" *(hōza)*, members refer to specific doctrines or passages from the *Lotus Sutra* to illustrate a point or justify their actions. Only seldom have I observed this use of the sutra in Reiyūkai.

In its scripture for daily recitation before an ancestral altar, also an abridgement of the *Lotus Sutra*, Risshōkōseikai utilizes many of the same passages from the *Lotus Sutra* as Reiyūkai. As an introductory passage, Risshōkōseikai has substituted the three refuges for a repentance piece, as well as a few lines on the meaning of sutra recitation (the Dōjō concept, *dōjōkan*), and opening *gāthās (kaikyōge)*. Symmetry is created by merit transfer passages at beginning and end.

It would be interesting to investigate the process by which Reiyūkai and Risshōkōseikai composed their scriptures. Clearly Risshōkōseikai's owes much to Reiyūkai. Reiyūkai enlisted the services of the famous buddhologist Watanabe Shōkō (1907–1977) in the compilation of its *Maitreya Sutra,* and I suspect that its founders may have sought similar "professional" advice in the compilation of the *Blue Sutra* as well. Models for abridgments of scripture to be used by lay people can be found in all the Buddhist schools. It seems likely that Risshōkōseikai's founders might also have sought academic aid in editing the scripture they inherited from Reiyūkai.

My observation of Risshōkōseikai is too limited to permit me to generalize with confidence, but I suspect that the group's concept

**The Construction of Risshōkōseikai's Scripture**
(An asterisk (*) indicates a passage identical to
or substantially similar to the corresponding
passage in Reiyūkai's *Blue Sutra*.)

The Three Refuges *(sankie)*
Invocation*
The Dōjō Concept *(dōjōkan)*
Merit Transfer *(ekōshō)*
Opening *Gāthā (kaikyōge)*
Sutra of Innumerable Meanings (excerpt)*
Expedient Devices*
Parable *(Hiyu)*
Devadatta*
Fortitude *(Kanji)*
The Life Span of the Tathāgata*
The Bodhisattva Never Disparaging*
The Supernatural Powers of the Tathāgata*
The Universal Gate of the Bodhisattva Avalokiteśvara*
The Encouragements of the Bodhisattva Samantabhadra*
Sutra of Meditation on the Bodhisattva Samantabhadra*
Merit Transfer

and practice of ancestor worship is changing. For its oldest generation, ancestor worship as seen in Reiyūkai may still be the main focus
of devotion. Observation of *hōza* at Risshōkōseikai headquarters and
in a local branch suggests, however, that managing family relations in
terms of an ethic derived from the family system (also a major concern in Reiyūkai) is more important. One hears less about punish-
ment *(bachi)* or guidance *(shidō)* from the ancestors, or about the
necessity of being grateful *(kansha)* to them or repentant *(sange)* in
Risshōkōseikai. Instead, members voice all these sentiments in relation to the founders, both of whom are hailed in the invocation in
the group's scripture. Between Naganuma and Niwano, there is a
tendency, much resented by her direct disciples, to shove Naganuma
into the background coupled with elevation of Niwano and his son
(the heir apparent). This trend is further linked to a tendency in second and succeeding generations of the new religions to establish a
sort of solidarity, a specious "male bonding," with secular society
through downgrading the importance of women and excluding them
from positions of leadership.

While both Reiyūkai and Risshōkōseikai include Kuonjitsujō in
their scriptural invocations, neither seems to have followed Butsuryūkō's choice of chapters of the *Lotus Sutra* exclusively from the second half of the scripture. It is notable that all three groups elected to
retain passages from chapter twenty, "The Bodhisattva Never Dis-

paraging." Nichiren believed himself to be a reincarnation of Sadā-paribhūta, the bodhisattva in question. The chapter prophesies that Never Disparaging will appear in the latter days, never despising anyone, no matter how often he himself is reviled and persecuted. Kubo believed with complete certainty in the idea of the latter days, and he also believed that he was an incarnation both of Nichiren and hence of Never Disparaging. At present there is little emphasis on the idea of the latter days in either Reiyūkai or Risshōkōseikai, however, and in the latter, this chapter of the sutra is now interpreted as an illustration of the no-self idea.[41]

Organizationally Butsuryūkō, Reiyūkai, and Risshōkōseikai have much in common. While Butsuryūkō never abolished ordination, it considerably diminished the difference between clerical and lay statuses. Both Reiyūkai and Risshōkōseikai are lay organizations entirely unaffiliated with any Buddhist ecclesiastical organization. Both consider lay members fully capable of performing all religious functions, including merit transfer, funerals, and daily and periodic ancestral rites. In all these rites sutra recitation is the main liturgical practice.

## The Vitality of the *Lotus Sutra* in Modern Japan

Nineteenth- and twentieth-century Japanese have used the *Lotus Sutra* principally in connection with the cult of ancestors, as a means of merit transfer and repentance. Clearly use of the sutra by large numbers depends on Japan's universal literacy and on aspects of lay centrality such as a decline in the prestige of Buddhist ecclesia, the appearance of vernacular renditions and abridgments of the sutra, and the encouragement of lay doctrinal study and lay liturgy.

Among these several factors, abridgment is particularly complex. An abridgment of a sutra carries the strong impress of the "editor," in this case the founders of a new religion and whatever academic "experts" they choose to consult. Abridgment represents two types of choices: positive choices in favor of incorporating certain ideas and images, and negative choices to subordinate material not included in the abridgment. Thus the several promises of supreme, perfect enlightenment to female devotees such as Yaśodharā, Mahāprajāpatī, and the daughter of the Sāgara Nāga (dragon) king may be known to Reiyūkai or Risshōkōseikai stalwarts who own and read the *Lotus* in its entirety, but not to novices who possess only an abridgment.

In addition to the significance of the actual doctrinal content of the

*Lotus* in the hands of lay devotees, the importance of the text as arti-
fact is not to be overlooked. Keeping, reading, reciting, copying, and
cherishing scripture are all attitudes the *Lotus* recommends, and millions of Japanese revere and treasure the sutra apart from any particular interpretation of its doctrines. It is a sacred book, and the words
written there are held to be gravid with potency.

Above all else, it is the use of the sutra in ritual and daily life that
maintains it as a living element in Japanese Buddhism and Japanese
culture generally. It is principally through implementing the sutra in
liturgy and in the context of messy, intransigent, personal problems
that the *Lotus Sutra* becomes part of a world-view. Here we must be
concerned not only with the sutra and its doctrinal content, but also
with the network of social relations formed within a religious organization.

Reciting an abridgment of the sutra daily, members receive advice
from leaders on personal problems. Leaders urge followers to apply
the sutra to a proper conception and disposition of illness, business
failure, inharmonious personal relations, and a variety of other com-
plaints. How to apply the sutra effectively, however, is not obvious or
self-evident. Followers are *taught* how to conceptualize and use the
sutra. In this process of socialization, they are exposed to the group's
interpretation of the sutra, and they are brought into the stream of
historical Japanese Buddhist tradition.

The history of Buddhism in Japan has produced a view of the religion as inseparable from the cult of ancestors. The lay groups discussed above take it for granted in addition that the sutra endorses
the role structure and values of the family, and many think of the
sutra as an endorsement of reactionary politics and extreme social
conservatism as well. Lay groups typically understand that correct use
of the sutra entails repentance and proselytization in the context of
social institutions and values they understand to be valorized by the
sutra.

A person who believes (and millions do) that a personal problem
has been solved or significantly ameliorated through use of the *Lotus
Sutra* comes to think not so much that a specific interpretation of the
*Lotus Sutra* as proferred by Reiyūkai or Risshōkōseikai, for example,
is right, but that the religion as a whole is good, and that the sutra in
its entirety is true and powerful. She or he becomes motivated to
associate further with the religious group, and inevitably will be
asked to proselytize and help others solve problems. Rank is awarded
for proselytization.

The satisfaction of rank achieved in these religious groups is hard to overemphasize, especially in the case of people unable to achieve comparable recognition in secular society on account of gender, class, or lack of wealth or education. These leaders guide converts to recapitulate the experience of solving problems through application of the *Lotus Sutra,* including sutra recitation, repentance, and accepting the guidance of leaders in construing and handling the problematic situation. Thus they perpetuate cycles of liturgy, interpretation, and implementation. It is the continuation of these cycles that accounts for the remarkable vitality of the *Lotus Sutra* in Japan today.

## NOTES

1. I regret that at this writing I have not had access to primary sources on Butsuryūkō.

2. Bunkachō, ed., *Shūkyō nenkan* (Tokyo: Gyōsei, 1984), 94–95.

3. Murakami Shigeyoshi, *Butsuryū kaidō Nagamatsu Nissen,* 30–47.

4. Ibid., 42.

5. Other Nichiren sects holding this view were the Honmonshū, the Hokkeshū, the Kenpon Hokkeshū, the Honmyō Hokkeshū, and Nichiren Shōshū.

6. Murakami, *Nagamatsu Nissen,* 43–44.

7. Ibid., 47.

8. Ibid., 50.

9. Ibid., 52–55.

10. Takeda Chōshū, *Nihonjin no ie to shūkyō, Nihonjin no kōdō to shisō* 27 (Tokyo: Hyōronsha, 1976), chap. 3.

11. Wada Ken'ichi, "Zaike Bukkyō sōsō shūzoku no shiteki ichikōsatsu," *Indogaku Bukkyōgaku kenkyū* 16, no. 1 (December 1967): 269–271.

12. Nihon shūkyōshi kenkyūkai, ed., *Fukyōsha to minshū to no taiwa, Nihon shūkyōshi kenkyū* 2 (Tokyo: Hōzōkan, 1968), 77.

13. Nichiren, "Ueno dono no haha ama goze gohenji."

14. Murakami, *Nagamatsu Nissen,* 57–60.

15. Ibid., 55–64.

16. This chapter mainly tells of the virtues of eye, ear, tongue, nose, thoughts, etc., that will come to one who preaches and reveres the *Lotus Sutra.*

17. Murakami, *Nagamatsu Nissen,* 56.

18. Ibid., 66.

19. Ibid., 77–78 and 90–92.

20. Ibid., 124–126.

21. Ibid., 132.

22. Kan Ken'ichi, "Butsuryūshū," in *Nihon kindai to Nichirenshūgi,* vol. 4 of *Kōza Nichiren,* 4 vols. (Tokyo: Shunbunsha, 1972), 210–214.

23. Murakami, *Nagamatsu Nissen,* 86 and 93–94.

24. Ibid.

25. Ibid., 81.

26. Ibid., 83 and 114.

27. Nishino Nikei, "Nagamatsu Seifu to Honmon Butsuryūkō," 40.

28. Murakami, *Nagamatsu Nissen*, 146.

29. Nishino, "Nagamatsu Seifu," 38–39.

30. Ibid., 41.

31. Ibid., 39.

32. Murakami, *Nagamatsu Nissen*, 157–158.

33. Ibid., 198–200.

34. Ikeda Eishu, *Meiji no Bukkyō—sono kōdō to shisō*, 15–18.

35. Ibid., 27–38, and chap. 2.

36. Ibid., chap. 3.

37. Tokoro Shigemoto, *Kindai shakai to Nichirenshugi*. On Tanaka Chigaku, see the essay by George J. Tanabe, Jr., in this volume.

38. Except where noted otherwise, my treatment of Reiyūkai herein is based on my *Lay Buddhism in Contemporary Japan: Reiyūkai Kyōdan*.

39. M. W. deVisser, *Ancient Buddhism in Japan*, 2 vols. (Paris: Librairie Orientaliste, Paul Guenther, 1928), 1:355–366.

40. Discussion of Risshōkōseikai herein is based mainly on fieldwork at the group's Tokyo headquarters and at its Yokohama church, carried out during the summer of 1984, and also on analysis of its scripture for daily recitation, "Kyōten."

41. Niwano Nikkyō, *A Guide to the Threefold Lotus Sutra*, 127–130.

# BIBLIOGRAPHY

## 1. English Translations of the *Lotus Sutra*

Buddhist Text Translation Society, trans. *The Wonderful Dharma Lotus Flower Sutra.* San Francisco: Sino American Buddhist Association, 1977.

Hurvitz, Leon, trans. *Scripture of the Lotus Blossom of the Fine Dharma.* New York: Columbia University Press, 1976.

Katō Bunnō et al., trans. *The Threefold Lotus Sutra.* New York: Weatherhill-Kōsei, 1975.

Kern, H., trans. *Saddharma Puṇḍarīka or the Lotus of the True Law.* New York: Dover, 1963.

Murano Senchū, trans. *The Sutra of the Lotus Flower of the Wonderful Law.* Tokyo: Nichirenshū Headquarters, 1974.

Soothill, W. E., trans. *The Lotus of the Wonderful Law.* Oxford: Clarendon Press, 1930.

Tamura Yoshirō and Miyasaka Kōjirō, trans. *Muryōgikyō, the Sutra of Innumerable Meanings and Kanfugengyō, the Sutra of Meditation on the Bodhisattva Universal Virtue.* Tokyo: Risshō Kōseikai, 1974.

## 2. Selected Works on the *Lotus Sutra* in Japanese Culture

Anesaki Masaharu. *Nichiren, the Buddhist Prophet.* Cambridge: Harvard University Press, 1916.

Ariga Yoshitake. "Hoke-kyō-e." In *Enryakuji Onjōji Saikyōji. Nihon koji bijutsu zenshū.* Vol. 10. Tokyo: Shueisha, 1980.

Chappell, David W., ed. *T'ien-t'ai Buddhism: An Outline of the Fourfold Teachings.* Tokyo: Dai'ichi shobō, 1983.

Chiba Shōkan. "Dengyō Daishi no sokushin jōbutsugi." *Tendai gakuhō* 24 (1982).

de Jong, J. W., Review article of Bunnō Katō, trans., *The Threefold Lotus Sutra,* revised by W. E. Soothill and Wilhelm Schiffer; and Senchū Murano, trans., *The Sutra of the Lotus Flower of the Wonderful Law.* In *Eastern Buddhist,* n.s. 8, no.2 (October 1975): 154–159.

Donohashi Akio. "Honkōji no Hoke-kyō hensō-zu." *Nihon bijutsu kōgei*, no. 457 (October, 1976): 15–24.

Dykstra, Yoshiko K., trans. *Miraculous Tales of the Lotus Sutra From Ancient Japan: The Dainihonkoku Hokekyōkenki of Priest Chingen.* Osaka: Kansai University of Foreign Studies, 1983.

Egami Yasushi. "Enryakujizō kingin kōsho Hoke-kyō *no* sōgonga." *Bijutsu kenkyū*, no. 309 (August, 1979): 1–18.

Eiki Giken. "Shinran Shōnin, Zonkaku Shōnin no Hoke-kyō ni taisuru taido." *Shinshūgaku*, no. 44 (1971).

Gotō bijutsukan, ed. *Koshakyō.* Tokyo: Gotō bijutsukan, 1971.

Grapard, Allan G. "Flying Mountains and Walkers of Emptiness: Toward a Definition of Sacred Space in Japanese Religion." *History of Religions* 21, no. 3 (1982): 195–221.

———. "Lotus in the Mountain, Mountain in the Lotus." *Monumenta Nipponica* 41, no. 1 (Spring 1986): 21–50.

Groner, Paul. *Saichō: The Establishment of the Japanese Tendai School.* Berkeley: Berkeley Buddhist Series, 1984.

Hardacre, Helen. *Lay Buddhism in Contemporary Japan: Reiyūkai Kyōdan.* Princeton: Princeton University Press, 1984.

Haruyama Takematsu. *Heianchō kaigashi.* Tokyo: Asahi shimbunsha, 1950.

Hayami Tasuku. *Heian kizoku shakai to Bukkyō.* Tokyo: Kikkawa kōbunkan, 1975.

Hioki Shōichi. *Nihon sōhei kenkyū.* Tokyo: Kokusho kankōkai, 1972.

Hirabayashi Moritoku. *Ryōgen.* Tokyo: Yoshikawa kōbunkan, 1978.

Hori Daiji. "Ryōgen to Yokawa fukkō." *Jinbun ronsō* 10 (1964): 24–55; 12 (1966): 1–34.

———. "Yokawa Bukkyō no kenkyū." *Shisō* 34 (March 1976): 26–42.

Hurvitz, Leon. "The *Lotus Sutra* in East Asia: A Review of *Hokke Shisō*." *Monumenta Serica* 29 (1970–1971): 697–792.

Ienaga Saburō. *Nihon Bukkyō shi.* 3 vols. Kyoto: Hōzōkan, 1967.

Ikeda Eishū. *Meiji no Bukkyō—sono kōdō to shisō.* Vol. 31 of *Nihonjin no kōdō to shisō.* Tokyo: Hyōronsha, 1976.

Inari Nissen. *Hoke-kyō ichijō shisō no kenkyū.* Kyoto: Heirakuji shoten, 1975.

Inoue Mitsusada. *Nihon kodai no kokka to Bukkyō.* Tokyo: Iwanami shoten, 1971.

Kabutogi Shōkō. *Hoke-kyō to Nichiren Shōnin.* Tokyo: Daitō shuppansha, 1985.

———. *Hokke hankyō no kenkyū.* Kyoto: Heirakuji shoten, 1954.

———. *Hokke hankyō no kenkyū.* Tokyo: Daitō shuppansha, 1983.

———. *Hokke shakyō no kenkyū.* Tokyo: Daitō shuppansha, 1983.

Kagawa Mitsuo and Fujita Seiichi. *Usa.* Tokyo: Mokujisha, 1976.

Kageyama Gyoō, ed. *Chūsei Hokke Bukkyō no tenkai.* Kyoto: Heirakuji, 1974.

Kageyama Haruki. *Hieizan.* Tokyo: Kadokawa shoten, 1975.

Kameda Tsutomu. "Heike Nōkyō no e to imayō no uta." *Bukkyō geijutsu*, no. 100 (February 1975): 105–119.

———. "Kyō-e ni tsuite." *Yamato bunka*, no. 50 (April 1969): 20–26.

Kan Ken'ichi. "Butsuryūshū." In *Nihon kindai to Nichirenshūgi.* Vol. 4 of *Kōza Nichiren.* 4 vols. Tokyo: Shunbunsha, 1972.

Kanakura Enshō, ed. *Hoke-kyō no seiritsu to tenkai.* Kyoto: Heirakuji shoten, 1974.

Kawada Tei. "Hoke-kyō-e ishō no tenkai." *Bukkyō geijutsu*, no. 132 (September 1980): 44–58.

Kawase Wakei. "Hoke-kyō to Shinshū." *Takada gakuhō*, no. 57 (December 1966): 18–29.

Komatsu Shigemi. *Heike Nōkyō no kenkyū*. 2 vols. Tokyo: Kodansha, 1976.

Kōyama Noboru. "Hoke-kyō-e." *Bukkyō geijutsu*, no. 93 (September 1973): 103–113.

———. "Saimyōji sanjūtōnai hekiga Hoke-kyō." *Bukkyō geijutsu*, no. 132 (September 1980): 59–76.

Kuroda Toshio. "Nihon chūsei no kokka to shūkyō." In Ienaga Saburo et al., eds., *Kokka to shūkyō*. Vol. 1 of *Nihon shūkyō-shi kōza*. Tokyo: San'ichi shobō, 1959; rev. ed., 1971.

———. *Nihon chūsei no kokka to shūkyō*. Tokyo: Iwanami shoten, 1976.

———. *Ōbō to buppō*. Kyoto: Hōzōkan, 1983.

Lai, Whalen W. "The Humanity of the Buddha: Is Mahāyāna Docetic?" *Ching Feng* 24, no. 2 (June 1981): 97–107.

———. "The Predocetic 'Finite Buddhakāya' in the *Lotus Sutra*: In Search of the Illusive Dharmakāya Therein." *Journal of the American Academy of Religion*, no. 49 (Spring 1981): 447–469.

———. "Seno'o Girō and the Dilemma of Modern Buddhism: Leftist Prophet of the *Lotus Sutra*." *Japanese Journal of Religious Studies*, no. 11 (March 1984): 7–42.

Lee, Edwin B. "Nichiren and Nationalism: The Religious Patriotism of Tanaka Chigaku." *Monumenta Nipponica* 20, no. 1 (Spring 1975): 19–35.

McMullin, Neil. *Buddhism and the State in Sixteenth-Century Japan*. Princeton: Princeton University Press, 1984.

———. "The Sanmon-Jimon Schism in the Tendai School of Buddhism: A Preliminary Analysis." *The Journal of the International Association of Buddhist Studies* 7, no. 1 (1984): 83–105.

Manaka Fujikō. *Kokubungaku ni sesshu sareta Bukkyō*. Tokyo: Bun'ichi shuppansha, 1972.

Matsumura Masao. "Hokke mandara." *Kokka*, no. 827 (February 1961): 66–71.

Meech-Pekarik, Julia. "Disguised Scripts and Hidden Poems in an Illustrated Heian Sutra: *Ashide-e* and *Uta-e* in the *Heike nōgyō*." *Archives of Asian Art* 31 (1977): 52–75.

———. "The Flying White Horse: Transmission of the Valāhassa Jataka Imagery from India to Japan." *Artibus Asiae* 42, nos. 1 and 2 (1981–1982): 111–128.

———. "Taira Kiyomori and the Heike nōgyō." Ph.D. diss. Harvard University, 1976.

Minamoto Toyomune. "Bukkyō bijutsu to bungaku to no ketsugō ni tsuite." *Bukkyō geijutsu*, no. 14 (November 1929): 24–40.

Miya Tsugio. "Hoke-kyō no e to imayō no uta." *Bukkyō geijutsu* no. 33 (September 1980): 21–43.

———. *Kinji hōtō mandara*. Tokyo: Kikkawa kōbunkan, 1976.

Miyazaki Eishū, ed. *Kindai Hokke Bukkyō no tenkai*. Kyoto: Heirakuji shoten, 1978.

Mochizuki Kankō, ed. *Kindai Nihon no Hokke Bukkyō*. Kyoto: Heirakuji shoten, 1979.

Mochizuki Kazunori. *Hoke-kyō to Shōtoku Taishi*. Tokyo: Dai'ichi shobō, 1975.

Morrell, Robert E. "The Buddhist Poetry in the *Goshūishū*." *Monumenta Nipponica* 28, no. 1 (Spring 1973): 88–100.

Murakami Shigeyoshi. *Butsuryū kaidō Nagamatsu Nissen*. Tokyo: Kodansha, 1976.

Murase, Miyeko. "Kuan Yin as Savior of Men: Illustrations of the Twenty-fifth Chapter of the *Lotus Sutra*." *Artibus Asiae* 33, nos. 1 and 2 (1971): 39–74.

Murayama Shūichi. *Honji-suijaku*. Tokyo: Yoshikawa kōbunkan, 1974.

Nakamura Zuiryū. *Hoke-kyō no shisō to kiban*. Kyoto: Heirakuji shoten, 1980.

Nara kokuritsu hakubutsukan, ed. *Hoke-kyō no bijutsu*. Nara: Nara kokuritsu hakubutsukan, 1979.

———. *Hoke-kyō: shakyō to sogon*. Tokyo: Tokyo bijutsu, 1987.

Nihon Bukkyō Gakkai, ed. *Bukkyō to seiji-keizai*. Kyoto: Heirakuji shoten, 1972.

Nishino Nikei. "Nagamatsu Seifu to Honmon Butsuryūkō." *Kindai shūkyō hyakunen no shogen,* special issue no. 2 of *Asoka* (1968).

Niwano Nikkyō. *A Guide to the Threefold Lotus Sutra*. Tokyo: Kōsei, 1981.

Nomura Yōshō, ed. *Hoke-kyō shinkō no shokeitai*. Kyoto: Heirakuji shoten, 1976.

Ōchō Enichi. "From the *Lotus Sutra* to the Sutra of Eternal Life: Reflections on the Process of Deliverance in Shinran." *The Eastern Buddhist* 11, no. 1 (May 1978).

———. *Hokke shisō no kenkyū*. Kyoto: Heirakuji shoten, 1975.

———. "Shinran to Tendaigaku." *Ōtani gakuhō* 46, no. 4 (February, 1967): 1–12.

———, ed. *Hokke shisō*. Kyoto: Heirakuji shoten, 1969.

Ōtake Junkō and Watanabe Shinkō. *Kunisaki bunka to sekibutsu*. Tokyo: Mokujisha, 1970.

Rosenfield, John M.; Cranston, Edwin A.; and Fumiko E. *The Courtly Tradition in Japanese Art and Literature*. Cambridge, Mass.: Fogg Art Museum, 1973.

Sakamoto Yukio, ed. *Hoke-kyō no shisō to bunka*. Kyoto: Heirakuji shoten, 1965.

Sakamoto Yukio and Iwamoto Yutaka, trans. *Hoke-kyō*. 3 vols. Tokyo: Iwanami shoten, 1965.

Satō Shin'ichi. *Nihon no chūsei no kokka to shūkyō*. Tokyo: Iwanami shoten, 1983.

Satomi Kishio. *Japanese Civilization*. Plymouth: The Mayflower Press, 1923.

Schopen, Gregory. "The Phrase 'sa pṛthivīpradeśaś caityabhūto bhavet' in the Vajracchedikā: Notes on the Cult of the Book in Mahāyāna." *Indo-Iranian Journal* 17, nos. 3/4 (November/December 1975): 147–181.

Shioiri Ryōchū. *Dengyō Daishi*. Tokyo: Nihon hyōronsha, 1937.

Shirahata Yoshi. "Hoke-kyō uta-e ni tsuite." *Bijutsushi gaku,* no. 88 (April 1944): 109–118.

Takada Jishō. "Shinran Shōnin no Hoke-kyō-kan." *Ryūkoku kyōgaku,* no. 12 (June, 1977).

Takagi Yutaka. *Heian jidai Hokke Bukkyō shi kenkyū*. 2d ed. Kyoto: Heirakuji shoten, 1978.

Tamura Yoshirō. *Hoke-kyō*. Tokyo: Chūō kōronsha, 1962.

Tamura Yoshirō and Kurata Bunsaku, eds. *Art of the Lotus Sutra*. Crawford, Edna B. trans. Tokyo: Kōsei, 1987.

———. *Hoke-kyō no bijutsu*. Tokyo: Kōseisha, 1981.

Tamura Yoshirō and Watanabe Hōyō, eds. *Hoke-kyō o ikiru*. Tokyo: Kodansha, 1984.

Tanabe, Willa Jane. "The Lotus Lectures: *Hokke Hakkō* in the Heian Period." *Monumenta Nipponica* 39, no. 4 (Winter, 1984): 393–407.

————. *Paintings of the Lotus Sutra.* Tokyo: Weatherhill, 1988.

Tanaka Chigaku. *Honge shōshaku ron.* Seventh printing. Miho: Shishi-ō Bunko Jimusho, 1914.

————. *Shūmon no ishin.* In Yoshida Kyūichi, ed., *Bukkyō: Gendai Nihon shisō taikei.* Vol. 7. Tokyo: Chikuma shobō, 1965.

————. *Tanaka Chigaku jiden.* 10 vols. 2d. ed. Tokyo: Shinsekaisha, 1977.

————. *What Is Nippon Kokutai?* Translated by Satomi Kishio. Tokyo: Shishi-ō Bunko, 1937.

Tanaka Ichimatsu. "Hoke-kyō emaki ni tsuite." *Kokka,* no. 684 (March 1949): 65–67.

Tanaka Kaidō. *Nihon shakyō sōkan.* Kyoto: Shibunkan, 1974.

Tanaka Kōho. *Tanaka Chigaku.* Tokyo: Shinsekaisha, 1977.

————. "Tanaka Chigaku no Nichirenshūgi to kokkakan." In *Nichirenshūgi no kenkyū.* Tokyo: Shinsekaisha, 1981.

Tokoro Shigemoto. *Kindai shakai to Nichirenshūgi.* In *Nihonjin no kōdō to shisō.* Vol. 18. Tokyo: Hyōronsha, 1972.

Tsuji Zennosuke. *Nihon Bukkyōshi.* 10 vols. Tokyo: Iwanami shoten, 1944.

Tsukamoto Keishō. "Daibahon no seiritsu to haikei." In Kanakura Enshō, ed., *Hoke-kyō no seiritsu to tenkai.* Kyoto: Heirakuji shoten, 1970.

Ueda Honsho. *Nichiren Shōnin ni okeru Hokke Bukkyō no tenkai.* Kyoto: Heirakuji shoten, 1982.

Umehara Kazuo. *Kunisaki hantō no rekishi to minzoku.* Oita: Saeki, 1974.

Yabuki Yoshiteru. *Nippon seishin to Nippon Bukkyō.* Tokyo: Bukkyō Rengōkai, 1934.

Yamada Ryūjō and Fukuhara Ryōgen. "Shinran kyōgaku to sono chōsakuchū no inyō-sho." *Ryūkoku Daigaku ronshō,* nos. 365 and 366 (December 1960): 257–309.

Yamagami Chusen. *Nihon bungaku to Hoke-kyō.* 1979.

————. *Rekisei Hokke bungaku monogatari.* Tokyo: Heibunsha, 1978.

Yamamoto Nobuyoshi. "Hokke hakkō to Michinaga no sanjikkō." *Bukkyō geijutsu,* no. 77 (September 1970): 71–84; no. 78 (October 1970): 81–95.

Yamasaki Keiki. "Saichō to Shinran." *Ryūkoku Daigaku ronshū,* nos. 400–401 (March 1973): 333–351.

Yanagisawa Taka and Suzuki Keizō. *Senmen Hoke-kyō.* Tokyo: Tokyo kokuritsu bunkazai kenkyūjo, 1972.

# CONTRIBUTORS

**Allan G. Grapard,** associate professor in the Department of Religious Studies at the University of California at Santa Barbara, has published *Kūkai: La Vérité Finale des Trois Enseignements* and articles on Japanese religion. His major study on the Kasuga cult is forthcoming.

**Paul Groner** is associate professor of religious studies at the University of Virginia. He is the author of *Saichō: The Establishment of the Japanese Tendai School.* His current research centers on the educational system of the Tendai sect.

**Helen Hardacre** specializes in modern Japanese religious movements and has written *Lay Buddhism in Contemporary Japan: Reiyūkai Kyōdan, Kurozumi-kyō and the New Religions of Japan,* and *Shinto and the State, 1868–1988.* She is associate professor in the Department of Religion at Princeton University.

**Kuroda Toshio,** professor of history and dean of the Faculty of Letters at Osaka University, has published important studies on the intellectual and institutional history of Buddhism, among them *Nihon chūsei no kokka to shūkyō, Jisha seiryoku,* and *Ōbō to Buppō.*

**Neil McMullin** is associate professor in the Department of Religious Studies at Erindale College, University of Toronto. He specializes in the relationship between religious and political institutions and has published *Buddhism and the State in Sixteenth-Century Japan.*

**Miya Tsugio** has a distinguished record of research in Japanese art, particularly of the Heian and Kamakura periods. Among his many works are *Ippen shōnin eden, Kinji hōtō mandala, Shōzōga,* and *Kasuga gongen kenki-e,* as well as numerous articles on the art of the *Lotus Sutra.* He is professor of art history at Jissen Women's University.

**Shioiri Ryōdō** has published extensively on the history and philosophy of Tendai Buddhism and is coauthor of *Kan minzoku no Bukkyō,* a study of folk Buddhism in China. He is professor of Chinese Buddhism and Tendai studies at Taishō University and director of the Sōgō Bukkyō Kenkyū-jo.

**Tamura Yoshirō,** professor at Risshō University, is author of many studies on Buddhist thought and philosophy, including *Kamakura shinbukkyō shisō no kenkyū,* and is coeditor of *Tendai hongaku ron.* In addition, he has translated the *Lotus Sutra* into modern Japanese and English, and has published *Lotus*-related studies such as *Hoke-kyō* and *Hoke-kyō no bijutsu,* which was recently translated into English.

**George J. Tanabe, Jr.,** is assistant professor of religion at the University of Hawaii. He has completed a major study of the thirteenth-century monk Myōe and has translated Myōe's diary of dreams. He is currently working on a history of sectarian Buddhism in twentieth-century Japan.

**Willa Jane Tanabe,** associate professor of art history at the University of Hawaii, has authored several catalogues for exhibitions of Japanese and Korean art at the University of Hawaii, and has recently published *Paintings of the Lotus Sutra.*

**Yamada Shōzen** specializes in the study of Buddhist poetry and its relationship to Buddhist philosophy. He is professor of Japanese literature at Taishō University and the author of several articles on poets of the esoteric Buddhist tradition, particularly Saigyō. He is currently doing research on *kōshiki,* Buddhist liturgical hymns.

# INDEX

**Production Notes**

This book was designed by Roger Eggers. Composition and paging were done on the Quadex Composing System and typesetting on the Compugraphic 8400 by the design and production staff of University of Hawaii Press.

The text typeface is Garamond No. 49 and the display typeface is ITC Garamond.

Offset presswork and binding were done by Vail-Ballou Press, Inc. Text paper is Glatfelter Offset smooth, basis 60. Insert paper is Glatco matte smooth, basis 60.